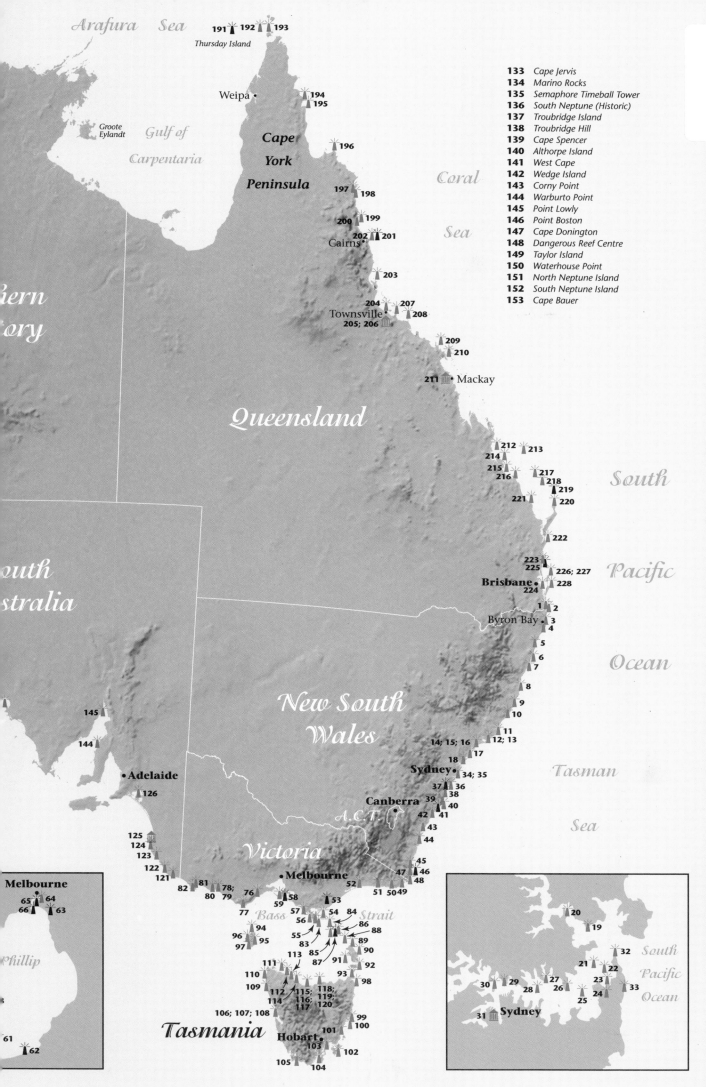

133 Cape Jervis
134 Marino Rocks
135 Semaphore Timeball Tower
136 South Neptune (Historic)
137 Troubridge Island
138 Troubridge Hill
139 Cape Spencer
140 Althorpe Island
141 West Cape
142 Wedge Island
143 Corny Point
144 Warburto Point
145 Point Lowly
146 Point Boston
147 Cape Donington
148 Dangerous Reef Centre
149 Taylor Island
150 Waterhouse Point
151 North Neptune Island
152 South Neptune Island
153 Cape Bauer

159 Four Bay
160 Cape Naturaliste
161 Casuarina Point
162 Woodman Point
163 South Mole Head (green)
164 North Mole Head (red)
165 Bathurst Point
166 Rottnest
167 Hillarys Boat Harbour
168 Guilderton
169 Escape Island
170 Pelsaert Island
171 Point Moore
172 Steep Point
173 Cape Inscription
174 Babbage Island
175 Point Quobba
176 Point Cloates
177 Vlaming Head
178 North West Cape
179 Jarman Island
180 Gantheaume Point
181 Red Bluff
182 East Lacepede Island
183 Cape Leveque
184 Caffarelli Island
185 Adele Island

Northern Territory
186 Charles Point
187 Emery Point
188 East Vernon Island
189 Cape Hotham
190 Cape Don

Queensland
191 Carpenteria Lightship
192 Booby Island
193 Western Hill
194 Restoration Rock
195 Chapman Reef
196 South Pipon Island
197 Grassy Hill
198 Archer Point
199 Low Isles
200 Island Point
201 Fitzroy Island
202 Little Fitzroy Island
203 South Brook Island
204 Townsville Leading Light
205 Wharton Reef (Historic)
206 Bay Rock (Historic)
207 Cape Cleveland
208 Cape Bowling Green
209 Eshelby Island
210 Dent Island
211 Pine Islet (Historic)
212 Great Keppel Island
213 North Reef
214 Cape Capricorn
215 East Point
216 Bustard Head
217 Lady Musgrave Islet
218 Lady Elliot Island
219 Breaksea Spit Lightship
220 Sandy Cape
221 South Head
222 Double Island Point
223 Point Cartwright
224 Cleveland Point
225 Caloundra Lights
226 Cape Moreton
227 North Point
228 Point Lookout

Lighthouses of Australia

Images from the End of an Era

John Ibbotson

Published By Australian Lighthouse Traders

First published in 2001 by Australian Lighthouse Traders
4/19 Elm Street Surrey Hills Victoria Australia.
Web address: www.lighthouses.com.au
e-mail address: lighthouses@mira.net

National Library of Australia cataloguing and publication data
Ibbotson, John, 1941 -
   Lighthouses of Australia Images from the End of an Era
   Includes 500 colour photographs of 220 lighthouses, 12 maps,
   index and a chronological list of over 400 Australian lighthouses

   ISBN 0 646-41674-X

Photographs, text and design by John Ibbotson
Cartography by Craig Molyneaux www.cartdeco.com.au
Scans by Unique Image Adelaide SA
Finished Art by Graeme Cogdell Imagart Adelaide SA imagart@ozemail.net.au
Printed in Australia by Openbook Publishers Adelaide SA www.openbook.com.au

First Edition
Reprinted, with corrections (particlarly to the Chronological List), 2004

Front cover photograph: **Sunrise, Whaler Point Lighthouse Portland Victoria**
Back cover photograph: **The Breaksea Spit Lightship CLS8 during routine
                         maintenance on 21st May 1994**

Endpapers: **Map of Australia showing the location of lighthouses appearing in the book
           with a numeric index in the front and an alpha index in the back**

Wholly produced in Australia

Acknowledgements

There have been many people over the years who have helped me in my photography and have provided information and inspiration. Without them and many others this book would never have been finished.

AMSA: Steve Andrews, Lindsay Gillies and the crew of the Cape Grafton on its maiden voyage, Beverley Atkins, Phil Badman, Laurie Campbell, Steve Clarke, Robert Cook, Alan Crossing, Clive Davidson, Jack Duvoisin, Maurice Glasson, David Gray, Rod Harris, Phil Hately, Malcolm McKenzie, Harry Nermut, Ian Oxley, Tony Ryan, John Sugarman, Geoff Welby, Ian Williams, Mark Wilson.

Lighthouse Keepers: Fred & Janet Armstrong, Owen & Brigitte Barrett, Mark & Elizabeth Bennett, Bob & Kim Carter, John & Christine Denman, Stan & Shirley Gray, Andy Gregory, John Hampson, Graeme & Jill Heynes, Richard Jermyn, Wayne, Leslie & Julie-Ann Kelly, Bob Kikwood, Pat & Judy, Travis, Shaun & Brett Howell, Steve Mundy, Ted, Anne & Alice Peers, Chris, Ailsa, Amanda, Tara & Nerissa Richter, Peter & Irene Scott, Denis Smith, Peter & Pat Sutton, David & Tina Cinzaro.

Others: John (Jack) & Jeannette Bruil, Stuart & Shirley Buchanan, Yvonne Cairns, Jack & Mary Clark, Jan Clasper, Cyril Curtain, Helen Deacon, Ron & Jill Harris, Frances Hunt, Marilyn Kenworthy, Malcolm McDonald, Grant & Tracy Maizels, Ross Meredith, Ivar Nelson, Bill & Nancy Stewart, Mark Tranter, Geoff White.

Bond Colour Laboratories who processed all my Fuji 220 transparencies and my associates at TABCORP who kept me motivated and functional after many early mornings of putting this book together.

Dedicated to the men and women who designed, built, staffed and maintained the lights.

WITH BEST WISHES TO
DEREK HARVEY

John Whitney

Cape Naturaliste Dunsborough Western Australia

Foreword

Lighthouses occupy a special place in the history of modern Australia. They stand as monuments to the transformation of the nation from a colonial outpost to a vibrant and prosperous society. For millions of people, lighthouses were the first sign of civilization after a long sea voyage to a new home. For others, they are grim reminders of the perils of the sea.

Modern technology has made many lighthouses redundant, but the buildings still evoke a special passion. They remind us of a time when ships ruled the world.

Over the past 20 years I have had the pleasure of setting foot in most of the lighthouses pictured in this book. When John Ibbotson presented his manuscript, the memories of all the people involved in building, maintaining, and manning these historic buildings came alive.

It is hard to fully appreciate the commitment and sacrifice that John has made to achieve what for him was an eight-year adventure as well as a labour of love.

John approached AMSA in 1993 determined to complete a new lighthouse pictorial history and has since circumnavigated the country by car, aircraft, ship and boat to achieve his goal.

Lighthouses of Australia, Images from the end of an Era is an invaluable collection of 500 beautiful photographs of lighthouses. It is a thoughtful and carefully compiled reference book that allows the enthusiast or casual reader alike to glean a wealth of information about Australia's lighthouses.

For anyone who is interested in the important part lighthouses have played in the development of modern Australia it will be an endless source of information. For the casual reader it provides a fascinating insight into the beauty of these picturesque landmarks.

Clive Davidson
Chief Executive Officer
Australian Maritime Safety Authority.
2001.

Preface

Lighthouse development has passed through three major cycles. The first that occurred during the first three thousand years was to build bigger, brighter and better lights that could withstand the elements and provide a reliable and powerful light. With the technology and fuels available these lights were labour intensive, costly and were limited to places where keepers could be stationed to tend them each night.

At the start of the twentieth century there was a significant change in the technology and with it the future direction of lighthouses. Gustav Dalen of Sweden perfected the storage of acetylene as a safe clean fuel and invented the 'Dalen Flasher' and the Sun Valve. These three items combined with the improvements in lenses and reflectors that occurred during the nineteenth century allowed lights to be automated. No longer were keepers required to keep the lights burning because now the lights only needed to be checked and re-fuelled every six or twelve months. This significantly reduced running costs. It also allowed lights to be placed on buoys and beacons and in places that were otherwise impractical. Even though there was an emphasis on cost reduction the number of lights proliferated during the twentieth century especially with the development of solar powered low wattage lights attached to prefabricated cabinets or buoys.

The third cycle started with the development of the first non-visual aids to navigation. These aids such as non-directional radio beacons (NDB's) that transmit a medium frequency signal in a horizontal band for up to 500km, the Decca Navigation System that uses low frequency signals and three transmission sites to provide accurate positioning information for ships and Omega that used very low frequency radio signals that could be picked up by ships or planes anywhere on earth were the first of the electronic aids. With the development of the satellite based Global Positioning System (GPS) that is used with sophisticated computer navigation systems or with simple and economical hand held devices, visual aids to navigation are really no longer necessary. As we go into the twenty first century lighthouses are approaching their use-by-date. They will not disappear as quickly as the slide rule but like the ocean going sailing ships they will gradually become less and less relevant. It will be up to people who recognise the significant historical importance of these buildings to take them over and preserve them for future generations.

The original purpose of this book was to provide a pictorial record of most of the major and many minor Commonwealth and State lights in Australia as they were at the end of the twentieth century. Although its primary purpose continues to be photographs of the lights it also provides expanded captions that may inspire the reader to find out more about particular lights and their history. There is also a section on museums displaying lighthouse artefacts and operational lights that provide organised access as well as a chronological list of over 400 Australian lights.

The photographs that are arranged in an approximate geographical order by state include many modern lights as well as the classical towers. Although the modern lights are not very photogenic their locations are often quite spectacular. It also shows how, with modern technology it has been possible to economically place lights in difficult and inaccessible locations.

In compiling this text numerous references were used. Unfortunately some of them contained or gave conflicting information; for other lights there was little if any information available.

The new (1996) GRP cabinet and the classical (1838) tower – Cape Bruny Tasmania

Table of Contents

Title Page
Author Information
Acknowledgements
Foreword
Preface
Table of Contents

Part 1: **Introduction 2-19**
   The History of Lighthouses
   Australia's Lighthouses
   Explanations

Part 2: **New South Wales 20-67**
   Index and Map
   The Lights of New South Wales

Part 3: **Victoria 68-105**
   Index and Map
   The Lights of Victoria

Part 4: **Tasmania 106-139**
   Index and Map
   The Lights of Tasmania

Part 5: **South Australia 140-169**
   Index and Map
   The Lights of South Australia

Part 6: **Western Australia & Northern Territory 170-209**
   Index of Western Australia and Northern Territory
   Map of Western Australia
   The Lights of Western Australia
   Map of Northern Territory
   The Lights of Northern Territory

Part 7: **Queensland 210-249**
   Index of Queensland
   Map of Northern Queensland
   The Lights of Northern Queensland
   Map of Southern Queensland
   The Lights of Southern Queensland

Part 8: **Lighthouse Museums 250-265**
   Index and Map
   Museums and Lighthouses

Part 9: **Appendices, Bibliography and Index 266-282**
   Appendix I   Chronological List of Major Lights
   Appendix II   Glossary
   Appendix III   Conversion from Kilometres to
                   Nautical Miles and Statute Miles
   Bibliography
   Index

Timeball Tower 1875 – Semaphore South Australia

1

The History of Lighthouses

Lights for maritime navigation have existed for more than 3,000 years. Their purpose has been to show ships where they are and to guide them into safe harbours or to warn them of rocks and reefs that could destroy them. Although preventing loss of life has always been a consideration it has been the preservation of the ships and their cargos that has been the real driving force behind lighthouse construction. They evolved from a fire on a hilltop to towers engineered to withstand any force the sea could deliver. Their lights went from a smoky flame to beams of light that could be seen for 50km. The technology progressed from constant manual attention from dusk until dawn every night to reliable, cost effective, automatic lights that only need servicing every year or two. They reached their zenith during the first half of the twentieth century but by the end of the same century their future has become uncertain. Today satellite navigation technology combined with computers has replaced the lighthouse as the safe, economic and reliable way to navigate the oceans of the world. The following is a brief history of the development of lighthouses and their technology.

The Towers

The first primitive lights, fires in bronze baskets were used along the Nile delta as early as 1,000 BC. The Colossus of Rhodes may have been used as a guiding light with lights in his eyes and in his outstretched hand but this has never been clearly established. The Pharos of Alexandria in Egypt, one of the Seven Ancient Wonders of the World, is generally regarded as the first authenticated lighthouse. Designed and built by Sostratus between 300 and 280 BC for Ptolemy the ruler of Egypt it is also the largest lighthouse ever built. Not only was the tower 137m tall but it also sat on a 110m square base that was 70m high. The first 72m high section of the tower was square with 30m sides. The next section was an octagonal tower 35m high and 17m across while the final section was a 26m cylinder 9m in diameter. It was built of stone covered with white marble and must have been an imposing sight. The fire burning in the brazier at its top could supposedly be seen for 55km. It served as an aid to mariners for 1,600 years but finally succumbed to time, invasions and a major fourteenth century earthquake.

The oldest surviving lighthouse is The Tower of Hercules that stands on a hill overlooking La Coruna Harbour on the northwest coast of Spain. Built around 20 BC by Gaius Sevius it served as a lighthouse at least through the fifth century AD when it was abandoned as the

Romans left the area. It was relit by the Spanish in 1682 and has been in service ever since. The Spanish also made extensive alterations to it removing the external ramp that wound up the outside of the tower, installing an internal staircase and strengthening the external walls. Early in the 1800's lamps and reflectors replaced the braziers. These were superseded in 1847 by a Fresnel lantern and lens with a diameter of 3.2m that is still being used.

The first lighthouse in England was built by the Romans in their fortress on the cliffs of Dover around 40 AD. Its remains can still be viewed in the precincts of Dover Castle. On the other side of the Dover Straits in France the lighthouse at Boulonge known as the Tour d'Ordre was built in 44 AD to commemorate the victory by Caligula (a mad Roman Emperor) over Neptune. The 38m 12 section octagonal tower built from red bricks and yellow and grey stone lasted for 1600 years until in 1644 it collapsed when the cliff on which it stood gave way.

In Italy the best-known lighthouse is at Genoa. Built during the twelfth century it was demolished in 1544 and rebuilt as a square, two-section brick tower. In 1449 one of the keepers was Antonio Columbus, Christopher's uncle and it may have been Antonio who piqued Christopher's interest in the sea because the rest of his family were weavers. With a total height of 61m (200') it is the tallest active classical lighthouse in the world.

(The tallest structure in the world with a navigation light on it is Tower 11 at the *Naval Communication Station Harold E. Holt* at Exmouth in Western Australia. The light is 120m (400') up a 304m (996') tower that is also used to transmit low frequency radio signals.)

The light at Meloria also in Italy and built in 1157 was the first rock or wave washed lighthouse. Although it no longer exists it was the forerunner to the famous rock lighthouses of Brittany in France and the English and Scottish lights in Great Britain. They included Grand Lejon, Pierres Noires, La Viielle, Ar-Men, Kereon and La Jument (the tower in the famous photo by Jean Guichardin of the wave breaking around the tower while the keeper stands at the door) Brittany and Bell Rock, Skerryvore, Chicken Rock, Bishop Rock, Fastnet Rock and the Eddystone lighthouses (all five of them) in Great Britain.

The first two Eddystone lights were built by Henry Winstanley. The first was a square wooden tower on a badly anchored stone base. After its first winter a second tower was built around the first. This tower lasted for five

years until it disappeared during a violent winter storm along with Winstanley who was visiting the tower at the time. John Rudyerd built the third tower in the same way that a ship's hull was constructed. The secure stone base and tower was sheathed in hardwood cladding that was caulked with oakum and covered with pitch. This tower lasted for 46 years until it burnt down. The fourth tower was built by John Smeaton. Its interlocking granite blocks and concave curves that swept the waves up and away from the tower may have lasted forever but the reef on which it was built started to disintegrate. After 122 years of service Smeaton's tower was dismantled and taken to Plymouth Hoe. The fifth tower designed by James Douglas used many of Smeaton's ideas and even improved on some such as using three dimensional interlocking granite blocks. This tower built in 1882 still stands, the only change being a helipad added to the top of the tower.

Another site that is almost as well known as Eddystone is the Bell Rock or Inchcape Rock lighthouse off the east coast of Scotland. It was the first lighthouse designed and built by the Stevenson family who over the next 150 years constructed 81 lighthouses along the Scottish coast including a number of rock lighthouses. They were also involved with the 'perfection' of the Fresnel lens continuing its development after the death of Augustin Fresnel. All of the Stevenson family were involved with the construction of lighthouses except for the 'black sheep' of the family Robert Louis Stevenson who preferred to write novels.

The next challenge in lighthouse construction was to find a way to build towers in shallow waters above a soft or sandy seabed. This was achieved with the development of pile lighthouses. These were made from either wood or iron with the piles being driven into the seabed. A platform was then built on top of the piles and the light tower and if appropriate keepers' quarters were added. At times driven piles were not feasible or satisfactory. This limitation was overcome by the invention of the Screw Pile by Alexander Mitchell an Irish engineer. This involved putting a screw-blade 1.2m in diameter at the end of the iron pile. A gang of labourers then wound them down, like a giant auger into the soft seabed. Generally there were nine screw piles, one in the centre surrounded by eight others in an octagonal pattern. The first tower of this type was built in 1841 at Maplin Sands at the mouth of London's Thames River. The USA became the largest user of the screw pile light building them in Chesapeake Bay, the Carolinas and along the Gulf coast.

Cape Otway Victoria – Chance Brothers First Order Lens

The Telescopic Tower is another and more modern way of placing a lighthouse in open water that was developed in the 1950's by Robert Gellerstad a Swedish engineer. Similar to the techniques used for building oilrigs it involves constructing the lighthouse on shore, launching it like a ship and then floating it to the site where it is sunk. The inner sections of the telescope are then raised or floated to the required height. The base is then filled with sand or concrete. Towers of this type have been placed in waters up to 18 metres deep. They are also used in waters that freeze during the winter where the tower not only has to withstand the pressures created by sea ice but they also have to resist being pushed around by the moving ice.

The dilemma of providing more navigation aids from ever diminishing budgets was partially overcome early in the twentieth century with the introduction of automated acetylene powered lights and prefabricated steel towers. It was found that steel framed towers were a fast and economical method for constructing lighthouses. Initially corrosion was a problem that was overcome with the discovery and use of stainless steel instead of the mild steel. In northern Australia frame towers along the Great Barrier Reef could easily be mistaken for telecommunication repeater stations. Replacing the acetylene cylinders though was still an expensive operation.

The next development in tower construction was the ubiquitous Glass Reinforced Plastic (GRP) cabinet that was first deployed in the

A modern 4m GRP cabinet with a solar powered Vega VRB25 acrylic lens

mid 1960's. This allowed new lights to be built on headlands, reefs or islands in just a few days. It involved the pouring of a concrete pad followed by the bolting together of the GRP panels and the installation of the light. Initially acetylene powered lights were installed but these have been replaced by the solar powered injected moulded acrylic ('Tupperware') lights. The GRP cabinets were also added to existing frame towers to hold the electrical components of today's solar powered lights. They have even been built next to existing classical towers so that the old towers with their huge lenses could be converted into museums.

Worldwide (with the exception of Russia, China and Korea) there are some 25,000 manned and unmanned lighthouses and lit beacons. Four countries (Canada, Japan, Norway and the USA) have over half of them and of those four the most are in the USA.

In the USA the first lighthouse (and the first in the New World) was built on Little Brewster Island in Boston Harbour in 1716. The British destroyed the original tower in 1776. It was rebuilt in 1784. The oldest lighthouse still in operation is the Sandy Hook light in New Jersey that was built in 1764. The tallest at 60m (196') is the Cape Hatteras light built in 1870. One of the unique characteristics of American lighthouses, particularly along the east coast is their design. Wherever possible they have incorporated the tower and the keepers' quarters into a single structure so that they look more like a New England house than a lighthouse. Overall there were about 1,500 lighthouses built in the USA (with 220 on the US shores of the Great Lakes) although the most in operation at any one time was about 850. Today there are about 600 still in existence. At their peak around 1915 there were also 72 lightships at 55 locations.

There are places, out in open water where lighthouses were needed but the technology, time or capital to construct them was not always available. The problem was overcome by anchoring a ship, equipped with a light at the site. These were often old merchant ships at the end of their commercial life. Many were not suited for the task but performed admirably. By the 1830's ships designed specifically for the task were being built. They were designed to be much more stable while anchored in rough water making life for their crews a little more bearable. The problem of them breaking their hemp anchor lines was overcome in the 1820's with the development of chain (anchor) cables. Another improvement, developed by Gustav Dalen was to attach the light to a pendulum pivoted at the centre of oscillation of the ship. This meant that the light's beam would always

remain parallel to the sea no matter how much the ship moved. Although this system worked it was found that gimbal mounted lenses were more reliable. The ships though, like the lighthouses of the time still had to have a crew. It wasn't until the lights could be automated in the early twentieth century that the lightships could be demanned. As lightships can be regarded as big buoys many have since been replaced with buoys although some still exist where ease of access for maintenance is a factor.

The Lights

The intensity produced by a modern car headlamp on high beam, using two 60-watt filaments, a moulded acrylic lens and free form reflectors is 75,000-95,000 candelas. The most powerful lighthouse in the world is at Creach, Ile D'Ouessant in France where, on misty nights a carbon arc lamp is used. This light produces an intensity of 500,000,000 candelas the equivalent of about 6,000 car headlamps.

This is a dramatic improvement over the smoky wood fires lit on open hillsides that were the first illuminated aids to navigation. These bonfires were not very effective. Even when the wood was burnt in bronze braziers the light produced was generally inadequate. Lacking an alternative source of fuel wood and sometimes coal were used for more than 3,000 years. The last wood powered light in England was not extinguished until 1832.

The use of candles goes back as far as 1540 and although they were used for over 300 years they were not very effective. Multiple candles (the first Eddystone light used a chandelier with 24 tallow candles) were also used. Their effectiveness improved when used in conjunction with reflectors but as the candle burnt below the focus of the reflector the intensity of the light diminished. Also the smoke would rapidly dull the reflector's polished surface. Once reliable oil lamps were developed the use of candles rapidly diminished.

The first smokeless oil lamp was invented by Aime Argand from Switzerland in 1782. His lamp had a hollow circular wick that allowed the air to flow up both sides of the wick. It produced a light equivalent to seven candles. The lamp was enclosed in a glass chimney (invented in France by Quinquet) and the heat generated by the lamp produced an upward draught of air through the chimney. The lamp was placed in front of a silvered copper parabolic reflector, (the catoptric system) developed by Hutchinson in 1772 and was focused to produce the optimum light. To increase the power of the light even further, lamps with up to ten concentric rings of wicks were also produced. Whale Oil, generally from the head of the sperm whale was the preferred oil but it was expensive and the most widely used oil was Colza (made from wild cabbage or rapeseed cabbage). This in turn was replaced by kerosene that became available in the 1860's.

The catoptric system of oil lamps and reflectors gave an acceptable performance that would take a considerable leap in technology to replace. This happened in 1822 when a French optician Jean Augustin Fresnel (Fray-NELL) developed the Fresnel lens. The lens, which resembles a beehive, is made up of lenses and prisms that focus a central light into a strong horizontal beam. It consists of tiers of dioptric (refracting) prisms above and below a central lens. These prisms refract the light and direct it outward through a central magnifying lens that further intensifies the light. When rotated the light was seen as a flash. This technique for concentrating the light was effective up to 45 degrees from the axis but did not capture the oblique rays produced by the lamp. To make use of the light missed by the dioptric lenses he added catadioptric (refracting-reflecting-refracting) prisms that capture the oblique rays from the light source and reflect and refract them so they too become part of the beam.

Unfortunately Fresnel died before he reached the age of 40. The Stevenson family who built most of Scotland's rock lighthouses took over the further development of Fresnel's lens. They added sloping dioptric prisms that collected the oblique light and refracted it back on to mirrors behind the lamp that in turn reflected the additional light into the main beam. Replacing the reflector with prisms that reflected the collected light back into the light source further refined the lens's performance.

Although the lens was invented in France it was an English company, Chance Brothers that perfected its manufacture. Started by Robert and James Chance in 1824 the company made glass for windows. Aided by French experts they built their first lighthouse lens in 1851. To maintain the high standard set for their lenses they then went on to build everything associated with the light from the mounting frames, turntables and burners to lantern-rooms. They even supplied complete prefabricated lighthouses.

They also came up with a standard set of lens sizes known as orders. Originally there were six orders of lens. The first order was the largest (1.8ms in diameter, 2.6ms high and weighing four tonnes) the sixth order the smallest (30cm in diameter and 40cm high). The hyper and meso radial orders were added later. The lenses were made in both rotating and stationary models. The standard orders based on the distance from the lamp to the lens are:

Hyper-radial:	1330mm
Meso-radial:	1125mm
First order:	920mm
Second order:	700mm
Third order:	500mm
Fourth order:	250mm
Fifth order:	187.5mm
Sixth order:	150mm

There was also a seventh order lens that was referred to as a three-and-a-half-order lens or a third order (small type) of 375mm.

A Chance Brothers First Order Lens – From South Solitary Island NSW now displayed in the Coffs Harbour Museum

In 1872 James Chance started an association with Dr John Hopkinson. He developed the group-flashing lens by arranging the panels of the prisms with their axes off-centre so that the flash sequence or character was easily recognisable. He also proposed the use of mercury in the turntables of the massive rotating lenses to minimise the energy needed to turn the lens. During the next 100 years Chance Brothers supplied 76 countries with more than 2,350 lights and associated equipment. After Great Britain Australia was their largest customer. As the need for large optics diminished so did the company and although it continued making small lenses for another 30 years its main plant was closed in 1955.

Today high quality glass is a common everyday commodity like the sand, soda and lime that are its prime ingredients. Although it has been used by many civilisations and is found naturally (for example as obsidian), it was not until the late eighteenth century that processes were developed to produce clear, strong, blemish free glass suitable for lighthouse lenses. Thomas Rogers made lenses from low quality window or bottle glass during the early 1780's but the lenses were of such poor quality that they actually restricted instead of enhancing the output from the light. In America Winslow Lewis produced similar results.

In the late 1780's Pierre Guinand, a Frenchman made optical quality lenses up to 23cm in diameter and by the 1820's Fresnel was making the lenses for his lights. There was a choice of two types of glass for making lighthouse lenses, Flint Glass or Crown Glass. Flint glass (crystal) is a high dispersion variety with a refractive index of more than 1.60 and although it is colourless it has the disadvantage of being softer, heavier, slightly hygroscopic (that is it can absorb moisture) and likely to have more striae (wavy lines or patches). Crown glass is a low dispersion non-hygroscopic glass that is not only harder, lighter and has less striae than flint glass but is cheaper to manufacture and easier to mould, shape and polish. In spite of having a green tinge crown glass had become the standard for the larger lenses while both types were used for the smaller ones. Chance Brothers used a glass made of French sand, lime, carbonate of soda, nitrate of soda and arsenic (that reduced the number of bubbles and the green discolouration). It had a refractive index of about 1.51.

By the end of the nineteenth century further improvements had been made to reduce the green tinge (caused by alumina and iron oxide) and to increase the refractive index to 1.54. When viewed today the lenses that were quite clear when manufactured, tend to have a yellow or amber cast. This is due to sunlight and ultraviolet light reacting with the trace elements (such as manganese and arsenic) added to the glass during the manufacturing process.

By the end of the nineteenth century the construction of classical towers and their lenses had been perfected. What was still needed was the ability to reduce the cost of running the lights hence the driving force behind lighthouse development and operation became construction and running costs. As these costs are generally paid for by commercial shipping they were anxious to have those costs reduced. It is still the major consideration today facing the deployment and operation of navigational aids. It was one of the factors motivating Gustav Dalen as he set out to automate lighthouse operations.

It was recognised in the late 1800's that acetylene (produced when calcium carbide and water are mixed) was a cleaner brighter and more reliable fuel than oil or kerosene for lighthouse lamps but it was dangerous to transport and burning it 24 hours a day wasted too much fuel. It was a number of inventions by Gustav Dalen, born in Sweden in 1869, that overcame these limitations and meant that lights at sea could be safely and reliably automated. First Dalen perfected the method of purifying and drying acetylene and then storing it in acetone so that it could be safely transported. Secondly in 1906 he invented the 'Dalen Flasher' a device that only took gas during the flash of the light although a small pilot light was constantly burning. This reduced gas consumption by more than 80%. His third invention in 1907 was the 'Sun Valve' a device that turned off the gas during daylight hours thus reducing gas usage by a further 50%. These three developments meant that lights only needed to be serviced once or twice a year with the result that lightships and many lighthouses could be demanned and that lit buoys could be deployed. This equipment was sold through Dalen's company 'AB Gasaccumulator' better known as AGA. Until the advent of solar cells and microelectronics Dalen's devices were the standard for lighthouse lights. In 1912 Dalen's work on the Sun Valve earned him the Nobel Prize for Physics. Unfortunately before receiving the award an experiment went wrong and left him permanently blind. Even with this handicap he continued inventing and innovating at AGA up until his death in 1937. Some of his later inventions included an automatic mantle changer and a rotating array that was turned by the pressure of the gas coming out of the cylinder.

The first electrically powered lighthouse was at Dungeness in England where, in 1862 an on site generator powered a carbon arc lamp. By 1893 there were at least 13 installations in France, six in Britain and the Macquarie light in Australia that had their own generators. As they were not economical most were replaced with kerosene or acetylene lamps.

The first electric filament light to be installed in England was at South Foreland in 1922. This was the start of the next phase of lighthouse development and cost reduction. Kerosene and acetylene lights were, wherever possible converted to electricity. The electric lights could be run off city power or if they were in remote sites comparatively small diesel generators could be used to generate the necessary power. As the light source was now quite small but up to ten times as powerful as the lamps they replaced, the large lenses were no longer required although many were adapted to the new lamps. The power of the lamps is infinitely variable too and ranges from less than ten watts for buoys up to 3,000 watts for major landfall lights. Enclosed Xenon discharge lamps are also used. At Tiri Tiri lighthouse in Auckland New Zealand a 2,000-watt lamp produces an intensity of 11,000,000 candelas while one in Florida USA produces 27,000,000 candelas. The most powerful light in Australia is Cape Byron that produces 2,200,000 candelas from a 1000 watt lamp.

The next step was to find a way to provide electric power to lights and buoys that could not physically or economically be powered by city power or generators. The answer was the solar cell used in conjunction with the small self-contained acrylic apparatus irreverently referred to as a 'Tupperware' light. The solar panel revolution started during the 1970's with the first one in Australia being installed at Hammond Island in Queensland in 1981. By the late 1990's all Australian lights and buoys were either mains or solar powered, a complete transformation in less than 20 years. This story has been repeated many times over around the world.

Other Devices

As well as lights there have been a number of other non-optical aids used to assist mariners. The first were **foghorns** that were developed late in the nineteenth century. They were used where lights could be obscured by low cloud or fog. Chance Bothers was one of the companies involved in the manufacture of these powerful air driven devices and one of their few remaining foghorns in operational condition is at Low Head lighthouse in Tasmania.

Next came **non-directional radio beacons** (NDB's). They transmit a medium frequency signal in a horizontal band for up to 500km over water. When picked up by a receiver on a ship it could be used as a homing beacon or, if the signal from two or more beacons could be read it allowed the ships position to be calculated. They have, in general been replaced by GPS navigation aids. Another radio signal device was the **Decca Navigation System** that uses low frequency signals and three transmission sites to provide accurate positioning information for ships up to 500km from the transmitters. Two of these systems were set up at the Pilbara region of Western Australia to guide the giant bulk carriers through the shallow approaches to the ports in the area. These have now been replaced by a chain of buoys that extend out along the channels to deep water.

**The Goose Island Tasmania Apparatus –
Now displayed in the Maritime Museum of Tasmania**

The **Omega Long Range Navigation System** used very low frequency radio signals to provide relatively accurate (within 4 km) location information to ships (or planes) anywhere around the world. This was achieved by the ship or plane reading the unique time co-ordinated signals from three or more of the eight transmission stations. From each pair (one station could be common to both) it could calculate where it was on a curved line between the two stations. Its position was where the lines crossed. The eight transmission towers (that were up to 430 metres tall) were located in Norway, Liberia, Reunion Island, Japan, Argentina, Australia and Hawaii and North Dakota in the USA. With the introduction and acceptance of the GPS system it was determined that Omega was no longer needed. It was closed down in 1997 and a number but not all of the towers were demolished. The Australian tower at Darriman in Victoria (that is still the tallest man-made structure in the Southern Hemisphere) is now being used to transmit messages to naval ships in Australian waters.

Marine Radar Beacons or **Racons** can only be used over a comparatively short distance (20–40km) but are useful where the surroundings are featureless or where there is a confusing profusion of nav aids. The racon has an ultra high frequency radar receiver/transmitter. On receiving a pulse from the ship the racon returns a similar pulse of a higher power along with an inbuilt identification code. This allows the ship to accurately display the position of the racon on its radar screen. Where the cost of a racon is not justified **Passive Radar Reflectors** are often installed on buoys or beacons that ensure that a radar signal is bounced back to its source. They are flat panels added to the buoy or beacon whose regular surfaces are usually rounded and not suitable for reflecting radar signals.

The Global Positioning System (GPS)
GPS is a satellite based navigation system that provides precise position, velocity and time information. Developed by and for the United States Department of Defence during the 1980's at a cost of 10 billion dollars it is now available to the public. The basis of the GPS system is twenty-four 863kg NAVSTAR satellites that orbit the earth twice daily at a radius of approximately 17,700km. Of these 21 make up the operational system while the remaining three are spares that can be moved into position as replacements when required. The other part of the system are the system control centres and the receivers that are on ships or planes, taxis or in backpacks and which cost as little as a hundred dollars.

Essentially GPS is based on satellite ranging or triangulation using four or more of the satellites. To do this the exact position of the satellite must be known. As they are constantly moving in their twice-daily orbit it is crucial that time can be measured precisely so that their position is always known. This is done with one of the four on-board atomic clocks that are accurate to better than 1/100th of a second. As well as keeping track of where they are the satellites are also continuously transmitting a unique code that can be read by the receiver.

The GPS receiver measures the time of arrival of the signals from the four satellites yielding a pseudo-range measurement to each. The receiver then solves for latitude, longitude, altitude and exact time. For triangulation three satellite readings should be enough for the receiver to calculate its exact three-dimensional position on the earth's surface. It's not. This is because the receiver's clock is not accurate (atomic clocks cost a lot of money and are bulky), nor would it be prudent to assume that the receiver's clock was synchronised with those in the satellites. To overcome this the reading from a fourth satellite is obtained so that the receiver can adjust its time until it is synchronised with those in the satellites. As ships already know their altitude and only need a two-dimensional reading they can get by using three satellites although a fourth satellite will improve the accuracy of the fix. The system gives a positional accuracy of about 15 metres.

The accuracy can be improved further by using **Differential GPS (DGPS)**. This involves using two or more receivers simultaneously one of which is a base station whose precise position is known. The base station calculates its position using the satellites and compares it to its known position. From this a correction factor can be calculated. It is then transmitted (usually via UHF/VHF/HF radios) to the DGPS receivers that can adjust their calculated position by the correction factor. This will be improved by having the base stations transmit the correction factors back through the satellites so that the receivers will no longer need separate data transmission devices. DGPS improves the positioning accuracy to around three metres.

Accurate marine charts are now available for literally the whole of the earth's watery surface. These charts have also been computerised and in conjunction with GPS can display the exact position of a ship on the screen. They can also sound alarms if the ship is approaching dangerous rocks or reefs. When connected to the controls of the ship it even allows the ship to be sailed on automatic pilot over any predetermined course in any kind of weather. The future is here.

Just as there were improvements in the visual navigation aids there have also been continual and rapid improvements in non-visual aids culminating with the GPS system. Although GPS and DGPS will continue to evolve they have already reached the point where all other forms of navigational aids are superfluous. It is only their existing momentum, sentimentality and resistance to change that keeps the visual navigation aids operational. It is indeed the end of an era.

Cave Point Lighthouse - Albany Western Australia

Macquarie Lighthouse Outer South Head Sydney NSW

Australia's Lighthouses

Australia was 'discovered' by Lt. James Cook in 1770 even though Dutch and Portuguese sailors had sailed along the west coast 150 years earlier and the Aborigines had been trading with the islands to the north for possibly thousands of years. It was Cook's voyage though that initiated the European settlement of Australia. The only way for people and supplies to reach Australia was by sea. Ships would leave England and sail out of sight of land for weeks or months. It is not surprising that on reaching land it was often difficult to know exactly where they were or how they could find their way safely into port. The notorious weather in the Southern Ocean did not help. As a result many ships and many lives were lost particularly around Tasmania and Victoria although a number of ships also foundered on the west coast. Once George Bass and Matthew Flinders found that there was a passage between Van Diemen's Land (Tasmania) and New South Wales (now Victoria) in 1798 the captains preferred to weave their way through the narrow island studded passage instead of taking the longer and rougher route south of Tasmania. Although it was obvious that lights were needed to guide the ships through the treacherous waters of southern Australia only ten landfall and highway lights were built during the first 60 years of settlement. After that the number built increased dramatically so that today there are still over 350 in operation.

Colonial Lights through 1860

The decisions relating to aids to navigation in Australian waters were, at least in theory made by the Colonial Office or the Board of Trade in London until the passing of the Commonwealth Navigation Act of 1912. Even when the eastern states were granted self-government in the 1850's (Western Australia remained a crown colony until 1890) navigation was still considered to be an imperial matter. This did have some merit as it ensured that the lights that were built were recorded at a central location and that they had unique operating and visual characteristics so that there could be no confusion as to the light's identity. The Board also had the power to levy taxes to be used for the construction and operation of the colonial lights. During this 70-year period the overall number of lights built was small with only 14 coastal and harbour lights being built in the first 60 years although by the end of the period ten years later the number had risen to 37. It usually took a major shipwreck to motivate the Board to act.

In Australia the first illuminated beacon was a fire in a tripod mounted iron basket erected at South Head in Sydney in 1794. Although a fire had been lit on South Head for the *Bellona* on January 15th 1793. The first lighthouse designed by the convict architect Francis Greenway was the Macquarie light built in 1817 and first exhibited on November 30th 1818. It was commissioned by the governor, Major General Lachlan Macquarie without approval from London. He also named it after himself. It was built from inferior sandstone that rapidly deteriorated and was replaced in 1883 by a nearly identical tower designed by James Barnet. Benjamin Boyd an early land developer built the next lighthouse tower in NSW in 1846. Unfortunately the light was never lit and the tower was only used for whale watching. It was not until 40 years after the Macquarie light was built that additional NSW lights were constructed. These lights, built in 1858 were Fort Denison in Sydney Harbour, Hornby on South Head and Nobby's Head in Newcastle. These were followed in the 1860's by the Lookout Point light in Eden and the Cape St George light on Jervis Bay that was, unfortunately built in the wrong place.

Surprisingly many of the early lights, six of the first dozen, were built in Tasmania. These were the Iron Pot in Storm Bay (built in 1832 and rebuilt in 1833), Low Head (1833), Cape Bruny (1838), Swan Island (1845), Goose Island (1846) and Deal Island (1848). The Iron Pot, a state harbour light is Australia's oldest tower still in existence and also the oldest lighthouse still in operation. The oldest coastal tower still standing is Cape Bruny and the oldest coastal light still in operation in its original tower is Swan Island's.

The first lights in Victoria were the Timeball tower at Williamstown (1840), the Shortland Bluff light at Queenscliff (1843) and the landfall light at Cape Otway (1848) that marks the entrance into Bass Strait. This was followed by Gabo Island (1853), the Eastern Light at McCrae (1854), Whaler Point in Portland, Middle Island at Warrnambool, Cape Schanck near Flinders, and South East Point at Wilson's Promontory all in 1859.

In South Australia the first lights were the Cape Willoughby (1852) and Cape Borda (1858) lights both on Kangaroo Island, the Troubridge Shoal light (1856) and the original Cape Northumberland tower (1859). In Western Australia there were the Rottnest Island light built in 1851 and the Breaksea Island and Point King lights built in 1858. Only two lights were built in Queensland by

1860 these being Cleveland Point near Brisbane built in 1847 and the Cape Moreton light in 1857. The first light in the Northern Territory, Charles Point, was not built until 1893.

The first lightship was a schooner called *Rose* that was moored at the northwest end of the Sow and Pigs Reef in Sydney Harbour in 1836. This was followed in 1842 by the *Ville de Bordeaux* an old whaling vessel stationed at the mouth of the Port River in Port Adelaide. In 1853 a lightship was positioned in the West Channel of Port Phillip Bay while in Queensland there was a lightship stationed at the mouth of the Brisbane River in 1857.

State Lights through 1915

Although London continued to be involved in decisions relating to lighthouses after the States were granted self-government in the 1850's it was the States that made the final determination as to when and where lights would be established. In the mid 1850's the eastern states (Queensland, New South Wales, Victoria and Tasmania) under the leadership of Sir William Denison the Governor of NSW attempted to create a single control body for the landfall and highway lights but failed due to difficulties on how the costs would be allocated. As a result each state was left to cover the cost of any lights along its own coast with some cost sharing for lights (such as Gabo Island) that were close to common borders. This still put an unfair burden on Tasmania that had a large number of lights that were, in general used by ships going to the other States. It took until 1873 until an acceptable compromise was reached. This included special consideration being given to the costs of the lights in Torres Strait, Bass Strait and the Cape Leeuwin and Tasman Island lights. With this agreement in place the States particularly NSW and Queensland undertook extensive building programs.

This was the era when Francis Hixson was president of the NSW Marine Board and James Barnet designed most of his lights including the new Macquarie light, Barranjoey Head, Seal Rocks, South Solitary Island and his last light, Smoky Cape. By 1900 the NSW coast was 'illuminated like a street with lamps'. In Queensland the lights included North Reef, Cape Cleveland, Dent Island, Double Island Point, Booby Island and the original Archer Point. All were lights of significant architectural, social and historical significance and it is essential that those still remaining be preserved for future generations.

After 1901 when it became clear that all the coastal lights were going to be taken over by the Federal Government the States went on a building spree knowing that the lights they built would be maintained by the Commonwealth. In Western Australia most of its lights including Cape Naturaliste, Cape Inscription, Gantheaume Point, Cape Leveque and Vlaming Head were built during this period. So by 1915 when the Commonwealth assumed responsibility for the coastal lights over 100 new lights had been constructed. This resulted in a nearly unbroken string of lights that stretched from the Eyre Peninsula in South Australia to Cooktown in Queensland. Although a number of lights were built along the Western Australian coast there were, and still are large stretches of the western coastline without lights. There were not any lights across the Great Australian Bight between Ceduna in South Australia and Esperance in Western Australia either but they were not needed.

The Commonwealth Lighthouse Service through 1990

Prior to Federation all lighthouses were the responsibility of the various States. In 1901 the Australian Constitution provided the Commonwealth with the power to make laws with respect to 'lighthouses, lightships, beacons and buoys' and allowed for the transfer of those facilities to the Commonwealth. The Lighthouse Act of 1911, that went into effect in 1915 achieved this although the States retained the ownership and responsibility for harbour lights. While the Commonwealth coastal and landfall lights were under the control of a single department the State aids to navigation were generally controlled and maintained by each individual port that reported to an overall state authority.

When the Commonwealth took over in 1915 it was responsible for 104 manned lights, 18 automatic lights and 57 other beacons and buoys. Since then with the development of automated lights and economical construction methods the number of lights around the coast effectively doubled. This has been achieved while costs have, in real terms actually decreased. The majority of the new lights have been for the ports serving the bulk ore ships in the west and along Torres Strait and the Inside Passage of Great Barrier Reef in the northeast. They are bland functional and soulless towers with names like Bramble Cay, Long Spit, Palfrey Island and Bet Reef. They are stainless steel frame towers, concrete blockhouses or GRP cabinets originally equipped with small acetylene lights that have now been converted to solar powered FA 251 or ML 300 (Tupperware) lights. From the 200 lights built

since 1915 there are only a small number that have the classical lines of earlier times.

Other Commonwealth initiatives included building and commissioning four unmanned lightships around 1920 that were replaced in the early 1980's and three purpose built lighthouse maintenance ships or tenders that were built in the late 1920's and that were replaced with three new ships in the early 1960's. Also since 1915 other navigational innovations that have come and gone including radio beacon transmitters, the Decca Navigation Chains in Western Australia and Omega the original worldwide navigation system. Still operational are the radar transponders (racons) and the GPS and DGPS systems. It also seemed that the name of the department changed as often as the technologies being used. Since starting out as the Department of Trade and Customs in 1915 the Administration went through ten name changes before adopting its current title of the Australian Maritime Safety Authority (AMSA) in 1991. Although the names and the technology altered the objective of the successive Administrations to provide reliable and cost effective aids to navigation for commercial shipping in Australian waters never wavered.

to navigation AMSA is responsible for ship survey and regulatory matters, crewing, safety, protecting the marine environment and co-ordinating marine search and rescue operations.

Since its inception AMSA have completed a number of navigation initiatives many of which have been in progress ever since the Commonwealth Lighthouse Service was established in 1915. These initiatives include:

- The electrification and automation of all lights in Australian waters using either mains power or solar energy
- The demanning and if necessary downgrading of all remaining manned lightstations
- The replacement of the three lighthouse tenders with a single ship
- The elimination of lightships
- The construction of appropriate DGPS ground stations
- The disposal of the lightstation properties to state or private ownership
- The outsourcing of all aids to navigation construction and maintenance operations, including the selling and leaseback of the lighthouse tender.

The 1990's and Beyond

In 1989 the Minister for Transport and Communications announced that a new statutory authority would replace the Commonwealth Lighthouse Service. The **Australian Maritime Safety Authority (AMSA)** commenced operation in January 1991. It brings together all of the activities relating to marine management. In addition to constructing, maintaining and upgrading aids

In 2001 there are more aids to navigation than ever before with Stainer Island and Maxwell Reef both in Queensland being built in 2000. With the increase in marine tourism along the Kimberley coast in northern Western Australia it is possible but unlikely that additional lights will still be added along that rugged coastline. Today's lights are more efficient and reliable than at any time in the history of lights. They are at their peak. Yet their ongoing maintenance has been structured so that they can go into decline as the need for them diminishes. The creeping darkness of extinguished lights will take place without a whimper.

Lighthouse Automation

From its inception the Commonwealth Lighthouse Service had a policy of reducing costs. The most savings could be achieved by replacing manned stations with automatic lights. This could only be done once a clean and reliable light source that could be turned on and off automatically was available. Acetylene gas and electric power, both discovered in the second half of the nineteenth century, had potential but it was not until early in the twentieth century that reliable ways of using them safely and economically were developed.

Acetylene was difficult and dangerous to transport and store until Gustav Dalen around the start of the twentieth century found that it could, under high pressure be dissolved in acetone. He also developed the 'Dalen Flasher' and the 'Sun Valve'. These three inventions made light automation possible. The technology was quickly adopted and implemented throughout Australia. The tungsten filament lamp that had been

perfected around the same time made electric lights a viable option as long as there was a reliable source of power. For lights that had access to mains power this was easily achieved. It was also cost effective to install generators to power the large landfall lights. But it was not possible to power the small remote lights and buoys with electric lamps until solar panels and acrylic lenses (Tupperware lights) were developed. In 1981 Hammond Island in Torres Strait Northern Queensland was the first light in Australia to be powered by solar panels.

As a result, during the 1920's and beyond a large number of lights were automated and demanned. Those that continued to be manned were generally major landfall lights that used diesel powered generators to provide the power needed to service the large and powerful Fresnel style lights with their high wattage lamps. With a continued pressure to reduce costs and the availability of reliable and efficient solar cells it was decided to automate and if necessary reduce the range of the remaining manned lights even if this resulted in the need to build additional lights. Generally it involved the installation of a small solar powered Tupperware light in the existing tower although in some cases a new tower was built beside the old one. In two instances a completely new light had to be built between two existing lighthouses to fill in the void created by the downsizing of the

adjacent lights whose looms no longer overlapped. These were the Little Rame Head light built between Gabo Island and Point Hicks in Victoria and the Whales Head light between Bruny Island and Maatsuyker Island in Tasmania.

Demanning

Commercial ships that no longer need to use the visual aids to navigation cover many of AMSA's costs for these devices. Two of the most effective ways to reduce costs was to convert all the lights to electrical power and to finish demanning the remaining manned lights. When AMSA took over in 1991 there were still 25 lights out of the original 104 that had lighthouse keepers. The following schedule was established to complete the demanning process.

Although some delays, usually involving the future ownership of the lights, were encountered all the lights were demanned before the end of 1996. The last official head keeper, Chris Richter retired from Maatsuyker Island on 22nd August 1996 and was given a farewell by AMSA on 21st March 1997. Since then there have been non-AMSA people living at these lightstations. Some have been involved in collecting weather data, some as tour guides or private accommodation operators and many are National Park employees. None are Lighthouse Keepers.

Cape Nelson Portland Victoria

Demanning Schedule

Year	Station	Target Date	Factors to be Considered.
1991/92	Althorpe Island, SA	Dec 91	
	Double Island Point, Qld	Feb 92	
	Green Cape, NSW	Jun 92	Build a new lattice tower
	Deal Island, Tas	Jul 92	Build new lights at North East and Southwest Islands
	Cape Willoughby, SA	Aug 92	
	Booby Island, Qld	Aug 92	
	Cape Leeuwin, WA	Sep 92	
1993/94	Point Hicks, Vic	Dec 93	Build a new light at Little Rame Head
	Low Isles, Qld	Dec 93	
	Gabo Island, Vic	Dec 93	Build a new light at Little Rame Head
	Wilsons Promontory, Vic	Dec 93	
	Cape Bruny, Tas	Dec 93	Build a new GRP tower
			Build a new light at Whales Head
	Point Perpendicular, NSW	Dec 93	Build a new lattice tower
	Cape Otway, Vic	Dec 93	Build a new GRP tower
	Cape Moreton, Qld	Feb 94	
	Sandy Cape, Qld	Mar 94	
1994/95	Eddystone Point, Tas	Jul 95	
	Cape Schanck, Vic	Jul 95	
	Cape Naturaliste, WA	Jul 95	
	Sugarloaf Point, NSW	Jul 95	
	Norah Head, NSW	Jul 95	
	Smoky Cape, NSW	Jul 95	
	Low Head, Tas	Jul 95	
	Cape Nelson, Vic	Aug 95	
	Maatsuyker Island, Tas	Dec 95	Build a new GRP tower

Lighthouse Tenders

Prior to the Commonwealth taking over the responsibility for the landfall and highway lights State Government steamers carried out the construction, maintenance and resupply of all offshore and remote onshore aids to navigation. To provide periodic maintenance to the lights that were otherwise inaccessible three lighthouse tenders were built in the Cockatoo Island Shipyard in Sydney between 1925 and 1931. The three ships were the *Cape York* and the *Cape Leeuwin* built in 1925 and the slightly smaller *Cape Otway* built in 1931. They were based in Brisbane, Melbourne and Fremantle. It was planned to build these ships starting in 1914 but World War I delayed their construction. During the interim the Commonwealth chartered and then bought the Victorian lighthouse tender, *Lady Loch* in

1915 and the South Australian lighthouse tender *Governor Musgrave* in 1916. It also acquired the *Kyogle* in 1924. In addition two smaller ships, the *A. H. Swingle* and the *Wallach* were constructed during the 1940's for service in Torres Strait and Papua New Guinea. They were replaced in 1974 by the *Lumen* that was based in Cairns and the *Candela* based in South Australia.

The 1920's Cape ships were replaced with the *Cape Don* and the *Cape Moreton* in 1963 and the *Cape Pillar* in 1964. They were built in the State Dockyard in Newcastle NSW. As the number of manned stations were automated and demanned, along with improvements in technology and the ability to service lights by helicopter the need for tender ships also diminished. The *Cape Don* and the *Cape Pillar* were sold off in 1990 and the *Cape Moreton* in

1993. The smaller ships were also decommissioned. Their tasks were taken over by the *Cape Grafton* that began service in April 1994. Built in Spain the *Cape Grafton* was originally going to be a Russian fishing trawler. Before leaving for Australia it was modified for use as a tender or as an oceanic research vessel. With the continued demanning, automation and installation of reliable solar powered lights even a single lighthouse tender was only being used for four or five months a year. Hence it was decided to sell the ship and then lease it back for the time required to carry out necessary work. So in June 2000 it was sold to P&O and then leased it back for 600 days over the next five years. P&O renamed the ship the *Southern Supporter*.

**The Crew of the Cape Grafton
on its maiden working voyage
18th May 1994 – 14th June 1994**

Rear: Lyn Carter, Steve Andrews (Captain), Bob Landsdowne, Steve Harris, Greg Sinclair, Merv Hagner, Brent Walpole, Rodney O'Leary, Ken Herble, Bryan Payne, Ivan McGuire, Phil Hutchinson
Front: Ian Mann, David Samulenok, Bernie Ruddy, Robert McKay, Barry Moore, John Baker, Darren McDonald, Ian Dickman, George Lilja, Ian McCarthy, Bruce Noble, Frank Rochford, Ian Workman
Not present: Bob McManamon and Philip Welland

The *MV Cape Grafton* (Above and top left) **and after being renamed the *Southern Supporter*** (Top right)

Lightships

Lightships or 'floating lighthouses' have been used around Australia from early in the nineteenth century. Some were only on site temporarily until a permanent lighthouse was built. Others were long time fixtures. The first lightship was a schooner called *Rose* that in 1836 was moored at the northwest end of the Sow and Pigs Reef in Sydney Harbour. A ship called *Bramble,* the first of two with that name replaced the *Rose*. A buoy finally replaced the ship in 1912.

In Victoria lightships were located at various points around Port Phillip Bay. One was stationed at the north end of the West Channel from 1853 until the West Channel Pile light was built in 1881. At the south end of the West Channel at Swan Spit there was a lightship there from 1856 until 1860, then a pile light, then two other lightships between 1881 and 1894. Three different ships were stationed at Gellibrand Point between 1859 and 1906 when the Gellibrand lighthouse was built. There was also a lightship at Bird Rock in the North Channel of Corio Bay Geelong from 1857 until 1893.

For Light's Passage at the mouth of the Port River in Port Adelaide South Australia two references gave two slightly different stories. The first indicated that the *Ville de Bordeaux* an old whaling vessel was the first lightship placed at Light's Passage in 1842 followed by the *Fitzjames* in 1851 that remained on site until 1869 when the Port Adelaide light was first exhibited. The second reference said that the *Lady Wellington* was moored near Light's Passage in 1840 followed by the former paddle steamer *Courier* and then by the *Ville de Bordeaux*. There were also acting lightships at Glenelg and Semaphore as well as one at Wonga Shoal from 1912 until 1926. In Spencer Gulf a lightship, the *Alexander* was stationed at Tipara Reef in 1865. It was replaced by a new vessel in 1872 that remained on site until the lighthouse was built there in 1877. There was also a lightship at Lowly Point prior to the lighthouse being built in 1883 and one at Middle Bank Shoal from 1896 until 1912.

Unlike the other states Queensland had coastal and harbour lightships. There were lightships in Moreton Bay at the Brisbane River Bar from 1857 to 1883 including the *Rose* that was originally stationed at the Sow and Pigs in Sydney Harbour. At Breaksea Spit north of Fraser Island there have been unmanned lightships or temporary buoys stationed there between 1918 and 1999. Near Rockhampton there was a lightship at Keppel Bay from the mid 1860's until the mid 1890's and also one at the Upper Flats in the Fitzroy River. Two were stationed at Claremont Island and Piper Island at the eastern tip of Cape York from the mid 1870's until 1918 and at Proudfoot Shoal in Torres Strait from 1883 until 1904. There was also one for a short period at the mouth of the Norman River in the Gulf of Carpentaria. There were unmanned lightships at Carpentaria Shoal southwest of Booby Island from 1918 until they were replaced by a buoy in 1999. In 1901 the Pipon Island light took over from the lightship stationed at Channel Rock in Princess Charlotte Bay that disappeared with all hands in 1899. In those early days all of the lightships were manned. Being on a ship, anchored for weeks or months on end, usually in a rough piece of water, must have been the hardest assignment for any lighthouse keeper. Fortunately with the advent of acetylene powered, automatic lights crews were no longer required.

When the Commonwealth took over the responsibility for non-harbour lights in 1915 one of its first actions was to commission the building of four unmanned lightships. These four ships (CLS1 – CLS4) were built at Cockatoo Island in Sydney between 1916 and 1918. They were stationed in Queensland at Breaksea Spit 43kms NNE of Sandy Cape, Carpentaria Shoal 94kms southwest of Booby Island and for a time at Merkara Shoal northwest of Booby Island. The fourth ship was kept in reserve.

On the 6th of June 1962 the *Breaksea Spit* was hit by the *Gladstone Star* and sank. It not only resulted in the Federal Government suing the ship's owners for 81,309 pounds but it also meant that a buoy was used at Breaksea Spit when the one lightship there was being serviced. Then during cyclone Greta in January 1979 the lightship at Carpentaria Shoal broke its moorings and was wrecked near Crab Island on the west coast of Cape York. This left two lightships, one at Carpentaria Shoal and one at Breaksea Spit. The latter was moved north to become the backup ship at Carpentaria Shoal and a buoy was stationed at Breaksea Spit. As the buoy was not as effective as a radar target the first permanent racon in Australia was installed at Sandy Cape.

During 1981-1983 four new lightships (CLS5 – CLS8) using an English design were built at the Ocean Shipyards in Fremantle Western Australia. Their acetylene powered third order Fresnel lights with ground glass lenses and prisms were visible for 19km. The light assembly was gimbal-mounted to provide stability during rough weather although the atrocious Bass Strait weather highlighted the limitations of this approach. As a result they were all converted to a fixed light with a range of 17km. They also had Racon capability. Two were stationed at Carpentaria Shoal and Breaksea Spit and two were used for traffic separation duties south of the Bass Strait oil fields. One of the old ships, CLS4 was also moved to Bass Strait as a relief vessel.

Once high-powered strobes and racons were installed on two of the drilling rigs in 1985-1986 the vessels were no longer required in Bass Strait. The two new lightships became the backup vessels at Carpentaria Shoal and Breaksea Spit while the old CLS4 was restored and moved to Darling Harbour in Sydney where it became the first floating exhibit at the Australian National Maritime Museum. The other remaining original ship, the CLS2 was also restored and is on display at the Queensland Maritime Museum in Brisbane.

During the early 1990's the lightships were converted to solar power. Increasing maintenance costs and commercial shipping acceptance saw another buoy replace the Breaksea Spit lightships in 1999. Until their fate was determined the ships, CLS7 and CLS8 were moored off Bundaberg. As it was not economical to move them to some maritime museum, let alone restore them they were donated to the Bundaberg and District Artificial Reef Association. The ships were then 'environmentally cleaned' and, on the 23rd September 2000 they were scuttled as part of the Cochrane Artificial Reef off Elliot Heads near Bundaberg.

Also in 1999 the Carpentaria Shoal ships CLS5 and CLS6 were removed from service and were replaced by a buoy. The ships were anchored in Normanby Sound adjacent to Goods Island until November 2000 when they were scuttled near the Great North East Channel to form part of another man-made reef. It is unfortunate that at least one of these last four vessels was not kept for restoration and display although the lanterns from the vessels were removed by AMSA prior to the ships being sunk. These are now being displayed at the Torres Strait Historical Museum on Thursday Island, the Burnett Shire Council Chambers in Bagara and at the Bundaberg Port Authority in Bundaberg.

Ownership Changes

Up until 1990 when lightstations were demanned the Commonwealth generally retained ownership of the lightstation. One notable exception was Swan Island in Tasmania that was sold to a private individual. When remote lightstations were demanned the infrastructure, except for the tower was often removed so that it would not deteriorate and

The Carpentaria Lightship prior to scuttling in 2000 (Top) **and the Breaksea Spit Lightship CLS 8 during maintenance in 1994** (Bottom)

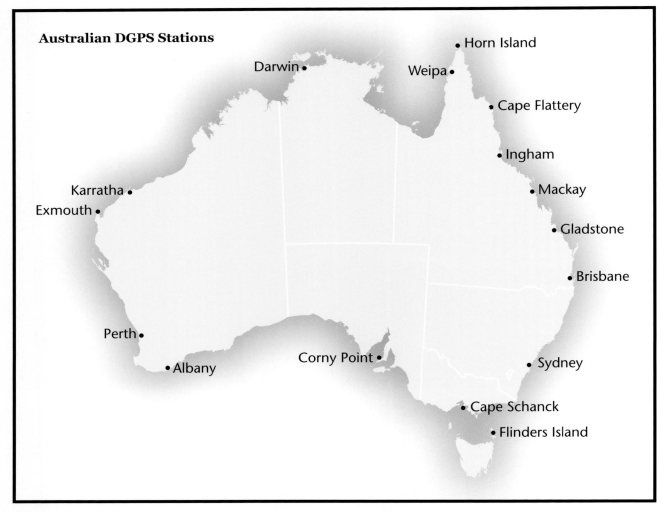

Australian DGPS Stations

Horn Island
Darwin
Weipa
Cape Flattery
Ingham
Karratha
Mackay
Exmouth
Gladstone
Brisbane
Perth
Corny Point
Sydney
Albany
Cape Schanck
Flinders Island

to Australian Maritime Systems (AMS) headquartered in Brisbane. Fortunately AMS is made up of people who had previously worked for AMSA's Operations and Engineering Business Unit so there is at least continuity associated with the maintenance procedures. Their contract commenced at the end of March 2001. As part of this consolidation the maintenance and re-supply vessel, the *Cape Grafton* was sold to P&O in June 2000 and contracted back for about four months per year. P&O renamed the ship the *Southern Supporter*. AMSA's role in relation to aids to navigation is now network planning and regulation.

The final years were hectic for the remaining staff. There was a concerted effort to ensure that all the lights and particularly the historical lights were in the best possible condition prior to the work being outsourced. Most lights were, as a minimum painted during this period. Other lights had extensive preventative maintenance done on them. Gabo and Cliffy Islands, two exceptional granite towers both had all their joints re-pointed with new mortar. For Gabo this was a nine-week undertaking.

become a hazard to people visiting the station. Examples of this are Point Charles in the Northern Territory, Cliffy Island in Victoria and Goose Island in Tasmania. When it came to demanning the accessible historic lights along the coastline it was decided to convey the lightstations, including their towers to state or private ownership. AMSA then leased back the towers except where a new tower was built for exhibiting the light. This was done at Point Perpendicular and Green Cape in NSW, Cape Bruny and Maatsuyker Island in Tasmania and Cape Otway in Victoria. Generally the stations were taken over by the States that in turn assigned them to their Park Authorities. (An exception was Point Lowly in South Australia that was taken over by the Whyalla City Council.) As a result the responsibility for preservation of these lightstations, most of which are on the Australian Heritage Commission's Register of National Estate has been handed over to the States.

DGPS

During the late 1990's and into 2001 AMSA installed a network of 16 Differential Global Positioning System (DGPS) stations around Australia that cover the critical areas of Australia's coast including the major ports, Bass Strait, Torres Strait and the Great Barrier Reef. The stations are located in Sydney, Cape

Schanck (the first station), Flinders Island, Corny Point, Albany, Perth, Exmouth, Karratha, Darwin, Weipa, Horn Island, Cape Flattery, Ingham, Mackay, Gladstone, and Brisbane. These stations provide coverage for most of Australia's major shipping routes and allow the ships to accurately determine their position to within three metres. With this kind of accuracy that can be determined in any kind of weather conditions the decreasing importance of lighthouses can be easily seen.

Outsourcing Operations and Engineering

From the outset one of the major activities for the Commonwealth Lighthouse Service was to build, maintain and resupply the lights. With automation, technological changes and demanning the effort required to fulfil these tasks has diminished. As a result there has always been a steady reduction in the size of the staff and facilities assigned to this task. By 1998 the number of Operations and Engineering Administrations for the whole of Australia had been reduced to one with the head office in Brisbane. There were still depots in Cairns, Brisbane, Melbourne, Hobart, Adelaide and Perth plus the lighthouse tender *Cape Grafton*. In 2000 it was announced that the whole maintenance and construction areas would be disbanded by March 2001 and the work outsourced. The contract was awarded

Phil Hately and Laurie Campbell carrying out external maintenance on the tower at Cliffy Island Victoria

The Future

The Deal Island tower is perched on a cliff top 280 metres above sea level. It is the highest lighthouse in the Southern Hemisphere. Although its height would appear to be an advantage it isn't. Even on clear nights cloud would often form around the tower obliterating the light for up to 40% of the time. As a result it was extinguished and replaced by two small lights on nearby islands.

In January 1995 a brush fire raced across the island and engulfed the light. It blew out the lantern room glass, burnt the outside woodwork and blackened the tower. Fortunately the lens was not damaged. Although it's a non-operational lighthouse AMSA undertook its repairs. A barge loaded with supplies headed out from Port Welshpool to the island, an overnight trip. As the barge approached Deal in the pre-dawn it was interesting to note that the helmsman was watching his computerised GPS chart even though four lights, Hogan Island, NE Island, SW Island and Craggy Island were clearly visible. Nobody would have even noticed if they were off. They were a superfluous anachronism of a bygone era.

It is inevitable that the funds allocated for maintaining the lights will continue to be reduced and in spite of intentions to the contrary the amount of maintenance carried out will diminish. The days of carefully removing and replacing the grout between the blocks in towers such as those on Gabo and Cliffy Islands are gone unless they are considered to be historically important and are funded accordingly. The long-term future of significant and historical lighthouses is now in the hands of people who are interested in the conservation and preservation of these unique and historical structures.

Transporting materials to repair the tower at Deal Island in Bass Strait after it had been damaged by fire

Cape Otway Victoria – Open Day 6th June 1994 after the main tower light was extinguished

Cape Otway

Apollo Bay Victoria

NEW: Ref: **2172**	Built: **1994**	Elevation: **73**	Tower: **2**	Range: **35W 28R**
OLD: Ref: ******	Built: **1848**	Elevation: **91**	Tower: **20**	Range: **46W 39R**

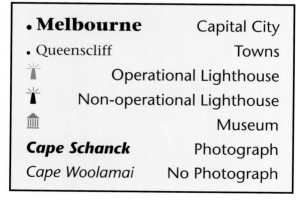

Map Symbols

Explanations

Tabulated Information:
Underneath each lighthouse name and location are a number of items of information. These are the:

Identification Number   **(Ref):**
This is the number used in the (British) Admiralty List of Lights and Fog Signals Volume K, the most complete list of aids to navigation that is readily available for Australian waters. **** indicates that the light is no longer in use and is included for historical or aesthetic reasons.

Date Built   **(Built):**
This is the year in which the tower was built, or first exhibited a light. Generally this date has been obtained from Australian Maritime Safety Authority (AMSA) documents.

Elevation   **(Elevation):**
The height of the light source above sea level in metres.

Height of Tower   **(Tower):**
The height of the tower in metres.

Nominal Range of the Light   **(Range):**
The approximate number of kilometres that the light is visible. Nothing after the range indicates a white light. Where there are multiple or non white lights **W** indicates a White light, **R** indicates a Red light and **G** a Green light. A Range of zero indicates that the light is no longer operational.

     Example: Ref: **2845**   Built: **1870**   Elevation: **25**   Tower: **20**   Range: **35W 20R**

Notes:
At times in the text a lighthouse may only be briefly referenced, for example '**Arden Islet** (Ref: 3285, a 13m metal frame tower built in 1982)'. If there is no description except for the reference number and date built, as in '**Williams Island** (Ref: 1873, built in 1964)' it means the light is just a GRP cabinet with a Tupperware light.

Volume K has been used for the Elevation, Height and Nominal Range figures, with the Range being converted from nautical miles to the nearest kilometre. These figures often vary from other sources but it is, at least, a constant reference.

A description of the lantern and lens (the apparatus) has only been included for major lights.
Although the lights may have once used sperm whale oil, gas, kerosene or acetylene all lights now use either mains electricity or solar panels to keep banks of batteries charged.

The location in latitude and longitude and the character of the light (eg Group Flashing (2) every 10 secs; Flash 0.01 secs; Short eclipse 2.49 secs; Long eclipse 7.49 secs) has purposely been excluded. It is available in the Admiralty List of Lights and Fog Signals Volume K.

Distances:
All distances in this book are in metres or kilometres. Where the measurement has been converted from nautical miles or statute miles the following formulae have been used:

One nautical mile (nm)	= 6,080ft	or 1.1515sm	or 1.8531km
One statute mile (sm)	= 5,280ft	or 0.8684nm	or 1.6093 km
One kilometre (km)	= 3,281ft	or 0.5396nm	or 0.6214 sm
One Foot (')	= 0.3047metres (m)		

See Appendix III for a table converting Kilometres to Nautical Miles and Statute Miles.

Index – New South Wales

Map	21
Point Danger	22
Fingal Head	23
Cape Byron	24
Clarence River	25
Ballina Head	26
North Solitary Island	28
South Solitary Island	28
Smoky Cape	30
Tacking Point	32
Crowdy Head	33
Sugarloaf Point	34
Nelson Head	36
Port Stephens	36
Steelworks Channel	38
Main Bar Lights	38
Nobby's Head	39
Norah Head	40
Barrenjoey Head	42
Hornby	43
Parriwi Head	44
Grotto Point	44
Western Channel Pile Light	45
Eastern Channel Pile Light	45
Vaucluse Bay Front	46
Vaucluse Bay Rear	46
Shark Island	47
Bradley's Head	47
Robertson Point	48
Fort Denison	49
Blues Point	49
Goat Island	49
Macquarie	50
Henry Head	52
Cape Bailey	52
Wollongong Head	54
Wollongong Harbour	56
Kiama Harbour	57
Crookhaven Head	58
Cape St George	59
Point Perpendicular	60
Warden Head	62
Montague Island	63
Burrewarra Point	64
Lookout Point	64
Ben Boyd's Tower	65
Green Cape	66

Wollongong Head Wollongong NSW

New South Wales

South Pacific Ocean

Tweed Heads • **Point Danger**
Fingal Head

Byron Bay • **Cape Byron**
Ballina Head
Evans Head

Yamba • **Clarence River**

North Solitary Island
Coffs Harbour • **South Solitary Island**

Smoky Cape

Port Macquarie • **Tacking Point**

Crowdy Head

Nelson Head **Sugarloaf Point**
Steelworks Channel **Port Stephens**
Newcastle • **Main Bar Lights;**
Nobby's Head
Norah Head
Barrenjoey Head
Palm Beach •
Sydney •
Henry Head
Cronulla • **Cape Bailey**
Wollongong Harbour
Wollongong • **Wollongong Head**
Kiama • **Kiama Harbour**
Crookhaven Head
Cape St George **Point Perpendicular**
Ulladulla • **Warden Head**
Brush Island

Burrewarra Point

Montague Island

Lookout Point
Eden • **Ben Boyd's Tower**
Green Cape

Canberra •

Sydney Harbour

Parriwi Head Clontarf
The **Grotto**
Spit **Point**
South

North
Head

Pacific
Mosman
North **Hornby** South Head
Sydney **Western**
Blues **Channel Pile**
Point **Eastern Channel Pile**
Robertson **Bradley's**
Goat **Point** **Head** **Vaucluse Bay Front**
Island Vaucluse **Macquarie**
Sydney **Fort** *Port Jackson* **Vaucluse Bay**
Harbour **Denison** **Shark** **Rear**
Bridge **Sydney** **Island**
Ocean

Woollhara

Point Danger Light

Captain Cook Memorial and Lighthouse, Tweed Heads NSW & Coolangatta Qld

Ref: **2845**   Built: **1970**   Elevation: **45**   Tower: **20**   Range: **35**

Lt. James Cook

Lt. James Cook named Point Danger in 1770 although the name was meant to apply to Fingal Head. To commemorate the 200th anniversary of his voyage a memorial was built by the Gold Coast and Tweed Heads City Councils, in conjunction with the Commonwealth Department of Shipping and Transport. It is strategically placed with the Queensland – NSW border passing through its centre. The four concrete columns connected at their top with sculptured steel are a fitting memorial and make an effective but unusual lighthouse. The world's first laser light, which had been tested at Cape Byron was installed in 1971. It was replaced with a conventional light after it was determined that the laser light offered no practical advantages. It is located at the end of Boundary Street in Coolangatta/Tweed Heads.

Fingal Head

Fingal NSW

Ref: **2844** Built: **1872** Elevation: **24** Tower: **7** Range: **32W 26R**

This cement-rendered brick tower is one of five visually similar towers built along the northern NSW coast. The others were Richmond River, Clarence River (replaced in 1955), Tacking Point and Crowdy Head although the latter two have an attached storeroom. Originally the Fingal light had a kerosene lamp but this was converted to automatic acetylene operation in 1920. The one keeper was withdrawn at the same time. The light can be accessed from the end of Lighthouse Parade in Fingal Head.

Cape Byron (Top, Opposite)
Byron Bay NSW

Ref: **2838**   Built: **1901**   Elevation: **118**   Tower: **22**   Range: **50**

Cape Byron is the most easterly point on the Australian mainland. The tower made of solid concrete blocks, was designed in the James Barnet style, by Charles Harding. It has a French 4.0m lantern and a two panel 920mm first order dioptric/catadioptric lens made up of over 700 lead crystal prisms. With an intensity of 2,200,000 candelas it is Australia's most powerful light. Watching the light dim as the sun rises is a magical experience, just you, the light and the early morning joggers. And as an alternative to trudging up the hill in the pre-dawn it is also possible to stay at two of the well maintained keepers residences that are at the end of Lighthouse Road in Byron Bay.

Clarence River (Right)
South Head, Yamba NSW

	Ref:	Built:	Elevation:	Tower:	Range:
NEW:	**2818**	**1955**	**41**	**17**	**30**
OLD:	********	**1866**	**28**	**7**	**26**

Matthew Flinders charted the Clarence River and South Head in 1799 although it took until 1866 for the first light to be built. The light was converted to acetylene in 1920 and the keeper was withdrawn at the same time. In 1955 a white concrete tower, similar in style to the Wollongong Head light was built and the original lighthouse was demolished. Since then a partial replica of the original structure, used as a community radio station has been built on the original foundations. The tower is on a headland at the end of Pilot Street in Yamba.

Ballina Head

Richmond River, Ballina NSW

Ref: **2834**   Built: **1866**   Elevation: **35**
Tower: **7**   Range: **26**

This masonry light is the second of the five small towers built along the northern NSW coast. The original 1866 light was converted to acetylene in 1920. The one keeper was withdrawn at the same time. The Chance Brothers 1.8m diameter flat panel lantern has since been converted to 240 volts mains power. The tower is in a small reserve off Lighthouse Parade in Ballina.

North Solitary Island (Right)
Coffs Harbour NSW

Ref: **2813**   Built: **1975**   Elevation: **58**   Tower: **4**
Range: **17**

Glass Reinforced Plastic (GRP) cabinets with Tupperware lights on them are uninspiring, bland and utilitarian. Yet in their own way they are the modern day version of the Fingal Head style of light, small, simple, reliable and cost effective. On remote and inaccessible sites using a helicopter, a helipad, lighthouse base and light can be built and made operational in about a week. As most of the lights in NSW were built before the advent of the GRP and solar power revolution there are only three in NSW. They are:

The mains powered **Evans Head** light (Ref: 2829, built in 1976), was established at the request of local fishermen.

The size 3, double height solar powered **North Solitary Island** light shown here.

The solar powered **Brush Island** light near Bawley Point (Ref: 2577.8, built in 1967) was established at the request of local fishermen.

Evans Head is accessible in the Dirawong Reserve on the southern side of the Evans River. The other two are not easily reached.

South Solitary Island (Below)

South Solitary Island

Coffs Harbour NSW

Ref: **2812** Built: **1880** Elevation: **58**
Tower: **20** Range: **28**

South Solitary Island (that is actually made up of four islands) is located 14km NE from Coffs Harbour. Building the James Barnet designed light started in 1878 and it was first exhibited in March 1880. The Chance Brothers first order dioptric lens with an intensity of 250,000 candelas was the first and the last light in NSW to use kerosene. The light was automated in 1975 and the station was demanned at the same time. The original lens that was replaced by a solar powered light in 1985 is now in the Coffs Harbour and District Historical Museum. Since demanning the keepers' houses have deteriorated significantly and, due to the harsh and inaccessible location and the cost it is unlikely that they will ever be restored. Boat tours around the islands are available from Coffs Harbour.

Smoky Cape
South West Rocks NSW

Ref: 2796 Built: 1891 Elevation: 128 Tower: 17 Range: 46

Smoky Cape with its gracefully proportioned, Barnet designed octagonal tower is one of the last lighthouses to be built in Australia that still combined aesthetics and function. Built of poured concrete it has a Chance Brothers 4.0m, nine-panel lantern with a 920mm first order catadioptric revolving lens. Initially it had an intensity of 100,000 candelas. In 1912 the original kerosene system was replaced with a pressurised kerosene system that increased the intensity to 316,000 candelas. This was converted to electric power in 1962 and that boosted the light output to 1,000,000 candelas. The head and assistant keepers' residences are in excellent condition and can be rented. The light is in the Hat Head National Park at the end of Lighthouse Road that turns off from the Jerseyville-Arakoon Road.

Tacking Point
Port Macquarie NSW

Ref: **2788** Built: **1879** Elevation: **34**
Tower: **8** Range: **30**

Matthew Flinders named Tacking Point during one of his survey voyages. The cement-rendered brick tower, with an attached storeroom is the fourth of the small towers built along the northern NSW coast. The original fixed catadioptric light was converted to acetylene in 1919 and the one keeper was withdrawn at the same time. In 1972 the light was converted to 240 volts mains power. The original Chance Brothers lantern has since been replaced with an acrylic Tupperware lens. The light is at the end of Lighthouse Parade in Port Macquarie.

Crowdy Head
Crowdy Head NSW

Ref: **2784**   Built: **1878**   Elevation: **61**
Tower: **7**   Range: **30W 24R**

This painted stone tower and storeroom is the last of the small towers built along the northern NSW coast. The original oil light was converted to acetylene in 1920 and the one keeper was withdrawn at the same time. In 1972 it was converted to 240 volts mains power. Although the original Chance Brothers fourth order lantern is still there the lens has been replaced with an acrylic FA251 light.

Sugarloaf Point
Seal Rocks NSW

Ref: 2776 **Built: 1875** **Elevation: 79** **Tower: 15** **Range: 46**

Originally the tower was going to be built on Seal Rocks below Sugarloaf Point but as access to the rocks was difficult and dangerous it was decided to locate the tower on the point. The cement-rendered masonry tower with a wide bluestone balcony and gunmetal railings is probably the first tower designed by James Barnet. It has a Chance Brothers 3.6m lantern and a 16-panel 920mm first order catadioptric lens with an intensity of 1,000,000 candelas. Its external staircase is quite unusual although other towers such as Cape Moreton and Sandy Cape also have external staircases that provide entry to the tower above the tower's storage room. The head and assistant keepers' residences are in excellent condition. The light is accessible by road from the Seal Rocks village.

Red Sector Light

Nelson Head (Right)
Nelson Bay NSW

Ref: 2771   Built: 1872   Elevation: 39
Tower: 3   Range: 19W   11R

Nelson Head is a harbour light in Port Stephens. Adjacent to the original keepers cottage built in 1875 are two new buildings that look like two corrugated-iron water tanks with windows cut into them. The actual light that was turned off early in 2003, was on a pole further down the hill. It is used as tearooms and a museum. In 1990 the Royal Volunteer Coastal Patrol was appointed trustee and are responsible for the maintenance of the beautifully kept reserve. Due to similar names visitors often mistake this light in Halifax Park that overlooks Port Stephens and is easily accessible by road, with the Port Stephens light at Fingal Bay that is much more difficult to visit.

Port Stephens (Below)

Port Stephens
Fingal Bay NSW

Ref: **2770** Built: **1862** Elevation: **38**
Tower: **21** Range: **31**

The Port Stephens light, designed by the Colonial Architect Alexander Dawson and built from Hawkesbury sandstone is located on Fingal Point or Fingal Island depending on whether it is low or high tide. At low tide there is a sand spit that extends from the end of Fingal Bay beach to the island. At high tide the water across the spit is waist deep. The original kerosene light was converted to acetylene in 1922 and the light was demanned at the same time. It was converted to mains power in 1973 using a submarine cable across the spit. When it was converted to solar power in 1989 the original lens was donated to the Port Stephens Historical Society. There are plans to restore the keepers' quarters that have been severely damaged by vandals. The light is a pleasant walk, at low tide from the Fingal Bay beach.

Steelworks Channel, Directional Light (Left)

Newcastle NSW

Ref: **2760**   Built: **1986**   Elevation: **64**   Tower: **60**   Range: **26W 22R 22G**

At 60m this is the tallest light specific tower in Australia. The spiral stairway in the open frame tower looks like a giant auger ready to drill into the ground. It is one of the few laser lights being used in Australian waters and allows for very precise navigation in the channel. If a ship is more than 10m from the centre of the channel a red or green light replaces the central white light. As the channel is only four kilometres long the range of the lights could be considered excessive. The light can be seen from Cormorant Road on the north side of the Hunter River.

Main Bar Lights (Below)

Newcastle Harbour, Newcastle NSW

Ref: **2740**   Built: **1990**   Elevation: **32**   Tower: **15-24**   Range: **9**

Elsewhere in this book there are other examples of leading lights that look like classical lighthouses and that were, in some cases manned. These lights are quite different. There are three front lights and a single rear light with each one being a grey steel column with bright orange reflective panels. The current poles replaced steel lattice towers built in 1908. When the rear and the middle front light are aligned the ships are in the middle of the channel into the Hunter River. When the rear light is aligned with one of the outer front lights it indicates that it is at port or starboard limit of the channel. The lights are accessible from along the riverfront in Newcastle.

Nobby's Head
Newcastle NSW

Ref: **2728**	Built: **1858**	Elevation: **35**
Tower: **10**	Range: **45**	

Nobby's Head was originally a 90m high island. During the construction of the harbour 46m were removed from the island (leaving 44m) and it was joined to the mainland. It is now a 32m high headland, the last 12m being removed to make a suitable base for the lighthouse. The lighthouse was only the third one built in NSW after the Macquarie light in 1818 and the Hornby light that was also built in 1858. Prior to it being built coal fired beacons had been used to guide ships into the harbour. To ensure that the light could be readily distinguished from the Newcastle city lights its output was increased to 1,000,000 candelas. The light is at the end of Nobby's Road in Newcastle.

Norah Head

Norah Head NSW

Ref: 2712   Built: 1903   Elevation: 46
Tower: 27   Range: 50W 13R 15G

Norah Head, made from precast concrete blocks is the last of the James Barnet style of lights. At first glance the tower with its arches, turrets and domes looks more like a mosque than a lighthouse. It is actually quite similar to the Byron Bay and the Point Perpendicular lights that were built at about the same time. All three were constructed of pre-cast concrete blocks using local aggregate. It has a Chance Brothers 3.7m first order lantern and a 2-panel 700mm second order catadioptric lens with an intensity of 1,000,000 candelas. The keepers' quarters also built from precast concrete blocks are in excellent condition. The light is accessible by road from Norah Head.

40

Barranjoey Head (Left)

Palm Beach, Sydney NSW

Ref: **2702** Built: **1881** Elevation: **113**
Tower: **20** Range: **35**

Although temporary lights had been in use at Barranjoey since 1855 this was the first permanent structure to be constructed on the site. Built to guide ships into Broken Bay the James Barnet designed tower and keepers' quarters were constructed from local sandstone. The light, a Chance Brothers 700mm fixed optic was converted to automatic operation in 1932 and was demanned at the same time. After parking at the end of Barranjoey Road in Palm Beach it is a strenuous walk up to the lightstation.

Hornby Light (Opposite)

Inner South Head, Sydney Harbour NSW

Ref: **2636** Built: **1858** Elevation: **27**
Tower: **9** Range: **28**

The construction of the Hornby light was prompted by two shipwrecks that occurred in 1857, the *Dunbar* (with a loss of all but one of its complement of 122) and the *Catherine Adams* (with a loss of 21). Until it was built the Macquarie light on Outer South Head was the only NSW light out of the 14 lights that had been constructed to that time. The original kerosene light was converted to acetylene and then in 1933 to 240 volts mains power. The keeper was withdrawn at the same time. According to one source the tower was named after Admiral Sir Windham Hornby; another indicated it was named after Admiral Sir Phipps Hornby and a third said it was named by Sir William Denison, the Governor of the day after his wife whose maiden name was Hornby. The light can be reached by walking through the South Head Military Reserve.

Grotto Point and Parriwi Head

Entrance Leading Front, Sydney Harbour NSW

Entrance Leading Rear, Sydney Harbour NSW

FRONT: Ref: **2638** Built: **1911** Elevation: **19** Tower: **4** Range: **22W 17R 17G**

REAR: Ref: **2638.1** Built: **1911** Elevation: **43** Tower: **7** Range: **22**

Maurice Festu who also designed the Vaucluse leading lights designed the compact Grotto Point and the tall and graceful Parriwi that is also known as the Rosherville light. They define the safe passage through the Heads into Sydney Harbour. Red and green sectors on the Grotto Point light indicate the outer limits of the channel. A short walk through the Sydney Harbour National Park at Clontarf provides access to the Grotto Point light. The Parriwi light is situated in a small reserve on Parriwi Road near The Spit.

Western Channel Pile
Port Jackson, Sydney Harbour NSW

Ref: **2644**   Built: **1947**   Elevation: **10**   Tower: **10**   Range: **9R**

This small pile light is situated at the south western end of the Sow and Pigs Shoal. The current tower replaced the original one built in 1924. The light and the similar Eastern Channel Pile are called Sydney Harbour's Wedding Cakes. Originally the light was powered by acetylene but has now been converted to solar power. It can be easily seen from the Manly ferry or tour boats that ply the harbour.

Eastern Channel Pile
Port Jackson, Sydney Harbour NSW

Ref: **2652**   Built: **1947**   Elevation: **9**   Tower: **9**   Range: **9**

This light that is nearly identical to the Western Channel Pile is situated at the south eastern end of the Sow and Pigs Shoal. The first tower built in 1908 was replaced in 1947. Originally the light was powered by acetylene but has now been converted to solar power. It can be seen from tour boats that travel around the eastern side of the harbour.

Front   **Vaucluse Bay Leading Lights**   **Rear**

Vaucluse, Sydney Harbour NSW

FRONT: Ref: **2650**	Built: **1910**	Elevation: **16**	Tower: **8**	Range: **9**
REAR: Ref: **2650.1**	Built: **1910**	Elevation: **84**	Tower: **8**	Range: **9**

The Vaucluse Bay Leading Lights, also known as the Eastern Channel leading Lights, were first built in 1884. They were replaced by the current Maurice Festu designed 'Disney Castle' lights in 1910. They are used as leading lights for navigation through the Eastern Channel. Both the lights are located in Wentworth Road that winds its way down through Vaucluse from the New South Head Road. The rear light is in the front garden of a private home and is easily seen from the road. The front light is in the back garden of a house and is best viewed from a boat in Vaucluse or Parsley Bay.

Shark Island (Right)
Woollahra, Sydney Harbour NSW

Ref: **2656**   Built: **1913**   Elevation: **12**
Tower: **3**   Range: **11**

A wooden structure was first built on the reef extending from the northern end of Shark Island in 1890. It was replaced in 1913. The reinforced concrete tower is similar to the Robertson Point light but it has a larger base that was used to store the acetylene cylinders prior to it being converted to solar power. It can be seen from the Watson Bay ferry or the tour boats that travel around the harbour.

Bradley's Head (Right & Above)
Mosman, Sydney Harbour NSW

Ref: **2662**   Built: **1905**   Elevation: **7**
Tower: **7**   Range: **11**

Bradley's Head was named after William Bradley an officer on the *Sirius* guard ship of the First Fleet. The light is a mains power reinforced concrete tower that is 20m offshore from the southern end of Bradley's Head and is connected to the shore by a walkway. It is readily accessible from the end of the Bradley's Head Road in Mosman or can be viewed from the Manly ferry.

Robertson Point (Left)

Cremorne Point, Sydney Harbour NSW

Ref: 2664 **Built: 1910** **Elevation: 8** **Tower: 8**
Range: 9

Robertson Point light is a mains powered reinforced concrete tower connected to the shore by a walkway. It is of similar design and construction to Bradley's Head light but has a shorter walkway to the shore. It is a pleasant walk through a public reserve from the Cremorne Wharf or can be viewed from the Manly or Watson Bay ferries.

Fort Denison (Opposite, Top)

Potts Point, Sydney Harbour NSW

Ref: 2666 **Built: 1913** **Elevation: 19** **Tower: 5**
Range: 9

Originally called Rocky Island it was renamed Denison after Sir William Denison a Governor of NSW. It was first used as a high security prison. Due to the harsh conditions and the meagre rations handed out to the prisoners it also became known as Pinchgut. In the mid 1800's the top of the island was removed to just above high water level and the current fortress was built. The light built in 1858 in the middle of the main fortress was rebuilt and converted to acetylene in 1913. Prior to rebuilding it was electrically powered but as the power supply was not reliable it became one of the very few lights to be changed from electricity to another power source. The main tower at the northern end of the fort has a white light although it used to be red. There is also a small green light at the southern end of the fort. There are tours to the island or it can be seen from the Watson Bay or Manly ferries.

Goat Island (Opposite, Bottom)

Balmain East, Sydney Harbour NSW

Ref: 2695 **Built: 1990** **Elevation: 13** **Tower: 9**
Range: 6

Goat Island, like Fort Denison was levelled to just above the high water mark. This allowed the building of wharves and a powder magazine. The current light-on-a-pole replaced the original wooden octagonal structure built in 1904 and is used as an entrance light into Darling Harbour. It can be viewed from the Meadowbank ferries.

Blues Point (Above)

McMahons Point, Sydney Harbour NSW

Ref: **2688**   Built: **1993**   Elevation: **18**   Tower: **14**
Range: **11**

Blues Point, named after a Jamaican sailor Billy Blue is the first promontory on the western side of the Harbour Bridge. The white frame tower at the end of the point replaced the original eight-sided frame tower built in 1932. It is used in conjunction with lights on a radio tower as a front lead light for marking the passage under the centre of the bridge. It can be accessed from Blues Point Road McMahon's Point.

Macquarie
Outer South Head, Sydney NSW

OLD: Ref: ********   Built: **1818**   Elevation: **105**   Tower: **26**   Range: **0**

NEW: Ref: **2632**   Built: **1883**   Elevation: **105**   Tower: **26**   Range: **48**

In early 1794 there was an iron basket on a tripod erected near the lighthouse site in which a fire was lit every night. This bonfire beacon continued to be used until the first lighthouse was built. Its foundation stone was laid in 1816 and it was first exhibited on 30th November 1818. It was commissioned by the governor, Major General Lachlan Macquarie without approval from London. He also named it after himself. The tower, designed by the convict architect Francis Greenway was unfortunately constructed of inferior sandstone that rapidly deteriorated.

By 1878 the old tower was held together by a series of iron bands and it was decided to build a completely new tower. James Barnet designed the new tower in the same style as the original. Its Chance Brothers 3.7m lantern and a 250mm fourth order lens with double flashing panels with an intensity of 800,000 candelas was first exhibited in 1883. The keepers' quarters are in excellent condition but unfortunately are not open to the public. The lightstation can be accessed from Old South Head Road in Watson's Bay.

Henry Head (Above)

La Perouse, Botany Bay NSW

Ref: **2623**   Built: **1955**   Elevation: **27**
Tower: **4**   Range: **13**

The light at Henry Head, also known as the Endeavour Light is a small white concrete harbour light situated near the entrance to Botany Bay. Surrounded by wartime gun emplacements it is the only Australian light located on the grounds of a golf course. There is a private road through the NSW Club golf links in La Perouse to the light.

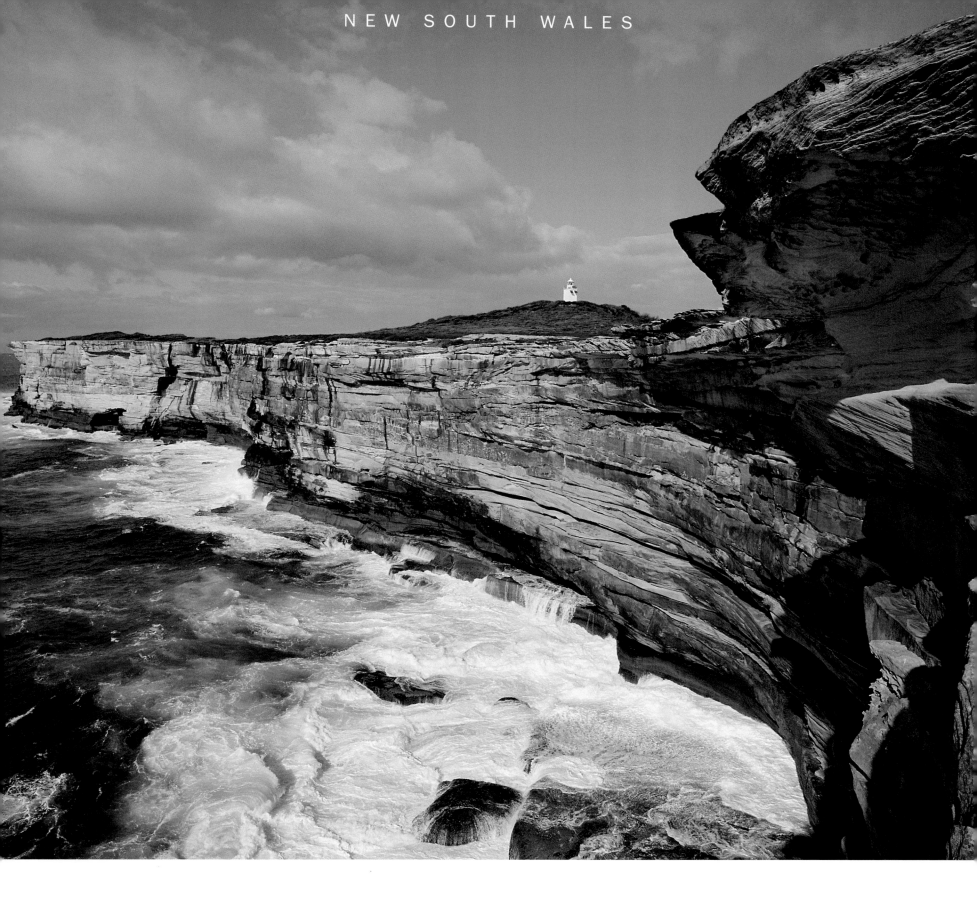

Cape Bailey (Opposite and Above)
Kurnell, Sydney NSW

Ref: **2622**   Built: **1950**   Elevation: **55**   Tower: **9**   Range: **24**

This squat square concrete tower sits at the edge of an imposing cliff on the Kurnell Peninsula near the entrance to Botany Bay. It is the first of five 'major' lighthouses that can be seen along the Illawarra Coast. Surrounded by coastal heath it appears to be on a remote and isolated site and yet it is only a few kilometres from the Kurnell industrial complexes. It can be reached by driving to the end of Sir Joseph Banks Drive, Kurnell and hiking along the cliff top to the light.

53

Wollongong Head

Flagstaff Point, Wollongong NSW

Ref: **2614**   Built: **1937**   Elevation: **40**   Tower: **25**   Range: **33W 28R**

This elegant reinforced concrete tower with a first order Chance Brothers catadioptric lens (ex Gabo Island) was the first fully automatic flashing light in NSW. (A temporary acetylene light was used for the first year until the permanent electric light arrived and was installed in 1938.) It is similar to the Clarence River light in Yamba. Located on a headland surrounded by old gun emplacements and close to the city and beaches it is a favourite meeting place and is often used as a backdrop for weddings. It replaced the harbour light in Belmore Basin that was eventually deactivated in 1947. It is accessible by road from Cliff Drive in Wollongong.

Wollongong Harbour

Breakwater, Wollongong NSW

Ref: **** Built: **1872** Elevation: **15**
Tower: **12** Range: **0**

The breakwater light, designed by Edward Moriarty was the first prefabricated wrought iron lighthouse constructed in New South Wales (the only other one being Warden Head at Ulladulla). It was replaced in 1937 by the Wollongong Head light although it was not turned off until 1947. In 1999 a program to repair the light was undertaken and it is now fully restored. It is also likely that the light will be relit for small boats entering the harbour. It is accessible by road from Cliff Drive in Wollongong.

Wollongong Harbour Light

Kiama Harbour (Right)
Blowhole Point, Kiama NSW

Ref: **2598**   Built: **1887**   Elevation: **36**
Tower: **15**   Range: **30**

Like Flagstaff Point in Wollongong Edward Moriarty designed this brick tower that is cement-rendered on the outside and plastered on the inside. Access to the lantern room is by three iron ladders. It is also a favourite meeting place for visitors and locals in Kiama. As with most Australian lights it has gone through a number of upgrades over the years. The original oil burner was converted to local coal gas in 1908. In 1920 it was converted to acetylene with the keepers being withdrawn at the same time. In 1969 it was upgraded to mains power. One of the old keepers' cottages was demolished but the other is still being used as a Tourist Information Centre. It is at the end of Terralong Street (the main street) in Kiama.

Crookhaven Head (Left)
Crookhaven NSW

Ref: **2594**   Built: **1904**   Elevation: **22**
Tower: **7**   Range: **15**

The original 1882 timber building was replaced by the current concrete structure in 1904. The new light used the lens from the decommissioned Cape St George light although that has now been replaced by an acrylic lens. Its light is used as a reference point by small boats entering the Shoalhaven River. The bottom photo includes a self-portrait of the photographer. The light is a one kilometre walk from the end of Prince Edward Avenue in Crookhaven.

Cape St George (Opposite)
Cape St George, Jervis Bay NSW

Ref: ********   Built: **1860**   Elevation: ——
Tower: ——   Range: **0**

Cape St George was the lighthouse built in the wrong place. The intent was to provide a light that could be seen by ships entering Jervis Bay but in reality it could not be seen at all by ships coming from the north and was of only marginal use for those coming from the south. Its location had not been officially approved and to make matters worse the builder erected the light about two kilometres from the selected site. This was done so that it was close to the sandstone quarry used to obtain building materials. In spite of its position the light was lit for 40 years until the new light was commissioned at Point Perpendicular. The lantern was then removed for later installation on the Crookhaven Head light. In 1913 the Navy used the tower for target practice effectively destroying it. The ruins are in the Jervis Bay National Park and accessible by road from Nowra.

Point Perpendicular

Beecroft Peninsula, Jervis Bay NSW

NEW: Ref: **2588**　Built: **1993**　Elevation: **95**
　　　　Tower: **19**　Range: **33**
OLD: Ref: ********　Built: **1899**　Elevation: **93**
　　　　Tower: **21**　Range: **48**

This light that replaced the one at Cape St George, was the first light in NSW to be built of cement-rendered concrete blocks. Others include Byron Bay and Norah Head. The light was first lit in 1899 although the glass panel above the doorway indicates its construction year of 1898. Over the years the intensity of the first order triple flashing dioptric light was increased from 100,000 to 1,200,000 candelas. The original light was decommissioned in 1993 and replaced by a solar powered light, with an intensity of 105,000 candelas on a white mild steel frame tower. At the time of its closure the lighthouse and the keepers' quarters were in excellent condition. The lightstation that is off the Nowra – Currarong Road is on a Department of Defence reserve that is used for training purposes. Check in Nowra to determine if the road to the lightstation is open.

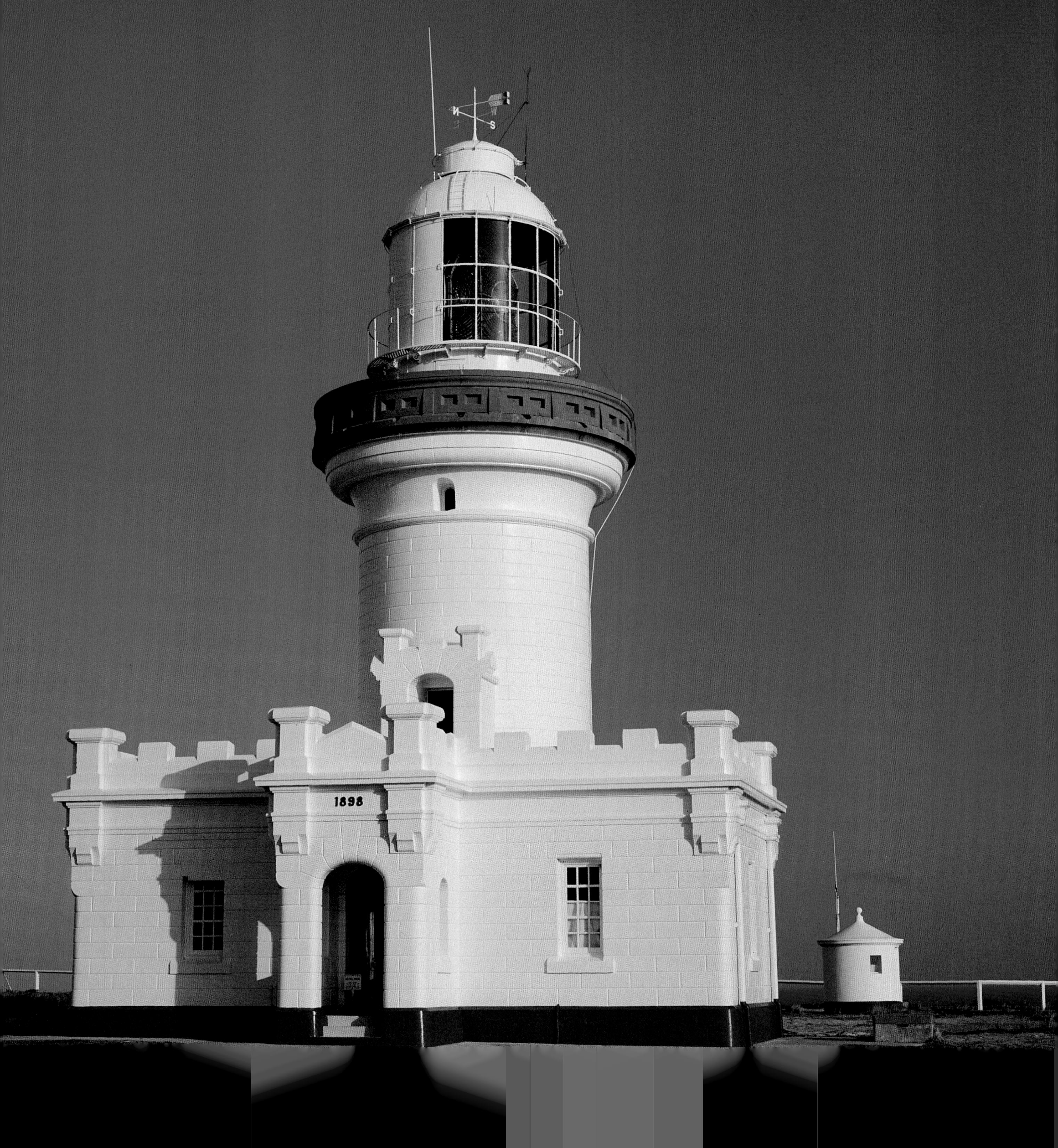
1898

Warden Head (Left and Below)
Ulladulla NSW

Ref: **2584**   Built: **1889**   Elevation: **34**   Tower: **12**   Range: **26**

Warden Head is the second of the two riveted wrought iron lights, designed by Edward Moriarty and made in NSW. (The first was the Harbour light in Wollongong.) Originally erected on the Ulladulla Breakwater in 1873 it was moved to its current location on Warden Head in 1889. After upgrading to acetylene in 1920 and being demanned the keeper's cottage was moved to Milton. The light was converted to electric power in 1964. It is accessible being at the end of Deering Street in Ulladulla.

Montague Island (Opposite)
Narooma NSW

Ref: **2576**   Built: **1881**   Elevation: **80**   Tower: **21**   Range: **37**

The lighthouse is built of grey granite (syenite) quarried from the north side of the island. A first order Chance Brothers lens was installed and was first exhibited in 1881. The keepers' quarters were built of cement-rendered brick with internal fittings of cedar. The intensity of the light increased from 45,000 to 250,000 and then to 357,000 candelas. On conversion to electricity the intensity reached 1,000,000 candelas. Then in 1986 it was converted to solar power and the intensity dropped to 120,000 candelas. The original light is now in the Narooma Lighthouse museum/Visitor Centre. Montague (sometimes spelt Montagu) Island is 82 hectares in area and is about five kilometres off shore from Narooma. As little as 8,000 years ago, during the last ice age it was a headland. As well as the lighthouse it is home to thousands of sea birds including a colony of fairy penguins and the only haul out site for Australian fur seals in NSW. It is accessible by tour boat from Narooma.

Burrewarra Point (Opposite, Top)

Guerilla Bay, Tomakin NSW

Ref: **2577.6**   Built: **1974**   Elevation: **62**
Tower: **10**   Range: **17**

This oval three section unpainted concrete tower is the only one of its type in Australia. It is surprising that a two or three high GRP cabinet was not used instead of poured concrete. It was converted from battery power to solar power in 1984. Like the small GRP Brush Island light at Bawley Point its main purpose is to aid local fishermen. It is accessible at the end of Burri Road that goes to Guerilla Bay from Tomakin.

Lookout Point (Opposite, Bottom)

Twofold Bay, Eden NSW

Ref: **2572**   Built: **1970**   Elevation: **39**
Tower: **14**   Range: **22W   17R**

The original frame tower was built in 1860 and first exhibited in 1862. The whole structure and lantern were the first of their kind to be completely manufactured in Australia. The old tower is long gone being replaced by the light-on-a-pole shown here that provides assistance to small craft entering the Eden Boat Harbour in Twofold Bay. It is accessible by road in Eden.

Ben Boyd's Tower (Right)

Eden NSW

Ref: ********   Built: **1846**   Elevation: **105**
Tower: **19**   Range: **0**

This tower was built and owned by Benjamin Boyd an early land developer. He wanted to build a 'city' on the southern side of Twofold Bay even though the Government had already decided that development would take place to the north. The tower was built at great expense using sandstone brought from Sydney in spite of there being ample supplies of local granite. Although it was built to be a lighthouse its only function was to be a lookout tower for whale watching. It is one of only two lighthouses in Australia that was never lit, the other being on Raine Island at the northern end of the Great Barrier Reef. To access the tower turn off the Princes Highway 19km south of Eden and drive to the end of Edrom Road.

Green Cape

Eden NSW

	Ref:	Built:	Elevation:	Tower:	Range:
NEW:	2570	1998	39	15	32
OLD:	****	1883	44	29	32

Green Cape, in the Ben Boyd National Park at the entrance to Disaster Bay is the tallest classical tower in NSW and the most southerly lighthouse in the state. The octagonal tower on a square base, designed by James Barnet was the first cast concrete lighthouse in Australia. Once poured it was cement-rendered. The Chance Brothers first order dioptric revolving light initially produced 100,000 candelas but by 1967 this had been increased to 1,000,000 candelas. Although the light was in operation the steamer *Ly-EE-Moon* ran aground on the cape in 1886 with the loss of 76 of the 91 on board. A single white cross in the cemetery and a plaque listing the names serves as a memorial to all those who perished. The keepers' houses with their numerous blue-topped chimneys make this one of the most picturesque light stations in Australia. A new lattice tower with a solar powered light with an intensity of only 37,000 candelas has now replaced the original lighthouse. Turn off the Princes Highway 19km south of Eden on to Edrom Road and then turn on to the Green Cape Road.

Index – Victoria

Map	69
Gabo Island	70
Little Rame Head	72
Point Hicks	72
Cape Conran	76
Mount Barkly	76
Omega Facility	77
Cliffy Island	78
South East Point	80
Citadel Island	82
Point Grant	82
Cape Liptrap	83
Cape Schanck	84
Monash Light	86
South Channel Pile	87
Eastern Light	88
St Kilda False Light	89
Port Melbourne Front	90
Port Melbourne Rear	91
Timeball Tower	92
West Channel Pile	93
Prince George Shoal	93
Coles Light	94
Wedge Light	94
Point Lonsdale	95
Shortland Bluff	96
Hume Tower	97
Queenscliff Low	97
Murray Tower	97
Split Point	98
Cape Otway	100
Flagstaff Hill Front	102
Flagstaff Hill Rear	102
Griffiths Island	103
Whaler's Bluff	104
Cape Nelson	105

Split Point Airey's Inlet Victoria

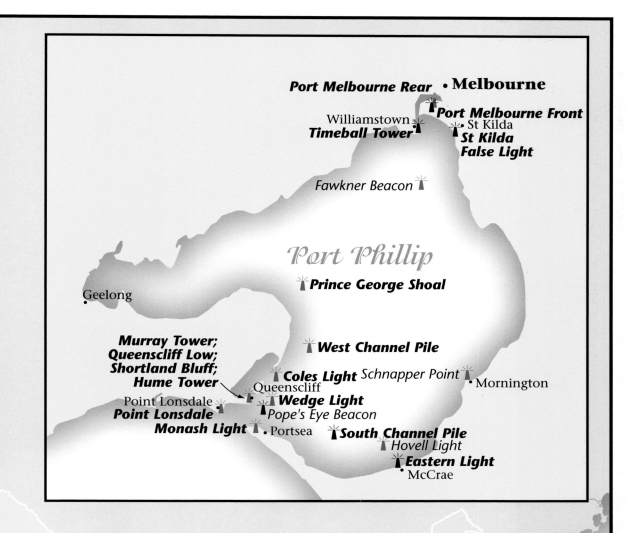

Port Melbourne Rear • **Melbourne**

Williamstown **Port Melbourne Front**
Timeball Tower • St Kilda
St Kilda
False Light

Fawkner Beacon

Port Phillip

Prince George Shoal

Geelong

West Channel Pile

Murray Tower;
Queenscliff Low;
Shortland Bluff; **Coles Light** *Schnapper Point*
Hume Tower Queenscliff • Mornington
Point Lonsdale **Wedge Light**
Point Lonsdale *Pope's Eye Beacon*
Monash Light • Portsea **South Channel Pile**
Hovell Light
Eastern Light
McCrae

Victoria

Tasman
Sea

Mallacoota
Cann
River
Mount Barkly Lakes **Gabo Island**
Breakwater Entrance **Little Rame Head**
Whaler's Bluff *Lights* **Griffiths Island**
Cape Nelson • Warrnambool **Cape** **Point**
Portland **Conran** **Hicks**
Queenscliff
Flagstaff Hill Front; **Split Point** **Cape** Flinders **Omega Facility**
Flagstaff Hill Rear Apollo Bay **Schanck** *Cape Woolamai*
Cape Otway **Point Grant;**
Round Island • Welshpool
Cape Liptrap *Lighthouse Point*
Cliffy Island
Citadel Island **South East Point**
TASMANIA

Bass *Strait*

King Island

Flinders Island

Gabo Island
Mallacoota Victoria

Ref: **2558**   Built: **1862**   Elevation: **55**   Tower: **47**   Range: **30**

There were a number of attempts made to build a lighthouse on Gabo Island. The first in 1846 failed. Next a prefabricated wooden tower was built in 1853. The current red granite tower was completed in 1862. Quarrying the granite for the tower was a painstaking process. Holes would be drilled by hand into the rock. There were two possible ways used to split the rock. One was to drive a wooden stake into the hole, wet it and let the expanding stake split the rock. The second and most likely way, was to place two semi-circular wedges into the hole and then drive a metal spike between the wedges. Once blocks were obtained they were chipped into the final shape required. After Cape Wickham on King Island the Gabo Island tower is the second tallest classical light in Australia. Initially it had a fixed first order lens. This was converted to a revolving light in 1913 and after upgrading to electrical power in 1935 produced 900,000 candelas. It was converted to solar power in 1992 and its intensity was reduced to 30,000 candelas. The keeper was withdrawn at the same time. It is accessible by boat or plane from Mallacoota.

Fairy Penguin

Little Rame Head (Below)
Mallacoota Victoria

Ref: 2557.5 Built: 1993 Elevation: 57 Tower: 2 Range: 33

When the Gabo Island and Point Hicks lights were converted to solar power their range went from 46 to 30 and 48 to 19 km respectively. As a result the loom of their lights no longer overlapped. To fill in this black hole a new light was built at Little Rame Head. Due to its elevation this one high GRP cabinet actually has a greater range than either Gabo Island or Point Hicks. The inland side of the light has been carefully blacked out to ensure that it does not disturb the wildlife in the Croajingolong National Park. Access is by a long walk through the park.

Point Hicks (Right, Opposite and Overleaf)
Cann River Victoria

Ref: 2556 Built: 1890 Elevation: 56 Tower: 38 Range: 19

The headland was named after Zachary Hicks who was the first man on Cook's 1770 voyage to sight mainland Australia. The name was then changed to Cape Everard in 1843 but in 1970 it reverted to its original name. The circular cement-rendered rubble tower has a Chance Brothers lantern with a first order lens. After conversion from kerosene to electricity its intensity was 1,000,000 candelas and could be seen for 48 km. Although the old light is still in place the active light, installed in 1991 is now a small Tupperware light bolted to the lantern room railing with an intensity of only 2,100 candelas. It looks quite out of place. A unique feature is the spiral staircase of 162 steps that is cantilevered from the walls instead of being attached to a central column. The weatherboard keepers' cottages are in good condition and can be rented. Until the 47km road was built from Cann River the lightstation was as isolated as any offshore light. When first built it was supplied by ship every three or four months. Now it is only a one-hour drive on a dirt road from Cann River.

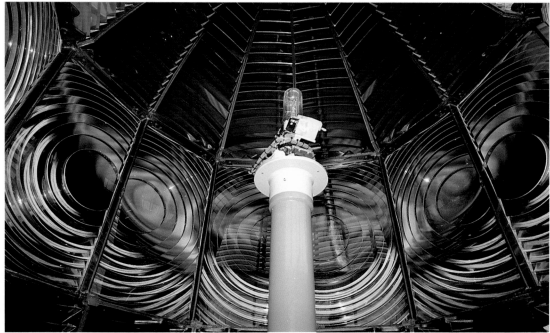

Point Hicks – The New and Old lanterns

Point Hicks

Point Hicks – (Top) **Looking Down the Staircase and** (Bottom) **Looking Up the Staircase**

Cape Conran

Orbost Victoria

Ref: **2555**　Built: **1966**　Elevation: **15**　Tower: **5**
Range: **17**

This frame tower, like the light at **Lighthouse Point** (Ref: 2502, a 24m steel frame tower built in 1944) at Corner Inlet on Wilson's Promontory, is used by local fishermen and recreational sailors. It is at the end of Marlo Road 31 kilometres out of Orbost.

Mount Barkly

Jemmy's Point, Lakes Entrance Victoria

Ref: **2544**　Built: **1923**　Elevation: **70**　Tower: **9**　Range: **32**

Like the tower further to the east at **Cape Conran** this light serves local fishermen and other small boats. In this case it guides them through the dangerous entrance channel into the Gippsland Lakes. It was named after Sir Henry Barkly a Governor of Victoria (1856 – 1863). It is only a short detour to the Jemmy's Point Reserve from the road into Lakes Entrance and provides spectacular views of the lakes.

Further west and just offshore from Port Welshpool are a number of Oil Platforms that have navigation aids including high-powered strobes and racons. They include **Kingfish B** (Ref: 2543.24, built in 1976), **Tuna** (Ref: 2543.8, built in 1980) and **Flounder A** (Ref: 2543.85, built in 1986).

Omega Facility

Darriman Victoria

Ref: ****   Built: **1982**   Elevation: **Not applicable**
Tower: **427**   Range: **Worldwide**

The Omega system is not a lighthouse. When it was fully operational it consisted of eight stations around the world that transmitted very low frequency radio signals. In addition to Darriman there were stations in Japan, Hawaii and North Dakota in the USA, Norway, Liberia, Argentina and on the island of La Reunion. Each station had a transmitter building containing two 150-kilowatt radio transmitters, a helix building that fed the signal to the antenna and a transmission tower. The 427m tower at Darriman, was and still is, the tallest structure in the southern hemisphere. By using a special receiver to pick up the signals from at least three of the transmitters ships and planes were able to fix their position anywhere in the world with an accuracy of about four kilometres. With the advent of the GPS satellite navigation system the need for Omega has, like the need for lighthouses, diminished. In 1997 the system was closed down and some of the stations have since been demolished. In Australia the Navy decided that the station here would be suitable for sending messages to its ships and submarines and bought the facility. The tower can be seen from the South Gippsland Highway between Woodside and Darriman.

Cliffy Island

Port Welshpool, Bass Strait Victoria

Ref: **2500**   Built: **1884**   Elevation: **52**   Tower: **12**
Range: **28**

Cliffy Island is the largest of a group of granite outcrops known as the Seal Islands north east of the Wilson's Promontory lighthouse. The granite tower is small but elegant. The stone walls that converge at the base of the tower seem to add to its stature. The original brick cottages were destroyed by fire in 1919 and were replaced with the cottage from Citadel Island that is on the other side of Wilson's Promontory. In addition a new brick cottage was built in 1927. When automated in 1971 the lightstation was demanned. All but one of the houses was demolished at the same time. The remaining one is in a sad state of disrepair. Access to the island was always difficult and unloading stores and people was a dangerous process. Generally people were transferred to and from the island by boarding a small boat that was then winched up and down the cliff face from a platform that protruded over the cliff edge. The platform is still in reasonable condition but the rest of the infrastructure has deteriorated. Today the only practical way to reach the island is by helicopter from Port Welshpool or Port Albert. The light was converted to solar power in 1989.

Cliffy Island's (Tupperware) APRB-251 light

South East Point

Wilson's Promontory Victoria

Ref: **2492**   Built: **1859**   Elevation: **117**   Tower: **19**   Range: **33**

To mark the passage around Wilson's Promontory that is the southernmost point on mainland Australia a number of options were considered including Rodondo and Cleft Islands and the Forty Foot Rocks. The most accessible was the promontory. It is a critical light because the shipping channel through this part of Bass Strait is quite narrow. Rodondo Island on the southern side of the channel is only nine kilometres from 'The Prom'. Interestingly the Victorian-Tasmanian border passes between them which means Tasmania is much closer to the mainland than is commonly imagined. Convicts, using local granite built the light and keepers' cottages between 1853 and 1859. The original parabolic mirrors were replaced in 1975 by a generator powered electric lamp array that was in turn converted to solar power in 1993. As there is no road to the lightstation all supplies have to be brought in by ship or helicopter. There are four keepers' houses. One was rebuilt in 1924 and two others were rebuilt in 1952 after being destroyed during a bushfire. Since the lightstation was demanned the refurbished houses can be rented although the undulating 18-kilometre walk to the lightstation is quite strenuous. The official name for the lighthouse is South East Point but it is much more commonly referred to as the Wilson's Promontory lighthouse.

Father Christmas arriving at South East Point (Wilson's Promontory) on December 23rd 1993. L to R with Santa: Michael Vanderzypp (pilot), Tara, Ailsa, Amanda, Chris and Nerissa Richter.

Citadel Island (Right)

Glennie Group, Bass Strait
Victoria

Ref: **2486**   Built: **1913**
Elevation: **117**   Tower: **4**   Range: **32**

Citadel Island is a mound of smooth granite boulders, twice as high as Cliffy Island but easier to access. It was the first automatic, Commonwealth funded light to be built. Although similar acetylene lights were already in operation in South Australia a keeper was stationed on the island for six months to ensure that it kept working. It was his weatherboard cottage that was moved to Cliffy Island in 1921. Even though it is quite high other islands in the Anser and Glennie Groups can obscure its light. In 1982 it was rebuilt using a two high GRP cabinet and converted to solar power. It is only accessible by helicopter.

Phillip Island Lights (Right)

Phillip Island Victoria

Cape Woolamai
Ref: **2476**   Built: **1928**   Elevation: **112**   Tower: **3**
Range: **22**
Point Grant
Ref: **2424**   Built: **1947**   Elevation: **52**   Tower: **19**
Range: **0**
Round Island
Ref: **2424.2**   Built: **1997**   Elevation: **31**   Tower: **3**
Range: **19**

There are lights at either end of Phillip Island. At the eastern end is the Cape Woolamai light, a small green cabinet that was the last remaining acetylene light in Victoria and possibly Australia. Located at the island's highest point it assists small boats sailing up the Eastern passage to San Remo and Newhaven. It can be seen during a walk to the Pinnacles near Newhaven. At the western end of the island is Point Grant. The original light, built in 1919 was replaced by a steel frame tower on top of a painted brick building in1947. This light, shown on the right was demolished in 1998 so that the Seal Rocks Tourist complex could be built. The new Round Island light that replaces it is so small it is even difficult to see it from the Nobbies lookout.

Cape Liptrap
Walkerville Victoria

Ref: **2482**   Built: **1951**   Elevation: **93**
Tower: **10**   Range: **30**

The first Cape Liptrap light, built in 1913 was an acetylene-powered light on top of a six metre high steel tower. Its light was first exhibited only four days after its neighbour, Citadel Island commenced operation. Like Citadel it was also an automated light but as a keeper was never stationed there it was really the first automatic Commonwealth funded light to be put into service. In 1951 the current octagonal concrete tower replaced the old steel structure. Its 400mm catadioptric drum lens produces 32,000 candelas. It is accessible by road from Fish Creek.

Cape Schanck
Flinders Victoria

Ref: **2423**   Built: **1859**   Elevation: **100**   Tower: **21**   Range: **35W 30R**

The limestone tower has a stone stairway instead of the usual wrought or cast iron one used in most lighthouses. Its original lens was replaced in 1915 with a Chance Brothers 3.3m lantern and a first order 920mm catadioptric lens whose intensity is 1,000,000 candelas. It was the first lightstation in Australia to be set up as a ground station for maritime DGPS. The head keeper's cottage built in 1859 is used as a museum while the two assistant keepers' cottages, built in 1859 and 1939 are available for overnight stays. As this is often considered to be the best preserved lightstation in Australia it is well worth an extended visit. It is located on the Cape Schanck Road Cape Schanck that is accessed from the Rosebud Flinders Road at the southern tip of the Mornington Peninsula.

Cape Schanck - Clockwork mechanism and a kerosene vaporiser unit.

Monash Light

Point Nepean, Melbourne Victoria

Ref: **2216.1**   Built: **1930**   Elevation: **48**   Tower: **4**   Range: **33**

The tower was named after Sir John Monash (1865-1931) a civil engineer and army commander. Constructed of reddish black clinker bricks it has had its front completely covered in the late 1990's with bright orange panels. The panels are about twice as high as the original structure. The brush and trees on the hillside were making it difficult to see the tower so the panels were added to make it clearly visible as a daymark. It is used in conjunction with the Wedge and the Coles light to mark the Western and Coles Channels in Port Phillip. As it is located on restricted military land it is not possible to visit the light.

To the north east of the South Channel Pile is the **Hovell Light** (Ref: 2324, an 11m pile light built in 1939 that replaced the original 1924 structure which was destroyed during a storm in 1938.) It marks the eastern extremity of the South Channel. The light is just offshore from McCrae and can be viewed from a small boat.

South Channel Pile

Rye, Port Phillip Victoria

Ref: **** Built: **1874/1998** Elevation: **9** Tower: **10** Range: **0**

The octagonal South Channel Pile was the front light marking the centre of the Southern Channel in Port Phillip. The Eastern Light at McCrae was the rear light. The light with two lighthouse keepers was one of the few manned lights in Australia that were built in the sea, two others being the Margaret Brock Reef and Tipara Reef lights in South Australia. The quarters built on the platform on top of the piles included a living room (with fireplace!), a four bunk bedroom and an office. The light that rose above the roof of the living quarters showed red and green sectors as well as white. Originally powered by kerosene it was converted to acetylene in 1925. It operated until 1985 when the light was extinguished and the station demanned. In 1998 Parks Victoria lifted the structure off its piles and transported it to Melbourne where it was faithfully restored. It was then mounted on new piles adjacent to the Rye Channel some three kilometres from its original site. There is no operating light in the restored structure although it is used as a daymark by small boats. Currently there is no access to the light except sailing around it in a boat but tours may be available in the future.

Eastern Light
McCrae, Melbourne Victoria

Ref: **2322.1**   Built: **1883**   Elevation: **45**
Tower: **34**   Range: **0**

The externally braced, riveted steel tower, the tallest light in the bay was built by Chance Brothers in England in 1874 but was not lit at McCrae until 1883. Its 1.5m central column has a 120-step spiral staircase leading up to the lantern room that contained dioptric, catadioptric, and holophotal lens systems. It replaced the old wooden structure built in 1854 that was moved to Arthur's Seat to be used as a lookout. The new light was used in conjunction with the South Channel Pile to guide ships through the Southern Channel. Even after the South Channel Pile was decommissioned in 1985 its light kept shining until 1994. It is now owned by the McCrae Foreshore Committee. It is located on the Point Nepean Road between Rosebud and McCrae.

Other lights along the eastern side of Port Phillip are:

Schnapper Point (Ref: 2330, a steel frame tower built in 1983 to replace the original 1870 tower.) It is located on the jetty at the end of Schnapper Point Drive in Mornington.

The **Fawkner Beacon** (Ref: 2337, a light-on-a-pole built in 1980) was named after John Fawkner the 'Father of Victoria'. The original light built in 1924 was demolished on two occasions, once in 1965 and once in 1980. The light located at the southern end of the Port Melbourne Channel is just offshore from Sandringham.

St Kilda False Lighthouse
St Kilda, Melbourne Victoria

Ref: ****   Built: **1965**   Elevation: **19**   Tower: **17**   Range: **0**

This fibreglass building is located on the St Kilda Marina breakwater. It was never meant to be a real lighthouse although small boats do find it useful as a daymark. It does function as a light pole to illuminate the surrounding area up until midnight and is an interesting and unusual sight from Marine Drive in St Kilda.

Port Melbourne Channel
Front (Opposite)

Port Melbourne, Port Phillip Victoria

Ref: **2338**   Built: **1924**   Elevation: **14**
Tower: **16**   Range: **0**

Located on piles between Princes Pier and Station Pier this wooden framed light, in conjunction with the Port Melbourne Channel Rear light would guide ships through Hobson's Bay into the Port Melbourne piers. At one time there was a walkway connecting the light to shore but this fell into disrepair and was removed. The light had not been exhibited for a number of years and needed to be repaired. In 1998 it was restored as part of the Beacon Cove housing development. It can be viewed from The Boulevard in Port Melbourne.

Port Melbourne Channel
Rear (Right)

Port Melbourne, Melbourne Victoria

Ref: **2338.1**   Built: **1924**   Elevation: **24**
Tower: **26**   Range: **37**

This concrete rear light is 500m north of the front light for the Port Melbourne Channel. It also has a directional light below the lead light that shows green, white and red lights 24 hours a day. Originally it was surrounded by a BP fuel distribution depot but the site was cleared in the early 1990's. The Beacon Cove housing development has now been built around it using the tower as a focal point. The light now shines down Beacon Vista to the port. As the light only has an arc of 1.5 degrees it does not disturb its new neighbours. It can be viewed at the end of Beacon Vista in Port Melbourne.

The top photos show the lights in 2001 while the bottom photos show the lights as they were in 1994.

Timeball Tower

Williamstown, Melbourne Victoria

Ref: ****   Built: **1849**   Elevation: **22**   Tower: **17**
Range: **0**

The first light in Victoria was exhibited from this site as early as 1840. The present tower of bluestone blocks was constructed in 1849 with a four-reflector light. The light was upgraded to a nine-reflector light in 1852. To provide ships in the harbour with the exact time each day the light was turned off at 19:58 and then turned on again at 20:00. When the light was extinguished in 1860 the 'Timeball' apparatus was erected on top of the lighthouse. It consisted of a large copper ball that was hauled to the top of an iron mast. At exactly 1:00pm each day the ball was 'dropped' thus allowing the chronometers on the ships to be calibrated. In 1926 the keeper of the Timeball died while on duty but it was ten days before anyone noticed that the ball had not been dropped. It was then realised that the ships were listening to the local radio stations to obtain the correct time and the 'dropping of the ball' was discontinued. It is one of the earliest examples of modern technology making visual observation obsolete. In 1934 a nine metre round brick extension was added to the tower. This and the light were removed in 1987. The tower, restored to its original state complete with a Timeball is easily visited from the end of Nelson Place in Williamstown.

Prince George Shoal

Portarlington, Port Phillip Victoria

Ref: **2236** Built: **1995** Elevation: **7**
Tower: **7** Range: **15**

The original light, built in 1931 was on top of a small cylinder that in turn was supported on piles. This was replaced by the current light-on-a-pole in the mid 1990's. It marks the outer edge of the shallow Prince George Bank that ships must go around when entering the Port Richards Channel on the way into the Port of Geelong. Just offshore from Portarlington it can be viewed from a small boat.

West Channel Pile

St Leonards, Port Phillip Victoria

Ref: **2232** Built: **1881** Elevation: **11** Tower: **12** Range: **26W 20R**

The current pile structure at the northern end of the Western Channel replaced a lightship that had been on duty at the site since 1854. The lantern and its support structure from the lightship were used in the construction of the permanent light. There is also a radar responder on the tower that sends back an identification signal when pinged. Just offshore from St Leonards it can be viewed from a small boat.

Coles Light

Queenscliff, Port Phillip Victoria

Ref: **2225**   Built: **1947**   Elevation: **5**   Tower: **5**   Range: **17**

The small white hut sitting on a pile structure is easily identified as it has 'COLES' in large letters painted on it. The light serves a dual function. In line with the Monash light on Point Nepean it guides ships into the Coles Channel. When in line with the Shortland Bluff Light in Queenscliff it guides ships into the northern entrance of the Western Channel. Just offshore from Queenscliff it can be viewed from a small boat.

Wedge Light

Queenscliff, Port Phillip Victoria

Ref: ********   Built: **1993**   Elevation: **3**   Tower: **3**   Range: **0**

The Wedge located on Pope's Eye Bank was built in 1993. It sits on top of a steel column next to the pile structure from the original light that was built in 1930. In line with the Monash light on Point Nepean it guides ships into the southern entrance of the Western Channel. The hut from the old light that was removed in 1993 is stored at the Queenscliff Maritime Museum. The pile structure was not removed as it is used as a nesting site by Australian gannets that build their nests on its concrete platform. Just offshore from Queenscliff it can be viewed from a small boat.

Point Lonsdale
Point Lonsdale Victoria

Ref: **2194**   Built: **1902**   Elevation: **37**   Tower: **21**   Range: **22W 19R**

Although there had been a number of navigational aids erected at Point Lonsdale it was not until the *Lightning* struck an uncharted rock near the entrance to the Bay that it was acknowledged that a light was needed. The first light was the original wooden Queenscliff low light. It was re-erected on the site in 1863 and painted with distinctive red and black bands. Although the tower was built in 1863 it was not lit until 1867. Up until then a temporary light was exhibited. The current concrete tower was built in 1902. In addition to identifying the entrance to The Rip it is also used by ships in the Bay's South Channel.

The octagonal signal station and observation room were added in 1950. In 1999 the signal station activities were demanned. As a result tours of the lighthouse are now available. The light is at the end of Point Lonsdale Road in Point Lonsdale.

Shortland Bluff

Queenscliff Victoria

Ref: **2200**   Built: **1863**   Elevation: **40**   Tower: **25**   Range: **26**

There are five lights that guide ships through the Heads (commonly known as 'The Rip') into Port Phillip. They are the Shortland Bluff (high light) and the Murray, Queenscliff and Hume (low lights) plus the Point Lonsdale Light. Although the heads are 3.05 kilometres wide the channel needed by the largest ships is only 200m across. Originally known as Whales Head it was renamed in honour of John Shortland, the first officer on the *Lady Nelson*. The bluff's first light, supposedly made of local sandstone was built in 1843 but deteriorated rapidly. The second light, constructed in 1863 was located 100m to the north and 30m to the west of the original light. Built of basalt blocks and equipped with a Chance Brothers lens it was a significant improvement over the original light. As the tower was left its natural colour it has become known as the Black Light. In 1885 the area became a military fortress and the keepers were moved to new houses built outside the fortress walls. Their original five brick and stone terrace houses inside the fort still exist. Those built outside the fort have since been demolished. Also of interest is the Signal Station next to the Black Light. Built in the mid 1800's the wooden structure was raised on to a new brick base in 1936. This was done to maintain a clear view of the sea over new housing that had been built on the fort. The fort is no longer a restricted area so tours of the fort, the old signal station and the lighthouse area are now available. All four Queenscliff lights are accessible from Fort Queenscliff on Gellibrand Street.

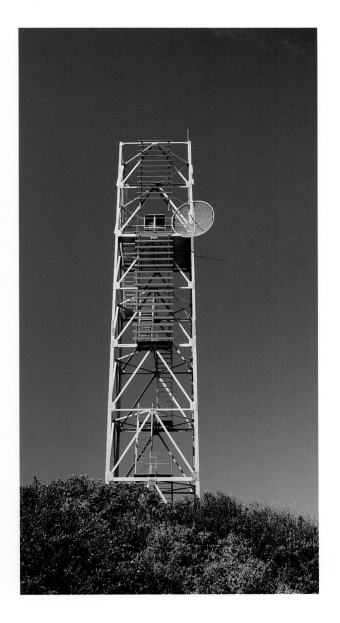

Hume Tower (Far left)
Queenscliff Victoria

Ref: **2199.9**   Built: **1924**   Elevation: **28**
Tower: **24**   Range: **20R**

During the early 1920's the channel through the heads was widened and deepened. The Hume Tower, a steel frame structure to the west of the White Light was constructed to mark the western boundary of the enlarged channel.

Queenscliff Low (Left)
Queenscliff Victoria

Ref: **2200.1**   Built: **1863**   Elevation: **28**
Tower: **20**   Range: **22W 20R 11G**

The first low light, a prefabricated wooden structure was built in 1854 and displayed a fixed red light. It was replaced with a new tower built in 1863 about 30m to the west of the original tower. It was also built with basalt blocks but as it was painted white it became known as the White Light. Once the new light was operational the original tower was removed and re-erected at Point Lonsdale where it remained in service until 1902. It was then demolished and used as firewood.

Murray Tower
(Left, Rightmost tower)
Queenscliff Victoria

Ref: **2204**   Built: **1975**   Elevation: **25**
Tower: **18**   Range: **9G**

This steel frame tower, to the east of the White Light was built to mark the eastern limits of The Rip. It replaced an unlit brick tower known as 'The Obelisk'. Once the light was in operation the obelisk was removed.

Split Point
Airey's Inlet Victoria

Ref: **2182**   Built: **1891**   Elevation: **66**   Tower: **34**   Range: **37W** **30R**

Originally called Eagles Nest Point its name was changed to Split Point in 1913. It is also known as the White Lady. The cement-rendered concrete tower has a Chance Brothers first order lantern and a 920mm focal radius lens. As with most lights of the era it started operation using kerosene. In 1919 it was upgraded to automatic acetylene operation and demanned. It was then converted to electricity in 1972. The light exhibits both red and white sectors. The accepted practice is for the white light to indicate a safe passage and red to indicate danger such as a reef. For some reason the colours were reversed and it was not until 1913 that the anomaly was corrected. The keepers' cottages, that were auctioned off in 1935 are in excellent condition and are available for rent. It is accessible by road.

In the photo on the left the entrance building attached to the tower was a temporary structure added for a TV show. The real entrance is shown in the photo on the right.

Cape Otway
Apollo Bay Victoria

NEW:
Ref: **2172**   Built: **1994**   Elevation: **73**   Tower: **2**
Range: **35W   28R**
OLD:
Ref: ****   Built: **1848**   Elevation: **91**   Tower: **20**
Range: **46W   39R**

Cape Otway is the oldest lighthouse in Victoria and the third to be established on the mainland although six had already been built in Tasmania. Cape Otway or Cape Wickham on King Island was often the first land that a ship would encounter some months and 20,000 kilometres after leaving England. As the gap between the two is only 84 kilometres wide it became known as the 'Eye of the Needle' or the 'Funnel'. The need for landfall lights on these two capes was obvious although the Cape Wickham light was not built until 13 years later. Constructed from local stone blocks the tower is still in excellent condition. The original catoptric lens was replaced by a Chance Brothers first order lens system in 1891. When converted to electrical operation in 1939 it produced 1,000,000 candelas. The first radio beacon in Australia was also installed at Cape Otway in 1939. When the lightstation was handed over to the State in 1994 a new solar powered 'Tupperware' light on a GRP cabinet with an intensity of only 87,000 candelas was built in front of the old tower. Having a separate operational light does mean that the magnificent first order lens can be viewed by the public and the original keepers' houses that were rebuilt in 1857 can be rented. The 17km road to the lighthouse turns off the Great Ocean Road 20 kilometres west of Apollo Bay.

The New tower (Below)

The photo above of the tower and its keeper, Peter Scott was taken on the 5th January 1994, the old tower's last night of operation

The photo to the right was taken during the 150th celebrations on the 29th August 1998.

Flagstaff Hill Leading Lights
Warrnambool Victoria

FRONT:	Ref: **2158**	Built: **1871**	Elevation: **27**	Tower: **8**	
		Range: **9W 9R 9G**			
REAR:	Ref: **2158.1**	Built: **1871**	Elevation: **33**	Tower: **7**	
		Range: **11**			

In the early 1850's there were two obelisks on Flagstaff Hill that acted as daymarks for guiding ships into Lady Bay. To complement the obelisks a light was constructed on Middle Island in 1859. It was used as a front light when lined up with a light on a wooden tower built on the beach in 1860. Unfortunately this system did not work very well particularly in rough weather when waves would obscure the beach light. In 1871 the Middle Island light was moved on to a new base on Flagstaff Hill at the site of the upper obelisk. At the same time the light from the Beach lighthouse was relocated to the top of the lower obelisk. The lights have been powered in more ways than any other lights in Australia. They have used colza oil, kerosene, town gas, acetylene, solar power and electric power. The lighthouse reserve, including the bluestone keepers' houses and signal station is now part of the Flagstaff Hill Maritime Museum. Although the lights are still operational it is possible to tour the upper light. The museum is on Merri Street in Warrnambool.

The Front light is on the right and the Rear light is shown below

Griffiths Island

Port Fairy Victoria

Ref: **2146**   Built: **1859**   Elevation: **12**   Tower: **11**
Range: **20**

This bluestone tower was built on Rabbit Island at the mouth of the Moyne River. Rabbit Island eventually became part of the much larger Griffiths Island. One of the unusual features of the light is its stairway. Each step is an elongated wall block that extends into the tower creating an unusual and functional spiral staircase. Unfortunately access to the tower and its interesting staircase are not currently available. A causeway, at the end of Gipps Street bridges the narrow channel to the island. From there the light is just a pleasant walk across the island.

Whaler's Bluff
Portland Victoria

Ref: **2138**   Built: **1889**   Elevation: **41**   Tower: **12**   Range: **28**

This bluestone tower with an English catadioptric lantern was originally built on Battery Point in 1859 and was known as the Portland Bay Light. Due to guns being installed on Battery Point it was moved in 1889 to North Bluff now known as Whaler's Bluff or Whaler Point. The old keepers' houses are privately owned. The light is in a small reserve at the end of Lighthouse Street.

Cape Nelson
Portland Victoria

Ref: 2136   Built: 1884   Elevation: 75   Tower: 32   Range: 39

Named after Lieutenant James Grant's ship the *Lady Nelson* this bluestone tower provides a point of reference for ships entering Western Bass Strait. Some literature mentions a square wooden tower that was built on the site in the 1870's but this has not been substantiated. The tower has a Chance Brothers 3.6m lantern and a 4-panel 250mm catadioptric rotating lens system. One of the features of the lightstation is the low rubble wall that surrounds the keepers' houses to help protect them from the wind. A higher wall extends from the storeroom and stables building to the tower. The storeroom and stables have now been converted into a spectacular restaurant. The three houses are in excellent condition and two are available for rent. The lightstation is 12km from Portland at the end of the Cape Nelson Lighthouse Road.

Index – Tasmania

Map	107
East Moncoeur Island	108
Hogan Island	108
North East Island	109
Deal Island	110
Goose Island	112
South West Island	112
Holloway Point	113
Cat Island	113
Cape Barren	113
Swan Island	114
Craggy Island	116
Cumberland	116
Cape Wickham	117
Stokes Point	118
Currie Harbour	118
Iron Pot Island	119
Eddystone Point	120
Cape Tourville	122
Chicken Point	122
Point Home Lookout	123
Tasman Island	124
Cape Bruny	126
Maatsuyker Island	129
Cape Sorell	130
Entrance Islet	131
Bonnet Islet	131
Sandy Cape	132
Bluff Hill	132
Highfield Point	132
Rocky Cape	133
Round Hill Point	133
Table Cape	134
Entrance Front Devonport	135
Entrance Rear Devonport	135
Mersey Bluff	136
Low Head	138
Middle Channel	139
She Oak Point	139

**Middle Channel Light Georgetown
Tasmania**

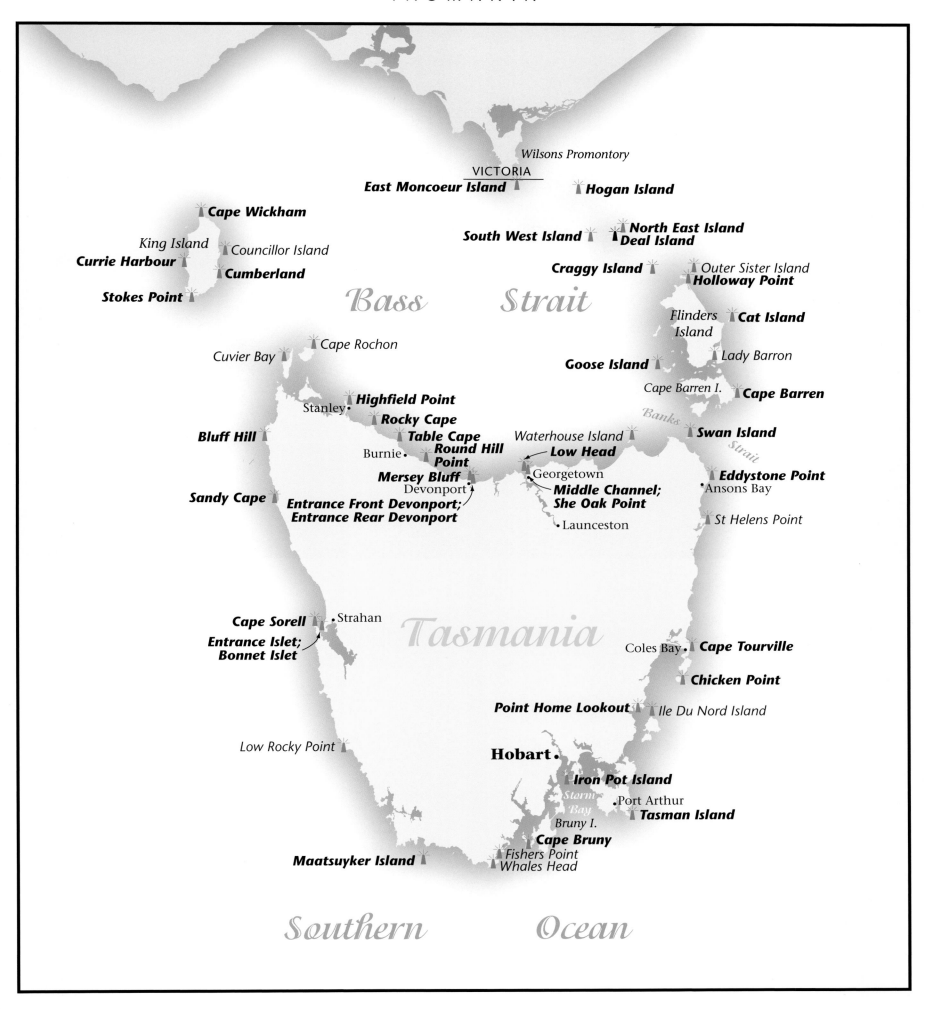

Wilsons Promontory

VICTORIA

East Moncoeur Island

Hogan Island

Cape Wickham

King Island
Councillor Island
Currie Harbour
Cumberland

South West Island
North East Island
Deal Island

Stokes Point

Bass *Strait*

Craggy Island
Outer Sister Island
Holloway Point

Flinders Island
Cat Island

Cape Rochon
Cuvier Bay

Lady Barron

Goose Island

Cape Barren I.
Cape Barren

Highfield Point
Stanley•
Rocky Cape
Bluff Hill
Table Cape
Waterhouse Island
Swan Island
Burnie•
Round Hill Point
Low Head
Banks
Mersey Bluff
Georgetown
Strait
Devonport
Middle Channel; She Oak Point
Eddystone Point
Ansons Bay
Sandy Cape
Entrance Front Devonport; Entrance Rear Devonport
•Launceston
St Helens Point

Cape Sorell
•Strahan
Tasmania
Entrance Islet; Bonnet Islet
Coles Bay•
Cape Tourville

Chicken Point

Point Home Lookout
Ile Du Nord Island

Low Rocky Point

Hobart•

Iron Pot Island
Storm Bay
•Port Arthur
Bruny I.
Tasman Island
Cape Bruny
Maatsuyker Island
Fishers Point
Whales Head

Southern *Ocean*

107

East Moncoeur Island (Above)
Bass Strait Tasmania

Ref: **2492.5**   Built: **1983**   Elevation: **102**
Tower: **2**   Range: **17**

Hogan Island (Left)
Bass Strait Tasmania

Ref: **2493**   Built: **1965**   Elevation: **136**
Tower: **4**   Range: **24**

These two GRP cabinets provide location markers amongst the many islands that dot Bass Strait. Although they are purely functional structures their contrasting locations highlight the varied terrain in which lights can now be placed. As they are small and can hardly be seen they do not make very good daymarks but the profile of the islands make the islands easy to recognise during daylight hours. Moncoeur is only accessible by helicopter while Hogan can also be accessed by boat.

North East Island

Kent Group, Bass Strait Tasmania

Ref: **2542.4**   Built: **1987**   Elevation: **107**   Tower: **4**   Range: **26**

The Kent Group is a cluster of four rugged islands, Deal, Erith, Dover and North East in central Bass Strait. The light on North East is a four metre GRP cabinet with a Tupperware light as are most of the lights on the Bass Strait Islands. Other northern Bass Strait islands in the vicinity with GRP cabinets are **Citadel** (Ref: 2486, built in 1913, replaced in 1982), **East Moncoeur** (Ref: 2492.5, built in 1983), **Hogan** (Ref: 2493, built in 1965), **South West** (Ref: 2542.3, built in 1987) and **Craggy** (Ref: 2542.5, built in 1981). The wide use of GRP cabinets in these remote nearly inaccessible places emphasises how simple, reliable and cost effective they are. The North East Island light was built, along with the light on South West Island to supplement and then replace the light on Deal Island. It is only accessible by helicopter.

North East Island is a typical 4m GRP cabinet with a solar powered FA-251 (Tupperware) lantern

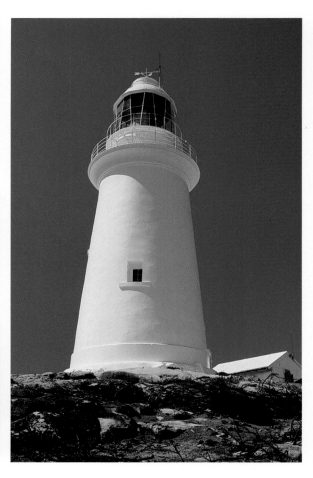

Deal Island

Kent Group, Bass Strait Tasmania

Ref: **** Built: **1848** Elevation: **305** Tower: **22** Range: **0**
(When operational the range was a nominal 45km or a geographical 70km)

The granite rubble tower perched on a cliff top 280m above sea level is the highest lighthouse in the Southern Hemisphere. Although its height would appear to be an advantage it was the opposite. Even on clear nights cloud would often form around the tower obliterating the light for up to 40% of the time. Upgrading the light to an electric first order Chance Brothers lens did not solve the problem so new lights were built on North East and South West Islands and in 1992 the Deal light was extinguished. Operating the lightstation was a formidable task. Supplies and fuel were landed in East Bay and were then moved three kilometres uphill to the tower. Originally this was done with a series of horse driven whims and Bullock drays, then with 4WDs and finally with helicopters. The keepers also had to provide much of their own food, as resupply in the early days was spasmodic. Growing vegetables was easy; protecting them from the local wallaby population was a challenge.

There have been a number of bush fires on the island. The original assistant keepers' cottages near the tower were destroyed in 1919 and another cottage was burnt in 1950. As a result the only original house still existing is the head keeper's cottage located on East bay. It is currently set up as a museum. Then in 1994 the lighthouse was badly damaged by fire. Even though the light was non-operational AMSA staff spent six weeks repairing the lantern room, replacing charred woodwork and repainting the tower. On the opposite page the lighthouse is shown before and after the fire and after it had been repaired.

Since the last long term residents left the island in 1998 the tower and residences have deteriorated. Access to the island is by boat or helicopter. The rough, boomerang shaped runway is an option as long as there are people around to chase the wallabies off it.

Goose Island (Right)
Flinders Island, Banks Strait Tasmania

Ref: **3600**   Built: **1846**   Elevation: **36**   Tower: **30**   Range: **33**

Goose and Swan Island lights were built to assist ships sailing through the Banks Strait to Launceston. In stark contrast to Deal Island the masonry rubble tower is on a low flat island. Before being taken over by the Public Works Department construction was being carried out by the Department of Roads who referred to it as the Goose Island Road Station a name as inappropriate as their ability to manage the building of it. As with other island stations resupply was spasmodic making life on the island difficult for the keepers. When it was converted to acetylene in 1931 the keepers were removed and the houses demolished. In 1985 it was converted to electricity using a wind generator and batteries. Due to high maintenance costs (enough wind was never a problem!) solar panels were installed in 1990 and the wind generator was removed. Located west of Whitemark on Flinders Island it is accessible by boat or helicopter.

South West Island (Below)
West of the Kent Group, Bass Strait Tasmania

Ref: **2542.3**   Built: **1987**   Elevation: **100**   Tower: **2**   Range: **19**

This is a two metre GRP cabinet with a Tupperware light. The light was built, along with the light on North East Island to supplement and then replace the light on Deal Island. It is only accessible by helicopter.

Cape Barren (Above)

Cape Barren Island, Bass Strait Tasmania

| Ref: **3601.6** | Built: **1967** | Elevation: **25** | Tower: **4** | Range: **15** |

Holloway Point (Top left)

North Coast, Flinders Island, Tasmania

| Ref: **3600.6** | Built: **1967** | Elevation: **9** | Tower: **4** | Range: **15** |

Cat Island (Bottom left)

Flinders Island, Bass Strait Tasmania

| Ref: **3600.8** | Built: **1967** | Elevation: **31** | Tower: **4** | Range: **26** |

The Furneaux Group consists of three large islands, Flinders, Cape Barren and Clarke plus a number of smaller islands. They effectively form a barrier across south eastern Bass Strait. To guide ships in the area there have been a number of GRP lights built. The three shown here were all built in 1967. All are four metre high GRP cabinets with solar powered lights. Although they are purely functional their location provides some appeal.

There is also **Waterhouse Island** (Ref: 3599, built in 1970) and **Outer Sister Island** (Ref: 3600.5, built in 1992). Holloway Point can be reached by road, the others can be accessed by boat or helicopter.

Swan Island
Cape Portland, Banks Strait Tasmania

Ref: 3602	Built: 1845	Elevation: 30	Tower: 27	Range: 33

Although construction of the masonry rubble tower commenced after the nearly identical Goose Island tower, the light was first exhibited some months earlier. It is the second oldest highway tower in Australia, after Cape Bruny. Like all Tasmanian lights constructed in this period the tower was painted white with a red lantern room. They are now all completely white. One of the unusual things about the island is its large population of tiger snakes, a fatter slower variety than their mainland cousins.

The housing for the keepers was inadequate until a new brick head keeper's cottage was built in 1908. The assistant keepers then used the original 1845 stone house until it was replaced by fibro-cement quarters in 1927.

When the station was demanned in 1986 a wind generator similar to Goose Island was installed. At the same time the island was sold, except for the tower and 1 hectare on the NE Point for $307,000. It was sold again in 2004 for about $2,000,000. The wind generator, replaced by solar power in 1990 is still used by the caretakers and visitors. The island is accessible by small plane, boat or helicopter. At one time the island's caretakers provided superb visitor accommodation but it is now on a more casual basis.

Craggy Island (Above)

Flinders Island, Bass Strait Tasmania

Ref: **2542.5**   Built: **1981**   Elevation: **114**   Tower: **2**   Range: **30**

Cumberland (Right)

King Island, Bass Strait Tasmania

Ref: **2191.8**   Built: **1965**   Elevation: **77**   Tower: **4**   Range: **13**

These two GRP cabinets highlight the varied terrain in which lights can now be economically placed. Craggy is a rugged, nearly inaccessible island between King and Flinders Islands while Cumberland is in the middle of a farm on eastern King Island. (The Craggy Island light is the white speck on the top of the rightmost peak.) Craggy is accessible by helicopter but Cumberland, being on private property is not readily accessible.

Cape Wickham (Opposite)

King Island, Bass Strait Tasmania

Ref: **2186**   Built: **1861**   Elevation: **85**   .Tower: **48**   Range: **45**

Cape Wickham or Cape Otway in Victoria was often the first land that a ship would encounter some months and 20,000 kilometres after leaving England. As it is only 84km between the two points it was obvious that landfall lights were needed so that ships could accurately determine their position. Even so the Cape Wickham light was not built until 13 years after the Otway light was first exhibited. Unfortunately some captains were not aware of the presence of the new light and thinking it was the Cape Otway light steered south and were wrecked on King Island. The light, at the northern tip of King Island is the tallest classical tower in Australia. Constructed from local granite it has 220 wooden steps leading up to the lantern room. In 1946 a small electric revolving light replaced the original first order catadioptric fixed lens. A panel from the lens is now in the Currie museum. When demanned in 1918 the keepers' cottages except for the mechanics residence were demolished. The light can be reached by road from Currie.

Stokes Point (Below)

Seal Bay King Island, Bass Strait Tasmania

Ref: **2190**   Built: **1971**   Elevation: **44**   Tower: **9**
Range: **19**

This uninspiring square white concrete tower with a Tupperware light, that replaced the original 1951 tower is located on wind swept farmland at the southern tip of King Island. It is accessible along a track that hugs the shore of Seal Bay. There are two other nondescript lights on King Island. Both are GRP cabinets on the east coast, **Cumberland** near Grassy (Ref: 2191.8, built in 1965) and **Councillor Island** (Ref: 2192, built in 1974). Neither of these is easily accessible.

Currie Harbour (Right)

Currie, King Island, Bass Strait Tasmania

Ref: **2189**   Built: **1880**   Elevation: **46**   Tower: **21**
Range: **41**

Although small boats use it as a harbour light it is also a landfall light for ships entering Bass Strait. Prefabricated in England by Chance Brothers, the 312 wrought and cast iron sections were reassembled on site. It is nearly identical with the East Light at McCrae in Port Phillip. In 1899 the original lens was replaced by a first order lens that in turn was replaced with a fourth order lens in 1940. In 1989 the light in the tower was extinguished and a light-on-a-pole took its place. After a public outcry by the people of Currie the old light was relit in 1995. The tower and the keeper's residence that is now used as a museum are within walking distance of Currie's main street.

Iron Pot Island

Storm Bay, Hobart Tasmania

Ref: **3622**   Built: **1833**   Elevation: **20**   Tower: **12**   Range: **19**

Sitting on a 0.4 hectare rock at the mouth of the Derwent River (officially known since 1884 as the 'Derwent Light') Iron Pot was the second light to be built in Australia and is the oldest still operating from the same tower. In 1832 a light, consisting of two poles and a cross bar was erected but for obvious reasons was not satisfactory and was replaced by the current stone rubble structure in 1833.

In 1884 the original oil powered reflector lamps were replaced with a Chance Brothers fourth order dioptric lens and in 1904 it was the first light in Australia to be converted to vaporised kerosene. The light was converted to acetylene in 1920, automated and the keepers were withdrawn. It was converted to solar power in 1977. During the 1860's the original two small stone cottages were demolished and replaced by two imposing wooden houses. After automation in 1920 these two houses were also demolished and the timber from them used by Hobart builders. Regular boat tours go around the island.

Eddystone Point
Ansons Bay Tasmania

Ref: **3606**   Built: **1889**   Elevation: **42**   Tower: **35**
Range: **48**

Unlike its famous namesake on a wave-swept rock off the English coast this Eddystone light is located well above the Tasman Sea. Both though are elegant granite towers. It still has its Chance Brothers 3.7m lantern with a 920mm first order focal radius catadioptric lens with an intensity of 1,200,000 candelas. The small light at the base of the tower was used to light Victoria Rocks but was extinguished when the station converted to electrical power. The three granite keepers' cottages were in good condition when the last keeper, John Denman, retired in 1994. Access is by road from St. Helens or Gladstone.

Cape Tourville (Right)

Coles Bay, Freycinet Peninsula Tasmania

Ref: **3608** Built: **1971** Elevation: **126**
Tower: **11** Range: **39**

Cape Tourville, along with Point Homes was built to replace the difficult-to-access Cape Forrestier (or Forestier) light. It is a concrete tower with a round utility building covered with granite rocks that blend in with the surrounding landscape. Located in the Freycinet National Park there are spectacular views of the rugged coast from the tower. It can be accessed by road from Coles Bay.

Point Home Lookout (Opposite)

Triabunna Tasmania

Ref: **3609.8** Built: **1971** Elevation: **57**
Tower: **14** Range: **33**

Point Home, along with Cape Tourville was built to replace the Cape Forrestier light. The concrete tower and round utility building, covered with granite rocks is nearly identical to the Cape Tourville light. Its main function is to guide ships bringing woodchips to the local pulp-mill. It can be viewed from the ferry that goes from Triabunna to Maria Island.

Chicken Point (Right)

Schouten Island, Coles Bay Tasmania

Ref: **3609.4** Built: **1970** Elevation: **44**
Tower: **4** Range: **15**

Located on the southern tip of Schouten Island in the Freycinet National Park this may only be a GRP cabinet but it is in a spectacular location. It overlooks the Tailefer Rocks a group of small outcrops also known as the Hen and Chickens. In contrast the GRP cabinet on **Ile Du Nord** Island (Ref: 3609.6, built in 1974) is located on low flat island just a few miles to the south. Both can be reached by helicopter or with difficulty by boat.

Tasman Island

Port Arthur Tasmania

Ref: **3614** Built: **1906** Elevation: **276** Tower: **29** Range: **33**

Tasman Island is the most spectacular lighthouse location in Australia, particularly when viewed from The Blade on Cape Pillar. It is the highest light in Australia being only 30m lower than the non-operational Deal Island light. The 29m tower is dwarfed by the 250m (830') high cliffs that rise abruptly out of the ocean on all sides of the island. The cast iron panels for the tower were prefabricated in England, shipped out to the island, hauled up the cliffs and assembled. To get the sections to the construction site they were unloaded from the lighthouse tender on to a launch. From there a flying fox moved them up on to a ledge about 30m up the cliff face. They were then hauled by an engine driven winch on a steep tramline to the top of the cliff and transferred to a horse-powered whim that moved them to the lighthouse. Until helicopters took over, supplies had to go through the same procedure. The original Chance Brothers first order catadioptric lens and lantern room were removed in 1976 and were replaced with a Tupperware light and a small lantern room that detracts from the overall symmetry of the tower. The original lens is now on display in the Australian National Maritime Museum in Sydney. A wind generator was also installed in 1976 and although it worked effectively it was replaced with solar panels in 1991. There are three solid brick Federation style keepers' cottages but unfortunately they have deteriorated since the tower was demanned in 1977. The only reasonable access is by helicopter.

Cape Bruny (Also overleaf)
South Bruny Island Tasmania

NEW: Ref: **3654**   Built: **1996**   Elev: **93**   Tower: **4**   Range: **35**
OLD: Ref: ****   Built: **1838**   Elev: **105**   Tower: **13**   Range: **48**

Cape Bruny juts out into Adventure Bay named by Tobias Furneaux in the 1750's. The light was the fourth lighthouse to be built in Australia and up until 1996 was the second oldest still operating from the same tower. It was designed by John Lee Archer and built, starting in 1836 by convict labour using local stone. The original reflector lights were powered with sperm whale oil then colza oil, coal oil and kerosene. The reflectors were replaced in 1903 with a second order Chance Brothers lens, sourced from Cape Sorell. In 1996 a new GRP cabinet was built and the original light was extinguished and the station demanned. When the lights at Cape Bruny and Maatsuyker Island were converted to the solar powered Tupperware lights their range went from 48 to 35 and 48 to 33km respectively. As a result the loom of their lights no longer overlapped. To fill in this dark space a new light was built at **Whale Head** on South East Cape near Ramsgate (Ref: 3655.3, built in 1997). The Cape Bruny lights can be reached by road and ferry from Hobart.

Cape Bruny, South Bruny Island

Maatsuyker Island

Ramsgate South Coast Tasmania

NEW:	Ref: **3656**	Built: **1996**	Elev: **140**	Tower: **2**	Range: **33**
OLD:	Ref: ********	Built: **1891**	Elev: **107**	Tower: **13**	Range: **48**

Named by Abel Tasman in 1642 the island has Australia's most southern lighthouse on it. It was supposedly named after Johan Maetsuyker. Another story says it was named Maatsuyker (which means 'mounds of sugar' in Dutch) after the profuse white tea tree flowers on the island that looked like - 'mounds of sugar'. Built with rendered red brick cavity walls it has a Chance Brothers first order lantern and a 920mm focal radius lens with an intensity of 1,000,000 candelas. Although the island has 250 wet days per year and is lashed by regular gales, it was quite a popular station. Until helicopters took over supplies were landed in a sheltered bay at the NE end of the island and hauled up to the lighthouse on a horse-powered whim. In 1996 a GRP cabinet replaced the old light that was then extinguished. After downgrading the looms of the Cape Bruny and Maatsuyker lights no longer overlapped so a supplemental light was built at Whale Head. The Federation style keepers' houses are being kept in good condition by caretakers stationed on the island. Maatsuyker can be accessed by helicopter or by sea (weather permitting).

Cape Sorell
Strahan Tasmania

Ref: **3660**   Built: **1899**   Elevation: **51**   Tower: **37**   Range: **26**

Proceeding up the west coast from Maatsuyker Island the next light ia a small GRP cabinet at **Low Rocky Point** (Ref: 3659, built in 1963). This is followed by Cape Sorell near the entrance to Macquarie Harbour. One of the most graceful towers in Australia Cape Sorell was designed by Hutchison and Hutchison in Hobart who also designed Maatsuyker and the Hells Gate lights. Originally powered by oil it was converted to diesel electric operation in 1935. The light was automated in 1971 and the keepers withdrawn at the same time. In 1988 a small solar powered APRB-251 Tupperware light replaced the original Chance Brothers apparatus. Unfortunately the quite large solid brick keepers' houses, trimmed with local hardwoods were demolished at the same time. Access to the tower is difficult.

Entrance Islet (Top)

Strahan Tasmania

Ref: **3664**	Built: **1892**	Elev: **10**
Tower: **8**	Range: **19W 15R**	

Bonnet Islet (Bottom)

Strahan Tasmania

Ref: **3668**	Built: **1892**	Elev: **14**
Tower: **8**	Range: **19W 4R 4G**	

These two six sided, wood framed, weatherboard clad harbour lights were built in 1892 to guide shipping through the 120m wide entrance into Macquarie Harbour that is, after Port Phillip the largest harbour in Australia. Sarah Island in the harbour was used as a penal colony for serious offenders and the conditions on the island were so harsh that the convicts entering the harbour referred to it as the Entrance to Hell or Hells Gate. The Entrance light is adjacent to the narrow entrance channel while Bonnet is on a small island just inside the harbour. Boat tours from Strahan go out to Hells Gate providing excellent views of the lights.

Sandy Cape (Right)

Kenneth Bay, West Coast Tasmania

Ref: **3676**   Built: **1953**   Elevation: **23**
Tower: **6**   Range: **15**

This white square concrete tower is on a remote headland midway along the western Tasmanian coast. It is only accessible by helicopter unless a week long hike is on the agenda.

Bluff Hill (Bottom left)

Arthur River Tasmania

Ref: **3677**   Built: **1982**   Elevation: **52**
Tower: **13**   Range: **30**

This white round concrete tower with a brown brick utility room is very similar to the Cape Tourville and Point Home lookout towers. It replaced the **West Point Light** (built in 1916) about 8km to the north that was then demolished. It uses mains power for its 400mm catadioptric lens. It is accessible by road the turnoff being 6km from Arthur River on the Marrawah Arthur River Road.

Highfield Point (Bottom right)

North Point, Stanley Tasmania

Ref: **3524**   Built: **1924**   Elev: **49**
Tower: **6**   Range: **19W   15R**

The current mains powered light looks like a GRP cabinet with a four metre tapered top attached. It replaced the original light built in 1924 whose lantern room is displayed in Stanley. As it is located in the middle of a farm it can only be viewed from a distance.

There are a number of islands to the NW of Stanley and there are GRP cabinets at **Cuvier Bay on Hunter Island** (Ref: 3518, built in 1924 and replaced in 1984) and **Cape Rochon on Three Hummock Island** (Ref: 3520, built in 1924 and replaced in 1983).

Rocky Cape (Above)
Detention River Tasmania

Ref: **3531**   Built: **1968**   Elevation: **64**   Tower: **9**   Range: **32**

This white square concrete tower sits on a spectacular headland in the Rocky Cape National Park. It has a mains powered Chance Bros 400mm catadioptric lens. It is accessible by road from Detention River.

Round Hill Point (Above, Below)
Burnie Tasmania

Ref: **3535**   Built: **1923**   Elev: **30**   Tower: **7**   Range: **33W 26R**

This squat square harbour light is used to guide ships into the Burnie Harbour. It has a Chance Brothers 2.4m lantern and a 400 mm focal radius lens. It can be viewed from the Burnie Devonport road.

Table Cape

Wynyard Tasmania

Ref: **3532**   Built: **1888**   Elev: **180**   Tower: **25**   Range: **33W   26R**

This classical white round masonry tower built at the edge of a sheer cliff has a Chance Brothers second order lantern and 700mm catadioptric lens. When converted to vaporised kerosene in 1913 the number of keepers was reduced to two and after conversion to acetylene in 1920 it was demanned. The keepers' cottages were demolished in 1926. In 1979 the lantern room was rebuilt and the light was converted to mains power. The tower is surrounded by farmland that is used for growing flowers and in spring the tulips, the tower and the sea provide a brilliant spectacle. The lighthouse reserve is accessible by road from Wynyard.

Entrance Lights

Mersey River, Devonport Tasmania

FRONT:
Ref: **3553**   Built: **c1960**   Elevation: **9**
Tower: **7**   Range: **19**
REAR:
Ref: **3553.1**   Built: **c1960** Elevation: **16**
Tower: **11**   Range: **19**

These leading lights are used to guide ships travelling up the narrow Mersey River, particularly the Devonport – Melbourne ferries.

Mersey Bluff

Devonport Tasmania

Ref: **3550**   Built: **1889**   Elev: **37**   Tower: **16**   Range: **32W 26R**

This white round brick tower with red vertical stripes (added in 1929) make it one of the most easily recognised lights in Australia. The Hornby light in Sydney is the only other light with multiple vertical stripes. Built of bricks on a stone base it has a Chance Brothers 700mm dioptric lens. It replaced a number of earlier navigation beacons, obelisks and the Don River light that had been used to guide ships into the Mersey River. It was converted to electric operation in 1920 and demanned. The keepers' cottages were let to local tenants until 1966 when they were demolished. It is easily accessible by road from Devonport.

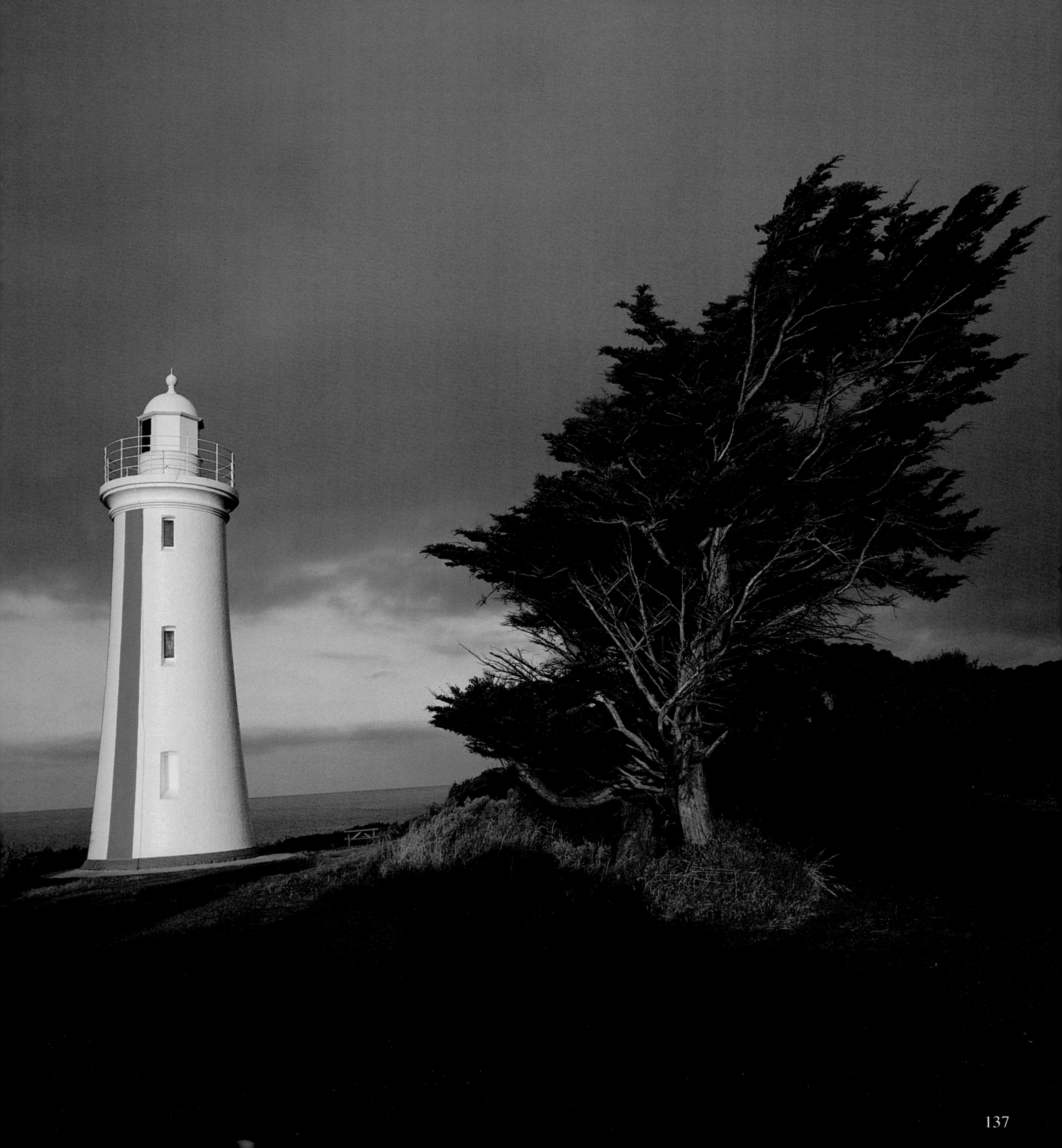

Low Head

Low Head Tasmania

Ref: 3566   Built: 1888   Elevation: 43
Tower: 19   Range: 43

The current double brick structure, designed by Marine Board architect Robert Huckson replaced the original 1833 stucco covered rubble tower that had been designed by Lee Archer. The original tower was demolished soon after the new tower was built. In 1916 its original oil lamp and parabolic reflector lens system was replaced with a Chance Brothers 3.3m lantern with a third order 375mm revolving catadioptric lens. It currently has an intensity of 500,000 candelas. The distinctive red band was not added to the white tower until 1926. An auxiliary red light to cover Hebe reef was added in 1898. It has since been removed. A foghorn (the only one in Tasmania and one of the only Chance Brothers fog signals still in existence) was installed in 1929 and operated until 1973. It is currently being restored. The four keepers' houses were built in 1833, 1891, 1920 and 1943. Although the station has been demanned for some years regular use of the keepers' cottages have kept them in good condition. The light is accessible by road from Georgetown.

Fog Horn Building

She Oak Point

Port Dalrymple, George Town Tasmania

Ref: **3570**   Built: **1881**   Elevation: **11**   Tower: **7**   Range: **17W 17R**

These leading lights also known as the Tamar River leading lights identify the channel into the Tamar River and Port Dalrymple. The She Oak Point light is a white rubble tower with a white light and a vertical red stripe (that has either faded or has been removed since the photo was taken). It serves as a front light for the Middle Channel rear light that is also a white

Middle Channel

Port Dalrymple, George Town Tasmania

Ref: **3569.9**   Built: **1881**   Elevation: **17**   Tower: **7**   Range: **17 R**

rubble tower with a vertical red stripe but it has a red light. Although they were originally manned the responsibility for the lights was handed over to the Low Head keepers and the two keepers' semi-detached stone cottages were sold. They are now used as a bed and breakfast. The towers and cottages are accessible by road from Georgetown.

Index – South Australia

Map	141
Cape Northumberland	142
Cape Banks	143
Point Malcolm	144
Cape Martin	145
Guichen Bay	146
Cape Willoughby	146
Cape St Albans	148
Snapper Point	148
Cape du Couedic	149
Cape Borda	150
Cape Jervis	151
Point Marsden	151
Marino Rocks	152
Troubridge Hill	153
Troubridge Island	154
Cape Spencer	156
West Cape	157
Althorpe Island Front	158
Althorpe Island Rear	158
Corny Point	160
Warburto Point	161
Point Boston	161
Point Lowly	162
Dangerous Reef Centre	164
Cape Donington	165
Taylor Island	166
Waterhouse Point	166
Wedge Island	167
Cape Bauer	167
North Neptune Island	168
South Neptune Island	168

Point Lowly Port Whyalla South Australia

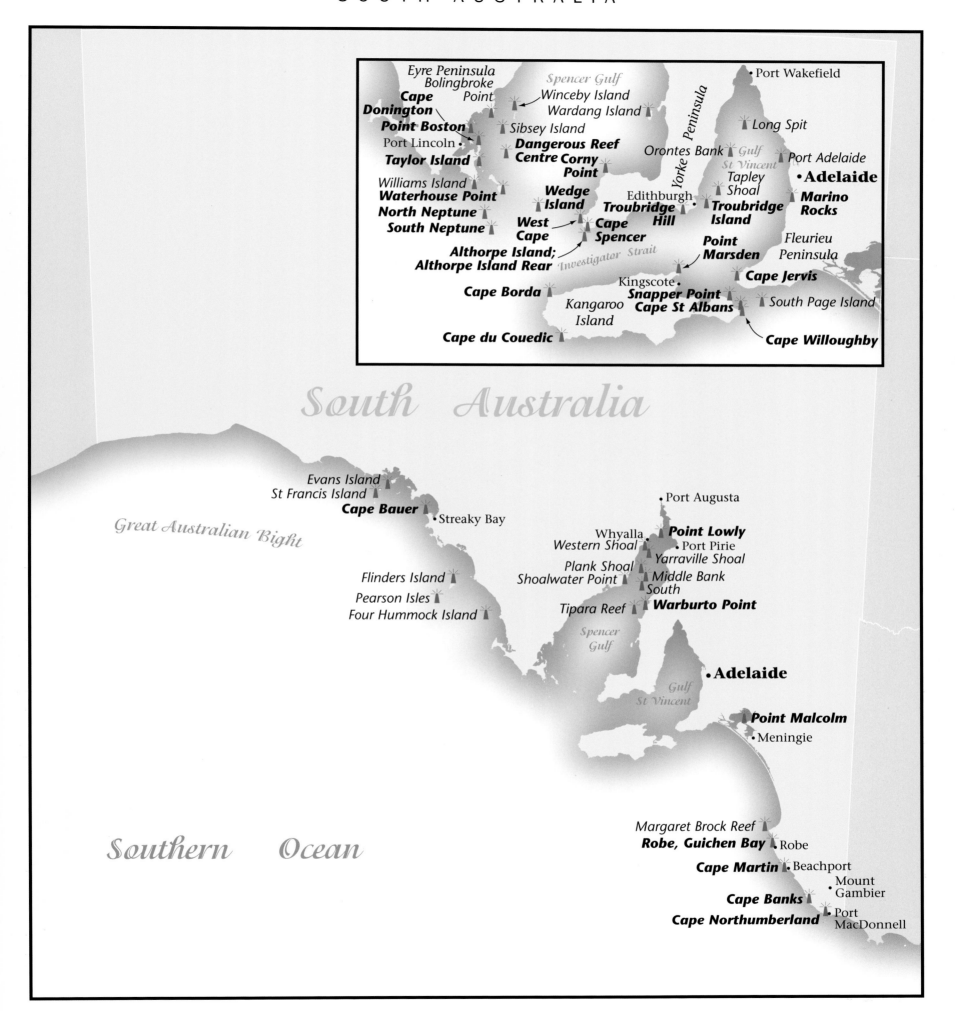

Eyre Peninsula
Bolingbroke Point
Cape Donington
Point Boston
Port Lincoln
Taylor Island
Williams Island
Waterhouse Point
North Neptune
South Neptune
West Cape
Althorpe Island;
Althorpe Island Rear

Spencer Gulf
Winceby Island
Wardang Island
Sibsey Island
Dangerous Reef
Centre Corny
Point
Wedge Island
Troubridge Hill
Cape Spencer

• Port Wakefield
Yorke Peninsula
Orontes Bank *Gulf St Vincent*
Tapley Shoal
Edithburgh
Troubridge Island
Point Marsden
• Long Spit
Port Adelaide
• **Adelaide**
Marino Rocks
Fleurieu Peninsula
Cape Jervis
South Page Island

Investigator Strait
Cape Borda
Kingscote •
Snapper Point
Cape St Albans

Cape du Couedic
Kangaroo Island
Cape Willoughby

South Australia

Evans Island
St Francis Island
Cape Bauer
• Streaky Bay

Great Australian Bight

• Port Augusta

Whyalla
Point Lowly
Western Shoal
• Port Pirie
Plank Shoal
Yarraville Shoal
Shoalwater Point
Middle Bank South
Tipara Reef
Warburto Point

Flinders Island
Pearson Isles
Four Hummock Island

Spencer Gulf

Gulf St Vincent

• **Adelaide**

Point Malcolm
• Meningie

Southern Ocean

Margaret Brock Reef
Robe, Guichen Bay • Robe
Cape Martin • Beachport
Mount Gambier
Cape Banks
Cape Northumberland
• Port MacDonnell

Cape Northumberland

Port MacDonnell South Australia

Ref: **2132** Built: **1882** Elevation: **45**
Tower: **17** Range: **37**

The original tower, built in 1859 only lasted for 23 years. Its location near the edge of a crumbling cliff resulted in it being replaced by the current limestone block tower, built on a concrete base about 400m to the east of the original site. The new tower was painted white with a red band around the centre of the tower. The solid keepers' houses that replaced the original ones around 1910 are in good condition. After conversion to electricity and demanning in 1980 the houses were leased to private individuals. It is easily accessible by road from Port MacDonnell.

Cape Banks
Carpenter Rocks South Australia

Ref: 2130   Built: 1882   Elevation: 25
Tower: 14   Range: 28

Cape Banks is a windswept headland named after Cook's naturalist Sir Joseph Banks. A number of reefs just offshore claimed eight ships before the light was built although another four were lost after the light was put into operation. The stone tower, manned until 1928 is unusual in that it is painted orange. Another unusual feature is its 14-sided DeVille lantern room. It can be reached by road from the small fishing village of Carpenter Rocks.

Point Malcolm

Lake Alexandrina, Meningie South Australia

Ref: ****   Built: **1878**   Elevation: **25**   Tower: **7**
Range: **10**

The Point Malcolm light, at the Narrung narrows between Lake Alexandrina and Lake Albert is the only inland lighthouse in Australia and possibly the Southern Hemisphere. It was built to assist ships that were passing through Lake Alexandrina on their way to Lake Albert or the ports on the Murray River. In 1931, due to the decline in river traffic and possibly the depression the light was turned off. With resurgence in commercial and recreational use an automatic light-on-a-pole next to the old tower has been installed. The concrete tower is in excellent condition but the keepers' cottage is deserted and dilapidated. To reach the light, turn off the Meningie Tailem Bend road at Ashville.

Cape Martin (Above)
Beachport South Australia

Ref: **2126** Built: **1960** Elevation: **38** Tower: **15**
Range: **33**

The first light in the area was built on **Penguin Island** in 1878. When converted to acetylene operation in 1918 it was demanned and the keepers' cottages removed. The light was abandoned in 1960 and its lantern was installed in the new light on Cape Martin. The island is now a bird sanctuary. Originally the new concrete tower was only 4.5m high but this was found to be inadequate and the tower was raised to its current height of 15m in 1980. The ruins of the Penguin Island light can be seen from the Cape Martin site in Beachport.

Penguin Island (Left)

145

Guichen Bay (Right)

Robe South Australia

Ref: **2122.8** Built: **1973** Elevation: **63**
Tower: **19** Range: **37**

The Robe light was built to replace the Cape Jaffa (**Margaret Brock Reef**) light that was moved to Kingston where it has been restored as a museum. It is an unusual white concrete tower made up of a three-sided star structure that widens out from 3.5m at its base to 5.0m at the top. The light also replaced the 12m **Cape Dombey obelisk**, built in 1855 to assist ships entering Guichen Bay. It is easily reached being located in Robe.

Cape Willoughby (Opposite and above)

Penneshaw, Kangaroo Island South Australia

Ref: **2112**   Built: **1852**   Elevation: **75**
Tower: **26**   Range: **43**

Cape Willoughby, named by Matthew Flinders is at the eastern end of Kangaroo Island. Originally known as the Sturt light after the explorer Charles Sturt this white granite and limestone tower was the first light to be built in South Australia. The original DeVille parabolic reflectors were replaced in 1923 with a Chance Brothers dioptric revolving lens that had previously been installed on the Tipara Reef light. In 1974 the lens and lantern room were removed and replaced with a smaller one that looks out of place on the tower. The old lantern and lens were installed on a stub tower at Hope Cottage a museum in Kingscote. The original keepers' stone houses were demolished in 1927 after being replaced. The new houses are in excellent condition and are available for rent. The light is accessible by road from Kingscote.

Cape St Albans (Above and top right)
Penneshaw, Kangaroo Island South Australia

Ref: **2110**   Built: **1908**   Elevation: **48**   Tower: **9**   Range: **26W 19R**

While Cape Willoughby was the first light built to mark the entrance to the Backstairs Passage, the narrow channel running between the Fleurieu Peninsula and Kangaroo Island there have since been two more constructed. One is the **South Page Island** light (Ref: 2114, built in 1980), a GRP cabinet on a small island in the middle of the Backstairs Passage. The other is the white masonry Cape St Albans tower (shown here). It is located in a farm on a picturesque headland and being on private property is not readily accessible.

Snapper Point (Above)
Kingscote, Kangaroo Island South Australia

Ref: **2108**   Built: **1978**   Elevation: **137**   Tower: **7**   Range: **15**

Overlooking central Backstairs Passage is this small light with a white daymark on a stainless steel framework tower. The light was decommissioned in 2003.

Cape du Couedic

Kingscote, Kangaroo Island South Australia

Ref: **2010** Built: **1909** Elevation: **103** Tower: **25**
Range: **32**

Cape du Couedic is on the rugged southwest corner of Kangaroo Island. Rock quarried at the base of the cliff below the tower was used to construct the tower and the spacious keepers' quarters. It has a Chance Brothers 3.7m lantern and a 375mm lens. A flying fox was used to bring supplies up to the station. It was demanned in 1957. The keepers' quarters can be rented and are accessible by road from Kingscote.

Cape Borda

Kingscote, Kangaroo Island South Australia

Ref: **2008** Built: **1858** Elevation: **155**
Tower: **10** Range: **39**

The cape, named after a noted French navigator and mathematician is on the northwest corner of Kangaroo Island. The square stone tower is unique for a major Australian lighthouse. It has a DeVille lantern room and a Chance Brothers fourth order flashing catadioptric lens. The canon was used to warn ships that approached too close to shore. When connected by telegraph to Adelaide in 1876 a signal station was established at the site. This in turn resulted in a postal officer and a schoolteacher being stationed there. All supplies were hauled up a steel railway from the base of the cliffs at nearby Harvey's Return. It was automated and demanned in 1988. One of the houses is now used as a heritage museum and the others can be rented. It is accessible by road from Kingscote.

Cape Borda Cemetery

Point Marsden (Above)

Kingscote, Kangaroo Island South Australia

Ref: 2094 **Built: 1915** **Elevation: 85** **Tower: 3** **Range: 30**

This small light is situated on North Cape on the northern most tip of Kangaroo Island. A white GRP hut has replaced the original structure. The fence is needed to keep the cattle, not people out and being on farmland is not readily accessible.

Cape Jervis (Top left)

Cape Jervis, Fleurieu Peninsula South Australia

Ref: 2092 **Built: 1972** **Elevation: 23** **Tower: 18** **Range: 33**

One hundred years after it was built the original seven-metre Cape Jervis light was replaced by a grey concrete, three-sided star structure that widens out from 3.5m at its base to 5.0m at the top. It is 'identical' to the Robe tower built at the same time. The original light was manned until 1927. The light marks the eastern entrance to the Backstairs Passage as well as being a harbour light for the ferries that run between Cape Jervis and Penneshaw on Kangaroo Island. It is easily accessible by road.

Base of the original Cape Jervis tower (Left)

151

Marino Rocks (Left)
Marino, Adelaide South Australia

Ref: 2087 **Built: 1962** **Elevation: 128** **Tower: 15**
Range: 48

This octagonal concrete tower is the latest and possibly the last of the 'Port Adelaide' lights that have had a convoluted history.

In 1869 a light was constructed at the entrance to Port River. This badly designed light replaced the lightship *Fitzjames* that had, in 1851 replaced another lightship the *Ville de Bordeaux*. Within three years the light had been upgraded and the height of the tower increased by nine metres.

In 1901 the 'unsightly' Port Adelaide light was partially demolished. The frame tower that had supported the light was used to construct a new light on South Neptune Island in Spencer Gulf. (In 1985 the South Neptune light was replaced with a small brick structure and the steel frame tower was taken back to Adelaide and erected at the South Australian Maritime Museum.) Its lantern and lens was installed on the new Wonga Shoal light that was opposite Semaphore just south of the entrance to the harbour. To replace the Port River light a buoy was moored nearby. This was replaced in 1904 with a fixed light on the remnants of the old tower. The structure has since been demolished.

Unfortunately in 1912 the Wonga Shoal lighthouse was knocked over by the sailing ship *Dimsdale*, destroying the structure, the lantern and killing the two keepers. This was replaced with a low powered beacon (Ref: 2055) that was upgraded in 1923 and is still operational.

The construction of the Marino Rocks light in 1962 once again provided a coastal light for ships approaching Port Adelaide. It has a rotating optical apparatus using glass parabolic reflectors that was developed in Melbourne. It was the first 'Searchlight Pattern Reflector' (or 'Headlamp') style of light installed in Australia. It produces 1,000,000 candelas. The light, in the Marino Conservation Park is easily accessible by road.

Troubridge Hill (Opposite)
Edithburgh, Gulf St Vincent South Australia

Ref: 2020 **Built: 1980** **Elevation: 62** **Tower: 33** **Range: 39**

This light was built to take over the coastal light function previously performed by the Troubridge Island Light. It is supplemented by a number of small (generally GRP) lights further into the Gulf of St Vincent. These include **Tapley Shoal** (Ref: 2025.3, built in 1982), **Orontes Bank** (Ref: 2030, built in 1925 and replaced in 1986) and **Long Spit** (Ref: 2048, built in 1925 and replaced in 1987). The Troubridge Hill tower was constructed from specially made red, wedge shaped bricks that did not require rendering. This technique was also used for the nearly identical Guilderton light in Western Australia. It has a Chance Brothers 250mm triple flashing catadioptric lens. The light is easily accessible by road from Edithburgh.

Troubridge Island

Edithburgh, Gulf St Vincent South Australia

Ref: **2022**   Built: **1856**   Elevation: **24**   Tower: **25**   Range: **19W 13R**

This was the second lighthouse to be built in South Australia and the first to use cylindrical cast iron segments prefabricated in England and assembled on site. When built the location was a low shoal but over time, possibly because of the presence of the lightstation, sand and seaweed have accumulated and vegetation has taken hold. At times though the reverse process occurs exposing the foundations of the tower and the keepers' cottages. The original light was upgraded in 1882 and again in the 1920's when a second order DeVille lamp and a Chance Brothers lantern was installed. In 1956 the output was increased to 480,000 candelas. So that the light could be automated and demanned a new light was built at Troubridge Hill in 1980 and the light's output was reduced to 1480 candelas. The light was turned off in 2003. Although the site is now a bird sanctuary it is possible to tour the island and even arrange for accommodation in the keepers' cottages.

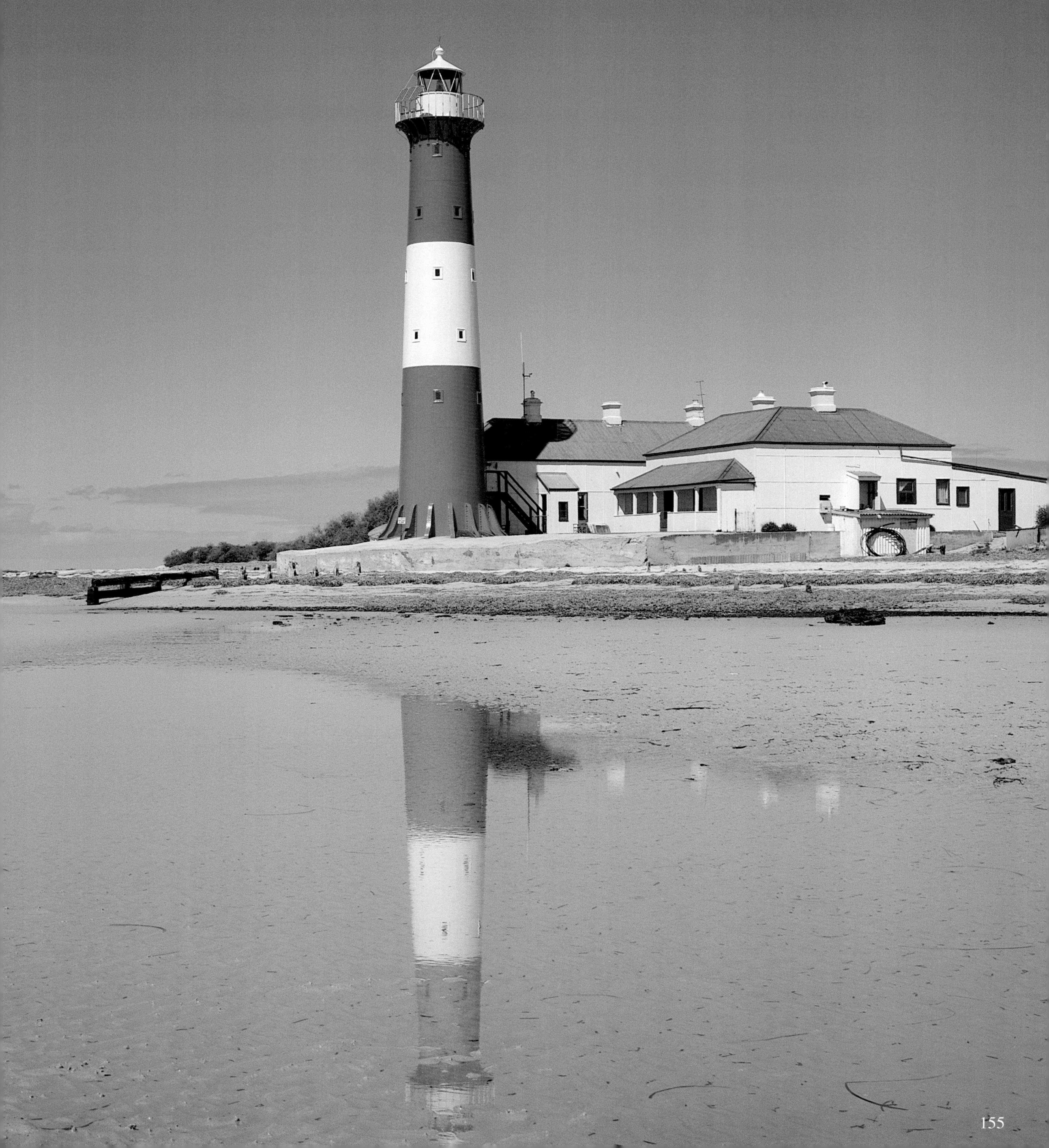

Cape Spencer (Opposite)

Stenhouse Bay, Yorke Peninsula South Australia

Ref: **2003**   Built: **1975**   Elevation: **78**   Tower: **9**   Range: **30**

The current and more powerful 400mm catadioptric drum lens in a square, concrete tower replaced the original light built in 1950. It overlooks Althorpe Island and it was probably upgraded with the intention of replacing the light on the island. The light is in the Innes National Park and is accessible by road.

West Cape (Right and below)

Stenhouse Bay, Yorke Peninsula South Australia

Ref: **2002**   Built: **1980**   Elevation: **67**   Tower: **9**   Range: **22**

West Cape is the first of three lights at the southwest tip of Yorke Peninsula that guide ships through Investigator Strait to the Gulf of St Vincent. The other two are Cape Spencer and Althorpe Island. It is a round stainless steel tower with a solar powered 400mm catadioptric drum lens. The light is in the Innes National Park and is accessible by road.

Althorpe Island Front (Top)
Investigator Strait South Australia

Ref: **2000**   Built: **1965**   Elevation: **86**   Tower: **2**   Range: **22W 17R 17G**

The small white brick hut on the western end of the island is used in conjunction with the main light to mark the channel between the island and Yorke Peninsular.

Althorpe Island Rear (Bottom and opposite)
Investigator Strait South Australia

Ref: **2000.1**   Built: **1879**   Elevation: **107**   Tower: **20**
Range: **30**

Named after the Earle of Althorpe by Matthew Flinders this rugged 91 hectare island sits eight kilometres off Cape Spencer on the southwest corner of Yorke Peninsula. The stone tower still has its 3.7m Chance Brothers lantern but the lens is a small solar powered Tupperware light. All people and supplies were carried to the top of the island from a small wharf by a flying fox. An airstrip was constructed on the top of the island that simplified resupply but once it was demanned in 1991 the airstrip became unusable due to mutton birds excavating their burrows in it. In 1901 there was a strong earthquake in the area that resulted in the lantern room catching fire and putting the light out of action for some weeks. The Troubridge Shoals and Corny Point lights were also damaged. Since the station was demanned the three keepers' houses have been maintained by the friends of Althorpe Island. The island is accessible by boat or helicopter.

Corny Point

Dunn Point, Yorke Peninsula South Australia

Ref: **1996**   Built: **1882**   Elevation: **30**   Tower: **15**   Range: **35W 28R**

The tower, constructed from local limestone was built for the benefit of grain ships heading south from the ports in Spencer Gulf. Its main function was to keep them away from Webb Rock and the shoals around Berry Bay and Daly Head. It has a Chance Brothers 2.7m lantern and a 500mm lens that currently produces 60,000 candelas. At one time the lantern room was going to be replaced but fortunately the original was retained. The keepers' two stone cottages were demolished after it was demanned in 1920. It is easily accessible by road.

Between Corny and Warburto Points there is another small light near Port Victoria on **Wardang Island** (Ref: 1986, built in 1909 and replaced in 1987).

Point Boston (Above)

Port Lincoln, Eyre Peninsula South Australia

Ref: **1879**   Built: **1990**   Elevation: **12**   Tower: **11**
Range: **28W 22R 22G**

Originally built as a frame tower in 1923 it was replaced by a light-on-a-pole in 1990. Although it is not an attractive light it is one of many small lights that dot the shoals and islands in St Vincent and Spencer gulfs. It is not easily accessible.

Warburto Point (Left)

Wallaroo, Yorke Peninsula South Australia

Ref: **1980**   Built: **1995**   Elevation: **36**   Tower: **32**   Range: **33**

Tipara, or **Tiparra Reef** (Ref: 1982), was first marked with a lightship in 1866 that was replaced by a manned pile structure in 1877. As it was difficult and expensive to service, the Warburto Point light was built to take its place. The Tipara Reef light was then demolished although there is a small beacon on the remnants of the platform. The new light consists of a white GRP hut at the top of a tall red frame tower. Although it is on farmland it can be easily seen from the back roads between Wallaroo and Moonta.

Point Lowly

Port Whyalla, Eyre Peninsula South
Australia

Ref: **1948**   Built: **1883**
Elevation: **23**   Tower: **25**   Range: **48**

Point Lowly was the first light built for ships sailing to Port Pirie and Port Augusta at the top of Spencer Gulf. Made from local sandstone it had an eight-sided catadioptric lens. In 1909 to improve the light's effectiveness the height was increased by eight metres providing, not only a better light but also a more graceful tower. The light was automated in 1973 and demanned. In 1993 AMSA determined that the light was no longer needed and it was extinguished. After two years of darkness the Whyalla City Council purchased the light and it was reactivated. The keepers' houses have been renovated and can be rented. The light is accessible from the Port Bonython Road near Whyalla.

Since Point Lowly was built a number of small lights marking shoals in the gulf have been built. This includes **Western Shoal** (Ref: 1931.5, built in 1985), **Yarraville Shoal** (Ref: 1931, built in 1951 and replaced in 1986), **Plank Shoal** (Ref: 1930.5, a 12m frame tower built in 1985), **Middle Bank** (Ref: 1930, an 11m frame tower built in 1912 and replaced in 1985), **South** (Ref: 1930.3, an 11m frame tower built in 1911) and **Shoalwater Point** (Ref: 1929, built in 1911 and rebuilt as a 15m column in 1986).

Dangerous Reef Centre (Opposite)

Port Lincoln South Australia

Ref: **1876**   Built: **1988**   Elevation: **11**
Tower: **6**   Range: **19**

The current light replaced one built in 1911. There are three reefs in the area and the light is on the central and largest reef. It can be accessed by boat or helicopter.

Cape Donington (Above and right)

Port Lincoln, Eyre Peninsula South Australia

Ref: **1878**   Built: **1905**   Elevation: **33**
Tower: **17**   Range: **33**

This six-sided, grey concrete tower, with a Chance Brothers 400mm lens is a major light for ships entering Port Lincoln. Located in the Lincoln National Park it is easily accessible by road.

Taylor Island (Right)
Port Lincoln South Australia

Ref: **1874**   Built: **1982**   Elevation: **76**
Tower: **9**   Range: **W20 R22 G22**

This light is one of the minor lights for ships entering Spencer Gulf on their way to Port Lincoln. It can be accessed by boat or helicopter.

Waterhouse Point (Below)
Thistle Island South Australia

Ref: **1872.5**   Built: **1983**   Elevation: **49**
Tower: **4**   Range: **19**

This light is one of the minor lights for ships entering Spencer Gulf on their way to Port Lincoln. It can be accessed by boat or helicopter.

166

Wedge Island (Left)
Spencer Gulf South Australia

Ref: **1870**   Built: **1990**   Elevation: **206**
Tower: **6**   Range: **32**

The original 1911 light was replaced with a grey concrete tower in 1990. With an elevation of 206m it is the second highest operational light in Australia. (The highest is Tasman Island in Tasmania.) The island is located midway between the Yorke and Eyre Peninsulas at the entrance to Spencer Gulf and is accessible by plane, boat or helicopter.

Others, that are all GRP cabinets in the Port Lincoln area are **Winceby Island** (Ref: 1890, built in 1911 and replaced in 1987), **Bolingbroke Point** (Ref: 1889, built in 1972), **Sibsey Island** (Ref: 1878.5, built in 1983) and **Williams Island** (Ref: 1873, built in 1964).

Cape Bauer (Above)
Streaky Bay, Eyre Peninsula South Australia

Ref: **1847**   Built: **1964**   Elevation: **84**
Tower: **2**   Range: **30**

On the western coast of Eyre Peninsula there are a number of lights although all, except Cape Bauer, are on offshore islands. They are all small GRP cabinets. They include **Four Hummock Island** (Ref: 1866, built in 1914), **Flinders Island** (Ref: 1858, built in 1914), **St Francis Island** (Ref: 1818, built in 1924), **Evans Island** (Ref: 1820, built in 1964) and **Pearson Isles** (Ref: 1856, built in 1968). Cape Bauer is in the middle of a wheat field. And being on farmland is not easily accessed.

North Neptune Island (Opposite top)

Spencer Gulf South Australia

Ref: **1872.3**   Built: **1983**   Elevation: **48**   Tower: **4**
Range: **19**

The light was built to augment the smaller South Neptune light once the old tower was removed. In 2003 it was turned off and dismantled.

**Old South Neptune Tower now in
the Adelaide Maritime Museum** (Opposite right)

South Neptune Island (Opposite, left and above)

Spencer Gulf South Australia

Ref: **1872**   Built: **1986**   Elevation: **43**   Tower: **5**   Range: **30**

The first light on the island, erected in 1901 was the old Port Adelaide tower. In 1985 a small brick tower replaced it. The station was demanned at the same time. The old tower was dismantled in 1984 and taken back to Adelaide where it was rebuilt and is now a focal point for the South Australian Maritime Museum. It is accessible by helicopter, plane or boat.

Index – Western Australia and The Northern Territory

Western Australia

Map	171
Breaksea Island	172
Cave Point	174
Eclipse Island	175
D'Entrecasteaux Point	176
Foul Bay	176
Cape Naturaliste	177
Cape Leeuwin	178
Casuarina Point	180
Woodman Point	181
South Mole Head (green)	182
North Mole Head (red)	182
Rottnest	184
Bathurst Point	185
Hillarys Boat Harbour	186
Guilderton	186
Escape Island	187
Pelsaert Island	187
Point Moore	188
Cape Inscription	190
Steep Point	192
Babbage Island	193
Point Quobba	193
Point Cloates	194
Jarman Island	195
Vlaming Head	196
North West Cape	197
Gantheaume Point	198
Red Bluff	199
East Lacepede Island	199
Cape Leveque	200
Caffarelli Island	202
Adele Island	202

Northern Territory

Map	205
Charles Point	206
Emery Point	208
East Vernon Island	208
Cape Hotham	208
Cape Don	209

Point Moore Geraldton Western Australia

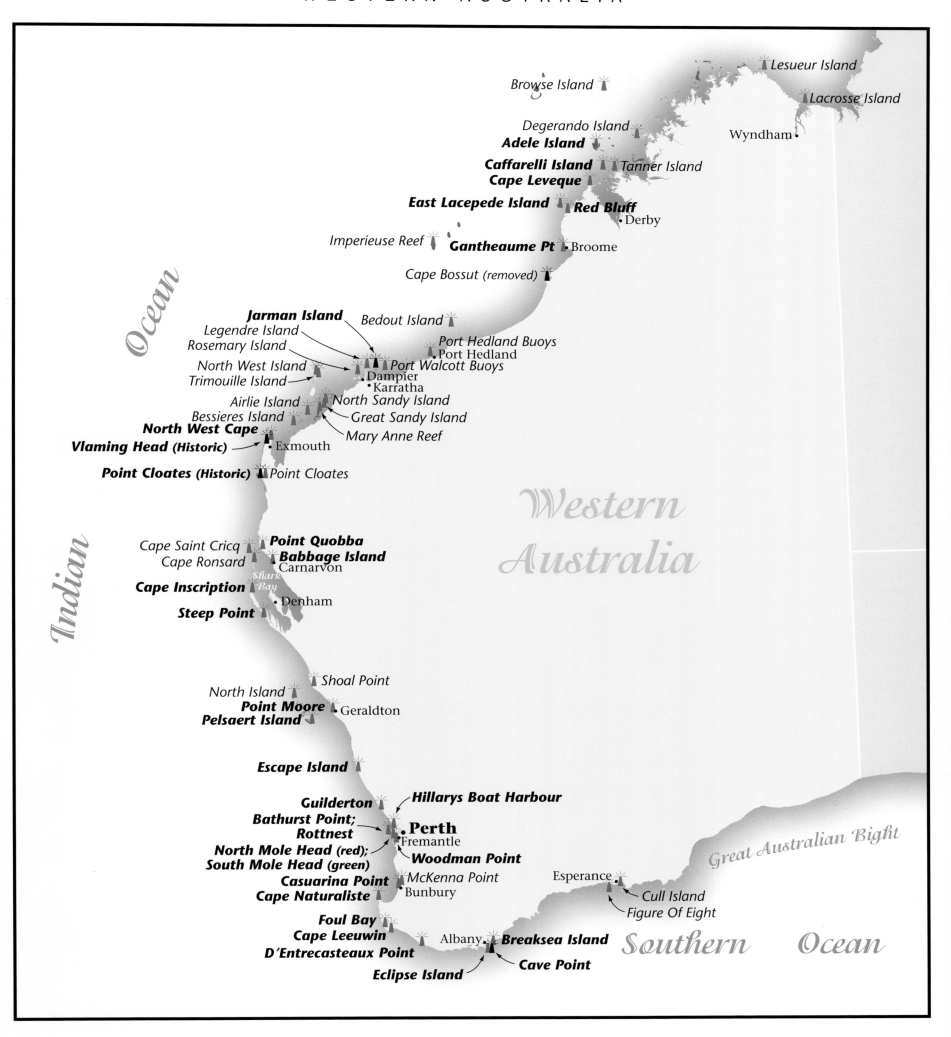

Lesueur Island

Browse Island

Lacrosse Island

Degerando Island

Wyndham

Adele Island

Caffarelli Island — Tanner Island

Cape Leveque

East Lacepede Island — *Red Bluff*

• Derby

Imperieuse Reef — *Gantheaume Pt* • Broome

Cape Bossut (removed)

Jarman Island — Bedout Island

Legendre Island

Rosemary Island — Port Hedland Buoys
• Port Hedland

North West Island — *Port Walcott Buoys*

Trimouille Island — Dampier
• Karratha

Airlie Island — *North Sandy Island*

Bessieres Island — Great Sandy Island

North West Cape — Mary Anne Reef

Vlaming Head (Historic) — • Exmouth

Point Cloates (Historic) — Point Cloates

Indian

Ocean

Cape Saint Cricq — *Point Quobba*

Cape Ronsard — *Babbage Island*

Carnarvon

Shark Bay

Cape Inscription

• Denham

Steep Point

Western Australia

Shoal Point

North Island

Point Moore — Geraldton

Pelsaert Island

Escape Island

Guilderton — *Hillarys Boat Harbour*

Bathurst Point; — • **Perth**
Rottnest — Fremantle

North Mole Head (red); — *Woodman Point*
South Mole Head (green)

Casuarina Point — McKenna Point
• Bunbury

Cape Naturaliste

Esperance — Great Australian Bight

Cull Island
Figure Of Eight

Foul Bay

Cape Leeuwin

D'Entrecasteaux Point — Albany • *Breaksea Island*

Cave Point

Southern Ocean

Eclipse Island

171

Breaksea Island
Albany Western Australia

NEW:
Ref: **1800**   Built: **1901**
Elevation: **119**   Tower: **16**
Range: **24**
OLD:
Ref: ********   Built: **1858**
Elevation: **117**   Tower: **14**
Range: **0**

There are no lighthouses across the Great Australian Bight. The most easterly ones in Western Australia are the small lights on **Cull (previously Gull) Island** (Ref: 1809, built in 1965) and **Figure of Eight Island** (Ref: 1808, built in 1965 and replaced in 1984) off Esperance. The first classical lights were built near Albany. A small square wooden tower was constructed on **Point King** in 1858 at the northern entrance to the harbour but it has, except for the walls of the keepers' cottage completely disappeared. The original prefabricated cast iron tower on Breaksea Island, located at the entrance to King Georges Sound was imported from England and erected by convicts. The octagonal granite living quarters surrounded the tower. The ruins of these structures are still evident. The new tower made of local granite has a Chance Brothers 3.4m lantern and a first order 920mm dioptric lens. In 1926 the light was automated and demanned. It is now solar powered. In 1883 a Lloyd's Signal Station was also established on the island. The two keepers' cottages have deteriorated significantly although the granite walls show little wear. Access is by helicopter or, with difficulty by boat (via a dilapidated jetty). The unusual sky colour in the photos is due to bush fire haze blowing out from the mainland.

Cave Point (Above and Opposite)

Albany Western Australia

Ref: **** Built: **1976** Elevation: **100**
Tower: **12** Range: **0**

The cylindrical concrete tower at Cave Point was built to replace the light on Eclipse Island that was difficult and expensive to maintain. Unfortunately it was found that Eclipse Island obscured the new light in a critical area so in 1994 the light was extinguished. The tower is now used as receiver station for the Australian Search and Rescue (AusSAR) organization. The tower is accessible by road from Albany.

Eclipse Island (Left and Above)

Albany Western Australia

Ref: **1798** Built: **1926** Elevation: **117** Tower: **14** Range: **28**

This reinforced concrete tower was the first Commonwealth light built in WA. It had a Chance Brothers lantern and first order lens that is now in the Albany Residency Museum. It now has a Tupperware light. Providing supplies and changing keepers was difficult as there is no suitable harbour at the island. A landing, 15m above sea level was constructed in a cove at the NE end of the island. A derrick on it was used to lift supplies and people from a small boat that was able to maintain a position close to the cliffs. Although a wicker basket was available for the transfer of people many would just stand on top of the supplies that were being lifted. For lighthouse keepers even getting to work could be hazardous! It was demanned after a fatal crane accident in 1976. Access is by helicopter.

D'Entrecasteaux Point
(Above)

Windy Harbour Western Australia

Ref: **1795**   Built: **1960**   Elevation: **111**
Tower: **3**   Range: **32**

This square, cream brick tower with a small Tupperware light is located on spectacular cliffs near Windy Harbour. At the time of conversion to a solar powered FA 251 beacon in 1989 it was the last acetylene light operating in the state. From Northcliffe the light is at the end of the Wheatley Coast Road.

Foul Bay (Right)

Augusta Western Australia

Ref: **1792**   Built: **1967**   Elevation: **92**
Tower: **6**   Range: **32**

This small brick tower has a 2.2m CLS lantern with a 375mm (3½ order) lens. Built to replace the **Hamelin Island** light it is a modern version of the small lights built on the northern NSW coast in the late 1800's. A rough sandy track leads to the light from the Caves Road near Augusta.

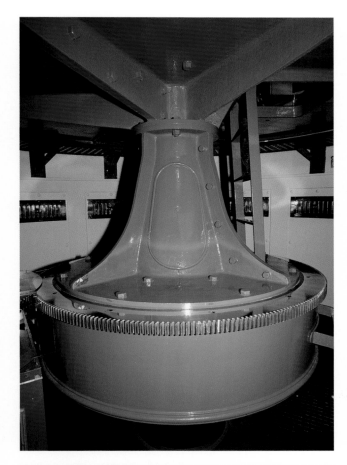

Cape Naturaliste

Dunsborough Western Australia

Ref: **1790**   Built: **1904**   Elevation: **123**
Tower: **19**   Range: **46**

This tower, built from local limestone has a Chance Brothers 4.3m lantern and a first order 920mm two panel catadioptric lens with a catadioptric-reinforcing mirror with an intensity of 930,000 candelas. The internal staircase is made of teak (with the steps end-grain up for long wearability) instead of the usual cast iron or stone. The three keepers' cottages, also built from local limestone are in excellent condition. One is used as a museum while another is available for visitor accommodation. The lighthouse reserve that abuts the Leeuwin-Naturaliste National Park is accessible by road from Dunsborough.

Cape Leeuwin

Augusta Western Australia

Ref: **1794**   Built: **1896**   Elevation: **56**
Tower: **39**   Range: **48**

Matthew Flinders named Cape Leeuwin after the Dutch ship *Leeuwin* (The Lioness) that rounded the cape in 1622. Built of local volcanic ironstone called tamala this landfall light is on the extreme southwest corner of Australia. It also is the arbitrary meeting point of the Indian and Southern oceans. It has a Chance Brothers 3.7m lantern and a first order 920 mm lens with an intensity of 1,000,000 candelas. Originally there was going to be a red light installed next to the main tower and although the foundations for it were poured the tower was never built. The radio beacon towers installed in 1955 are no longer used and have been removed. The three keepers' houses are in excellent condition and may, in the future be available for overnight accommodation. The light is eight kilometres by road from Augusta.

Casuarina Point

Bunbury Western Australia

Ref: **1782**   Built: **1971**   Elevation: **43**
Tower: **15**   Range: **35**

This most attractive light has a chequered history. In 1870 a three-metre wooden tower on Casuarina Point replaced the original wooden keg that had a lantern sitting on its lid. In 1901 a steel framework tower on Marlston Hill just south of Casuarina Point took over from the wooden structure. In 1904 it moved back to a braced lattice tower on Casuarina Point. In 1959 its height was increased. Then in 1971 the current tubular steel tower was built south of Marlston Hill that included a six-metre section from the old light. At the same time a light-on-a-pole was also erected at **McKenna Point** (Ref: 1784, built in 1971). There is now an architecturally interesting lookout on Marlston Hill. The Point Casuarina light is located on Ocean Drive in Bunbury.

Woodman Point

Munster Western Australia

Ref: **1774** Built: **1902**
Elevation: **37** Tower: **13** Range: **41**

This harbour light, built from limestone blocks with a first order dioptric lens is unique in Australia in that it has one side painted white while the other side has been left its natural stone colour. It is referenced by both northbound and southbound traffic using Gages Road into Fremantle Harbour. It was demanned in 1921. The two keepers' cottages are now privately owned. The tower is just off Coburn Road in Munster.

181

South Mole Head (Green)
Fremantle Western Australia

Ref: **1765** Built: **1903** Elevation: **15** Tower: **9** Range: **G20**

North Mole Head (Red)
Fremantle Western Australia

Ref: **1764** Built: **1903** Elevation: **15** Tower: **9** Range: **R20**

C. Y. O'Connor who also designed the Woodman Point light designed the green South Mole and the red North Mole lights. Constructed from cast iron panels these two lights, with fourth order fixed lenses are on the rock breakwaters constructed at the entrance to the Swan River. They are accessible by road from Fremantle.

Rottnest
Rottnest Island Western Australia

Ref: **1760**   Built: **1896**   Elevation: **80**   Tower: **38**   Range: **48**

Dutchman William De Vlamingh named Rottnest Island in 1696 after the quokkas on the island that he mistakenly referred to as 'a kind of a rat as big as a cat. There have been two main lighthouses on the highest point in the middle of the island. The foundation stone of the original 16m tower, the first lighthouse built in Western Australia was laid in 1842 but the light was not exhibited until 1851. It was made from local limestone and had a locally made light consisting of three oil lamps with silvered parabolic reflectors. Its keepers' quarters were built around the tower.

It is not known why the new tower, erected in 1896 just 15m to the west of the old one was built as there did not appear to be any problems with the first tower. It was constructed from local limestone with a Chance Brothers 3.7m lantern and a 920mm first order 8-panel holophotal revolving catadioptric lens that has a current intensity of 1,300,000 candelas. Its dome is unusual in that it was, at one time, painted gold. This was done for the America's Cup Challenge in 1987. The idea was to wrap a green banner around the tower and show "Green and Gold" when Australia retained the cup. The race series was lost, the green banner was never needed and the dome has since been repainted white. The old tower was demolished although some portions of the walls still remain. Rottnest Island can be reached by small plane or by ferry from Perth or Fremantle. The light is within walking or cycling distance from the point of arrival. There is also a bus service around the island.

Bathurst Point
Rottnest Island Western Australia

Ref: **1761.1** Built: **1900**
Elevation: **30** Tower: **19** Range: **26**

Located on the northeast corner of Rottnest Island and constructed from local limestone it also had a gold coloured dome for the America's Cup Challenge. Its second order dioptric fixed light was originally going to be installed on the lower light at Cape Leeuwin that was never built. The light was converted to acetylene in 1920 and demanned at the same time. The cottage was sold to the Rottnest Island Board and is used by its employees. It was converted to electric operation in 1986. Rottnest Island can be reached by small plane or by ferry from Perth or Fremantle. The light is within walking or cycling distance from the point of arrival. There is also a bus service around the island.

Hillarys Boat Harbour (Above)

Wanneroo Western Australia

Ref: **1758.3**　Built: **1986**　Elevation: **24**　Tower: **20**
Range: **22**

Hillarys Boat Harbour was built during the lead up to the America's Cup Challenge that was held in 1986-1987. The frame tower entrance light shown here has an AGA lantern that came from the original 1909 Bedout Island light. The harbour is accessible by road from Perth.

Guilderton (Right)

Guilderton Western Australia

Ref: **1757.5**　Built: **1984**　Elevation: **74**　Tower: **30**
Range: **41**

Slightly shorter but similar to the Troubridge Hill light in South Australia it was constructed from specially made red, wedge shaped bricks that did not require rendering. It has a 2.2m lantern that probably came from Hamelin Island and a 375mm lens. The light is accessible by road from Guilderton.

Escape Island (Left)
Jurien Western Australia

Ref: **1756** Built: **1980**
Elevation: **30** Tower: **24** Range: **19**

The original light built in 1930 was a 22m Stone Chance metal framework tower. It was replaced in 1980 by a stainless steel lattice tower similar to many others built along the Western Australian coast such as Bedout Island, Airlie Island, North Sandy Island and Gantheuame Point except that it doesn't have a lantern, just an ML 300 Tupperware light. It serves the Port of Jurien that is home to a large crayfish fishing fleet. It is accessible by helicopter or, with difficulty by boat.

Pelsaert Island (Left)
Abrolhos Islands, Geraldton
Western Australia

Ref: **1753.6** Built: **1974**
Elevation: **21** Tower: **20**
Range: **24**

The Abrolhos Islands that in Portuguese mean 'Keep your eyes open', were chartered and named by Don Jorge de Meneses in 1527 nearly 250 years before Cook visited Australia. It was on these islands that the *Batavia* was wrecked in 1629. The light on Pelsaert Island is an enclosed stainless steel column shaped like a rocket ship and is a smaller version of the ones on Imperieuse Reef also in WA and Frederick's Reef in Queensland. Other lights in the area are **North Island** (Ref: 1739.4, built in 1967) and **Shoal Point** (Ref: 1739, a square brick tower with a Chance Brothers lantern and lens built in 1958). There are boats that go out to resorts on the islands and these could no doubt detour past the lighthouse.

Point Moore

Geraldton Western Australia

Ref: **1740**   Built: **1876**   Elevation: **34**   Tower: **35**   Range: **43**

This tapered cast iron cylinder, made up of 16 tiers each containing 12 plates was prefabricated in England and assembled on site in 1876. The first site was found to be unsuitable so it was moved to its present location, five kilometres away, in 1878. It has a Chance Brothers 3.1m lantern and a 700mm second order, eight-panel catadioptric lens with an intensity of 410,000 candelas. The three original stone keepers' cottages were demolished in 1926 and were replaced by a single timber framed cottage on Chapman Road. After being automated in 1985 it was demanned and the keepers' cottage was sold. Its distinctive red bands were not added until 1969. The light on Wilcock Drive in Geraldton is accessible by car.

The first lights to operate in Geraldton were the Bluff Point Leading lights built in 1854. They were automated and demanned in 1943. In 1952 the lower tower was destroyed by fire and demolished. The Geraldton Historical Society now own the historic rear tower and keeper's cottage.

Cape Inscription

Dirk Hartog Island, Denham
Western Australia

Ref: **1724** Built: **1910**
Elevation: **39** Tower: **15**
Range: **22**

Dirk Hartog Island, the largest island in Western Australia, is 80km long and 15km wide with shifting sand dunes up to 200m high. It was named after the captain of the Dutch East India Company ship the *Eendraught* who, in 1616 landed on the island next to the lighthouse site and left a metal plate nailed to a pole. The concrete tower, located at the northern end of the island has a Chance Brothers 2.7m lantern and a 400mm catadioptric drum lens. To provide access to the light there was a five kilometre long, winch powered tramway from the lightstation to a 76m jetty built at Turtle Bay. The station was only manned for seven years with the keepers being removed in 1917 after a new acetylene light was installed. The original lens that came from Breaksea Island is now in the WA Maritime Museum. Only the walls of the keepers' houses remain but they may at some time in the future be restored. The light in conjunction with the **Cape St Cricq** light on Dorre Island (Ref: 1723, built in 1971) marks the entrance into the Naturaliste Channel and Shark Bay. Access to the island, used as a merino sheep station and wilderness resort is by small plane or boat. The light is then an enjoyable five-hour drive by 4WD from the homestead.

Steep Point (Above)
Shark Bay, Denham Western Australia

Ref: **1728**   Built: **1984**   Elevation: **70**
Tower: **4**   Range: **19**

The original Steep Point light built in 1960 was a round metal tower. The current light built in 1984 is a small GRP cabinet with an ML 300 solar powered lantern. Its location, on a treeless headland that overlooks the southern end of Dirk Hartog Island, is the most westerly point on the Australian mainland. It is the starting point of a 4WD rally that finishes at Cape Byron in NSW, the most easterly point in Australia. Steep Point is accessible by 4WD from Denham.

Babbage Island (Opposite, left)
Carnarvon Western Australia

Ref: **1718**   Built: **1965**   Elevation: **30**
Tower: **18**   Range: **W13 R9**

Originally constructed from wood in 1896 the kerosene powered light was damaged by fire a number of times before the current steel frame tower was built. The old lantern room with its distinctive red and white striped dome has been preserved on a small tower in the Gascoyne Historical Society grounds next to the light. The light that services the local fishing fleet was given a fresh coat of paint in 2000 simply because the Olympic Torch relay was scheduled to pass by it. The island is connected to the mainland and is accessible by road.

Point Quobba (Opposite, right)
Shark Bay, Carnarvon Western Australia

Ref: **1716**   Built: **1950**   Elevation: **64**   Tower: **18**
Range: **26**

With its Chance Brothers red domed 3.9m first order lantern that probably came from the original Point Cloates light, this modern concrete tower has distinctive classical lines. Its staircase also came from the Point Cloates light. When converted to a solar powered FA 251 Tupperware light in 1988 the old lens, that had originally come from Cape Wickham in Tasmania was given to the WA Maritime Museum. The light in conjunction with the **Cape Ronsard** light on Bernier Island (Ref: 1717, a steel cylindrical tower built in 1961) marks the entrance into the Geographe Channel and Shark Bay. Point Quobba is 50km along the Cape Cuvier road that exits from the main North West Coastal Road 25km north of Carnarvon.

Point Cloates (Left)
Exmouth Western Australia

	Ref:	**Built:**	**Elevation:**	**Tower:**	**Range:**
NEW:	1714	1966	39	2	32
OLD:	****	1910	50	8	0

Located on the 49,000 hectare Ningaloo sheep station the old sandstone tower, severely damaged in the mid 1930's was abandoned and sold to the station owners for five pounds. The damage could have been caused by an earthquake but is more likely to have been due to its poor foundations. In 1936 its replacement, a 22m steel lattice tower was built on Fraser Island, a sandy islet just offshore from Point Cloates. Unfortunately in 1966 the islet was blown away and the tower collapsed. At this stage a new GRP cabinet was built about a kilometre south of the original light and its name reverted back to Point Cloates. The cracked and unstable tower and the walls of the keepers' cottage are all that remain. The light is on private property but can be visited if permission is obtained from the owners.

Jarman Island (Opposite)
Cossack Western Australia

Ref:	**Built:**	**Elevation:**	**Tower:**	**Range:**
****	1888	99	9	0

The tower, prefabricated in England and constructed of cast iron panels bolted together was built to guide ships entering Cossack. It was a thriving port until the harbour gradually silted up in the early 1900's and ships started to use the port at Point Samson that has in turn been replaced by the port at Dampier. The light was extinguished and the island abandoned after the Cape Lambert light was built in 1985. The tower is now in a dilapidated condition and only the walls of the stone keepers' house remain. Fortunately with grants from the local mining and petroleum companies the lightstation is going to be restored. Hopefully it will be done as well as the restoration of the buildings in the village of Cossack. Jarman Island is about three kilometres offshore from Cossack and on calm days it is possible to go out to the island on a small boat that can be rented in the village.

Between Exmouth and Dampier there are a number of off shore lights on islands and reefs. **Airlie Island** (Ref: 1698, a 24m stainless steel frame tower built in 1980 to replace the original 1913 tower) was built for ships entering Onslow. **North Sandy Island** (Ref: 1694, a 20m stainless steel frame tower built in 1980 to replace the original 1913 tower), **Bessieres Island**, previously known as **Anchor Island** (Ref: 1702, built in 1913 and replaced in 1985), **Legendre Island** (Ref: 1690, built in 1927 and rebuilt in 1963 and 1989 (twice)), **Mary Anne Island** (Ref: 1696, originally built in the 1930's and replaced maybe 6 times since), **Great Sandy Island** (Ref: 1695, built in 1959 and replaced in 1986), **Rosemary Island** (Ref: 1690.4, built in 1965), **Trimouille Island** (Ref: 1691.99, built in 1968) and **North West Island** in the Monte Bello's (Ref: 1691.98, built in 1968) were built for general shipping entering Dampier and Point Samson.

Since the development of the Robe iron ore deposits and the gas fields offshore from Dampier, there have been an extensive number of buoys built to guide ships into the ports of Dampier and Walcott. The 13 **Walcott Buoys** (Ref: 1684.nn, built in 1984) are interesting in that they are a cross between a buoy and a beacon. They are known as star buoys. Instead of being attached to a cable that would allow the 10m long buoys to move up and down they are firmly attached by only two links to a 60 tonne concrete base. This keeps the top of them at a constant height above the seabed.

Vlaming Head (Left)

Exmouth Western Australia

Ref: **** Built: **1912** Elevation: **129** Tower: **10**
Range: **0**

This concrete tower with a Chance Brothers lantern and lens was built after the *Mildura* was wrecked on the North West Cape in 1907. It was damaged by a cyclone in 1953 and repaired but was then extinguished in 1967, being replaced by a light installed on tower 11 of the *Naval Communication Station Harold E. Holt*. The tower was sold to the Shire of Exmouth while the keepers' cottages became part of the Lighthouse Caravan Park. After being damaged again by a cyclone in 1999 funds were allocated to completely repair the tower during 2001. It is 17km by road from Exmouth.

North West Cape (Opposite)

Exmouth Western Australia

Ref: **1710** Built: **1967** Elevation: **129**
Tower: **304** Range: **46**

When the Vlaming Head light was decommissioned it was replaced by a 'headlamp' type of light installed about five km away in tower 11 at the *Naval Communication Station Harold E. Holt*. Installed at the same height above sea level as the old light it is still only one third of the way up the 304m (996') tower that can justifiably be called the tallest lighthouse structure in the world. The towers, clearly visible from the road to Vlaming Head used to be painted in red and white bands but are now totally white.

Port Hedland named after Peter Hedland who discovered the entrance to the bay has like Port Walcott been developed for handling iron ore carriers. Based on tonnage it is the busiest port in Australia. As the approach to the port is quite shallow for some distance from the coast the **Port Hedland Buoys** (Ref: 1676.nn and 1677.nn, built in 1986) a 78 km chain of 14 lights, have been installed to mark the outbound channel. Typically the single tubular steel piles are 30m long with six metres being above the mean high water level.

Since the **Cape Bossut** light built in 1914 was removed in 1995, **Bedout Island** (Ref: 1675, a 20m stainless steel frame tower built in 1980 to replace the original 1909 tower) is the only coastal light in the 500km between Port Hedland and Broome. There is a lighthouse on **Imperieuse Reef** (Ref: 1674, a 30m stainless steel frame tower built in 1970 to replace the original 1960 tower) but it is 300km offshore and could hardly be called a coastal light.

Gantheaume Point (Opposite)
Broome Western Australia

Ref: 1660   **Built: 1984**   **Elevation: 33**   **Tower: 24**   **Range: 32**

Two towers, one built in 1905 and one in 1917 preceded the current stainless steel lattice tower with a white lantern that except for its height is identical to other lights along the Western Australian coast such as Bedout Island, Airlie and North Sandy Island. The station was manned until 1922 when an automatic light was installed. Built on a spectacular red sandstone point at the entrance to Roebuck Bay it is accessible by road from Broome although during 'the wet' a walk down Cable Beach may be easier.

Red Bluff (Top)
Broome Western Australia

Ref: 1659   **Built: 1987**   **Elevation: 48**   **Tower: 4**   **Range: 28**

Red Bluff on the Dampier Peninsula opposite the Lacepede Islands is midway between Broome and Cape Leveque. The original light built in 1968 was replaced in the early 1980's by two buoys. The buoys were, in turn replaced in 1987 by the current light, a double height GRP cabinet with a FA 251 lantern. The light, in conjunction with the East Island light marks the Lacepede Coastal Channel. It is accessible from Broome by helicopter and possibly by boat or 4WD.

East Lacepede Island (Centre)
Broome Western Australia

Ref: 1658   **Built: 1984**   **Elevation: 25**   **Tower: 17**   **Range: 24**

This stainless steel, open lattice tower with tube columns and a solar powered FA 251 lantern replaced the original steel lattice tower built in 1968. It is used in conjunction with the Red Bluff light to mark the Lacepede Coastal Channel. It is accessible by boat or helicopter from Broome.

Cape Leveque

Broome Western Australia

Ref: **1650**   Built: **1911**   Elevation: **43**   Tower: **13**   Range: **41**

This bolted iron-plate tower, manufactured in Perth by Bela Makutz has a Chance Brothers 2.9m lantern. Although it has 1909 above the door the light was not exhibited until 1911. It was automated, converted to solar power and demanned in 1985. At the same time the original lens was removed and replaced with an AGA PRB 24/4 lamp array. The lightstation has been taken over by the Bardi People who operate the Kooljaman Wilderness Lodge. The two keepers' houses are used as staff quarters. It is 220km from Broome on a 4WD only road. Regular air charters also fly to the cape from Broome or Derby.

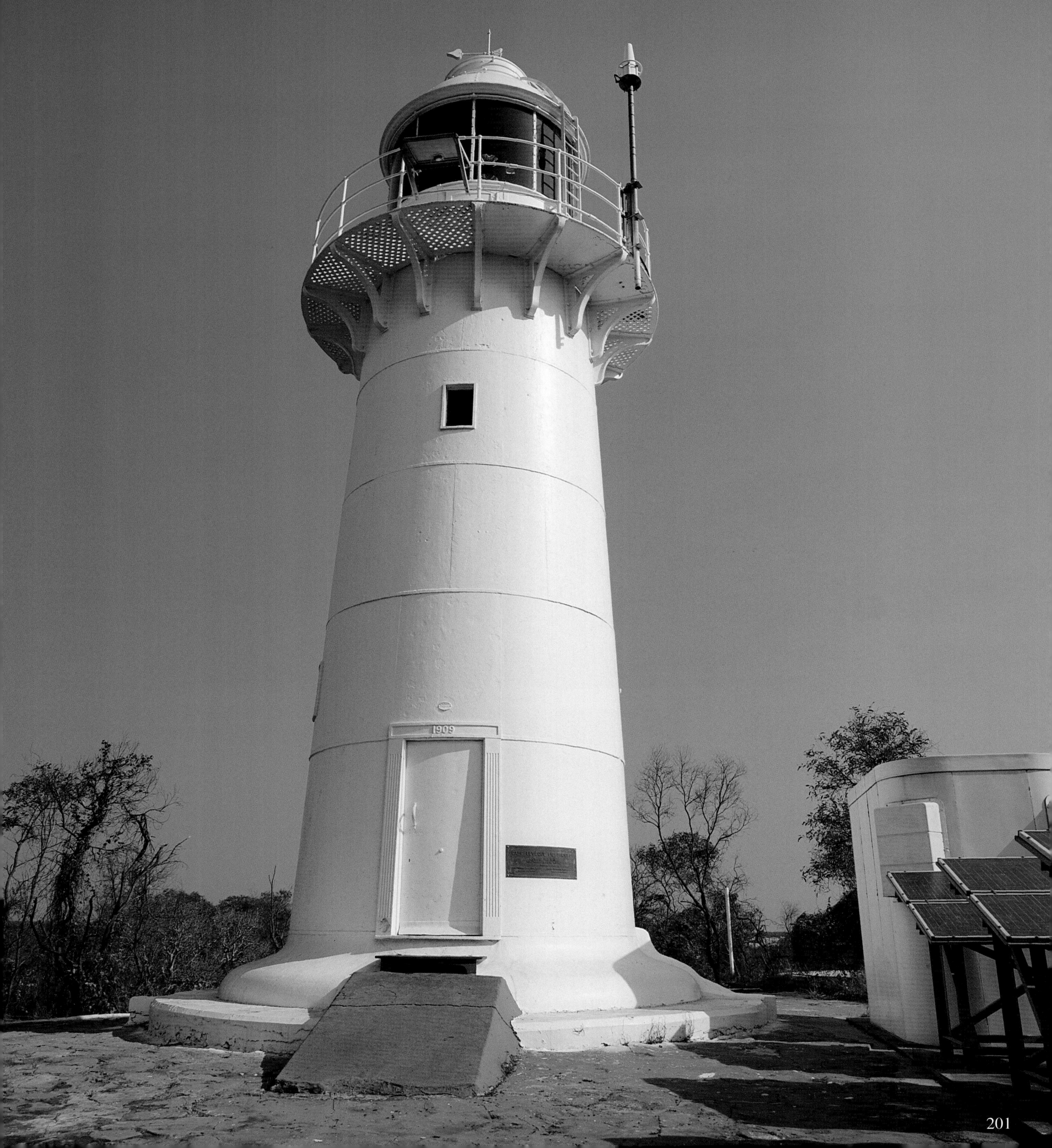
1909

202

Caffarelli Island

(Opposite Top)

Broome Western Australia

Ref: **1646**   Built: **1967**
Elevation: **68**   Tower: **6**
Range: **22**

To the east of Cape Leveque there are a number of offshore lights used by ships in King Sound. As well as the white cylindrical mild steel tower on Caffarelli Island (shown here) there is **Tanner Island** (Ref: 1643, a square concrete tower built in 1951). Both have catadioptric drum lenses. They are accessible with difficulty by boat or by helicopter.

Adele Island

(Opposite Bottom and Right)

Derby Western Australia

Ref: **1640**   Built: **1951**
Elevation: **31**   Tower: **30**
Range: **28**

To the north of Cape Leveque there are a number of offshore lights used by ships sailing through the Buccaneer Archipelago. As well as the red bolted steel framework tower on Adele Island (shown here) there is **Degerando Island** (Ref: 1641, a white cylindrical steel tower built in 1960) and **Browse Island** (Ref: 1642, a 30m white metal frame tower built in 1958 to replace the 1945 light). Adele and Browse have solar powered rotating beacon FA 251 (Tupperware) lights while Degerando has an electric lamp-change in the original AGA lantern. They are accessible with difficulty by helicopter or boat from Derby.

The only other major lights in Western Australia are **Lesueur Island** (Ref:1638, a 17m stainless steel lattice tower built in 1963) and **Lacrosse Island** (Ref: 1636, a cylindrical metal tower built in 1961). They are accessible with difficulty by helicopter or boat from Wickham.

1916

Cape Don Northern Territory

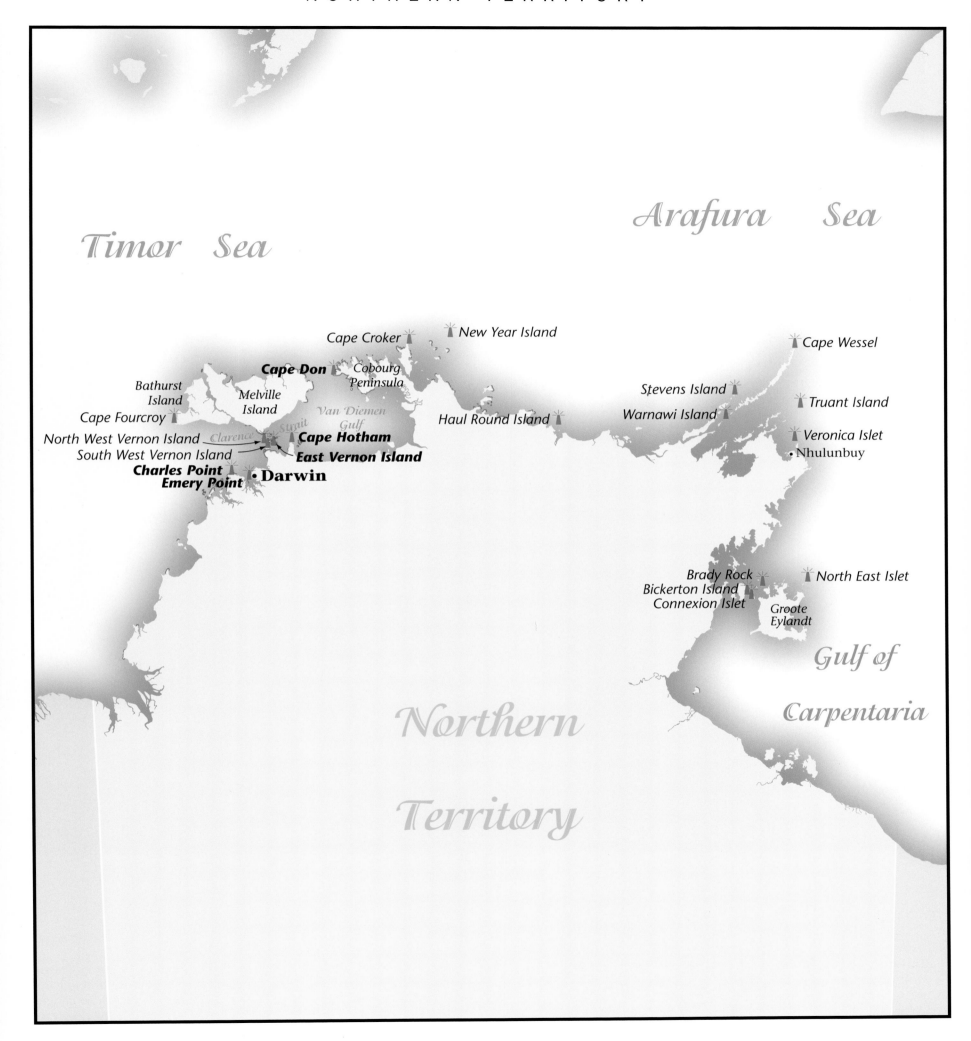

Timor Sea

Arafura Sea

Cape Croker

New Year Island

Cape Wessel

Cape Don

Cobourg
Peninsula

Bathurst
Island

Melville
Island

Stevens Island

Truant Island

Warnawi Island

Cape Fourcroy

*Van Diemen
Gulf*

Haul Round Island

Veronica Islet

North West Vernon Island

Clarence Strait

Cape Hotham

Nhulunbuy

South West Vernon Island

East Vernon Island

Charles Point

Emery Point

• **Darwin**

Brady Rock

North East Islet

Bickerton Island

Connexion Islet

*Groote
Eylandt*

Northern

Gulf of

Territory

Carpentaria

Charles Point
Darwin Northern Territory

Ref: **3322**   Built: **1893**   Elevation: **39**   Tower: **32**   Range: **32**

This iron skeleton or lattice tower is located on the Cox Peninsula just west of Darwin. In conjunction with **Cape Fourcroy** (Ref: 3318, a 15m white frame tower built in 1945) on Bathurst Island it marks the passage across Beagle Gulf into Port Darwin. When converted to automatic operation in 1933 it was demanned and the keepers' houses were demolished. It still has its Chance Brothers 3.7m lantern but its lens is now an FA 251 Tupperware light. The road to the light passes through the old Radio Australia facility and although the radio base no longer operates access is not permitted.

206

East Vernon Island
Darwin Northern Territory

Ref: **3316**   Built: **1928**   Elevation: **12**   Tower: **11**
Range: **11W   15R   15G**

There are a number of lights that mark the channel through Clarence Strait. These are **South West Vernon Island** (Ref: 3317, built in 1958), **North West Vernon Island** (Ref: 3317.5, built in 1987) East Vernon Island (shown here) and Cape Hotham. These lights replaced a number of buoys that were deployed in 1917. They are accessible by boat from Darwin.

Emery Point
Darwin Northern Territory

Ref: **3324**   Built: **1917**   Elevation: **18**   Tower: **9**   Range: **35W   26R**

This small white tower is the last of the lights built for ships sailing into Darwin from the east through Clarence Strait. Originally built by the South Australian Government in 1900 it was replaced by the Commonwealth in 1917. As it is located in an army reserve access is difficult.

Cape Hotham
Darwin Northern Territory

Ref: **3315**   Built: **1928**   Elevation: **17**   Tower: **16**   Range: **22W   17R**

This steel frame tower has a Chance Brothers 2.1m lantern and a 400mm catadioptric drum lens. It marks the eastern end of Clarence Strait. It is accessible by boat from Darwin.

Cape Don
Cobourg Peninsula Northern Territory

Ref: **3314**   Built: **1917**   Elevation: **50**   Tower: **36**   Range: **41**

This landfall light was built from reinforced concrete using materials, including the gravel that was shipped all the way from Melbourne. It took three dry seasons to complete construction. It has a Chance Brothers 3.3m lantern and originally had a third order dioptric lens. When it was automated in 1983 a high intensity light, the first of its kind to be powered by solar cells replaced the original lens. It was demanned at the same time. As the lightstation is in the Gurig National Park the keepers' houses were handed over to the Northern Territory Conservation Commission

although 'Cape Don Experience' is using two of the houses as a wilderness lodge. The lightstation is accessible by small plane from Darwin but as it is 15km from the airstrip access must be arranged through the lodge.

Other Northern Territory lights across the top of Arnhem Land are **Cape Croker** (Ref: 3313.4, built in 1988), **New Year Island** (Ref: 3313, a 30m white frame tower built in 1962) and **Haul Round Island** (Ref: 3312.8, built in 1987).

Warnawi Island (Ref: 3312.6, built in 1984), **Stevens Island** (Ref: 3312.5, built in 1984) and

Cape Wessel (Ref: 3312, a 30m stainless steel frame tower built in 1966) are on the Wessel Islands that reach out into the Arafura Sea from the north eastern corner of Arnhem Land.
Truant Island (Ref: 3311, a 15m round metal tower built in 1975) and **Veronica Islet** (Ref: 3310, built in 1982) are on the eastern side of Arnhem land while **Brady Rock** (Ref: 3308, built in 1966), **Connexion Islet** (Ref: 3307, built in 1966), **Bickerton Island** (Ref: 3306, built in 1975) and **North East Islet** (Ref: 3305, built in 1966) are on Groote Eylandt. Access to these lights is difficult.

Index - Queensland

Northern Queensland Map   211

Booby Island   212

Western Hill on Goods Island   214

Restoration Rock   215

Chapman Reef   215

South Pipon Island   215

Grassy Hill   216

Archer Point   217

Low Isles   218

Island Point   220

Fitzroy Island   221

Little Fitzroy Island   222

South Brook Island   222

Cape Cleveland   223

Southern Queensland Map   225

Cape Bowling Green   226

Eshelby Island   227

Great Keppel Island   227

Dent Island   228

North Reef   230

East Point   233

Lady Musgrave Islet   233

Cape Capricorn   234

Bustard Head   235

Lady Elliot Island   236

South Head   238

Breaksea Spit Lightship   239

Sandy Cape   240

Double Island Point   242

Caloundra Lights   243

Point Cartwright   244

Cape Moreton   246

North Point   247

Cleveland Point   248

Point Lookout   249

Point Danger   249

Leading Light Townsville Queensland

Bramble Cay
Dalrymple Islet
East Cay

Twin Island
Harvey Rocks
Sue Islet
East Strait Island
Wednesday Island

Arden Islet
Dove Islet
Bet Reef
Hammond Island;
Hammond Rock
Kirkcaldie Reef
Booby Island
Tuesday Islet
Carpenteria Lightship-Buoy
Wyborn Reef
Goods Island;
Western Hill
Albany Rock
Eborac Island
Thursday Island

Cairncross Islets

Hannibal Islands

Clerke Island

Moody Reef
Inset Reef
Piper Islands
Eel Reef
Duyfken Point
Middle Reef
Restoration Rock
Lockhart River
Wye Reef
Chapman Reef

Waterwitch Reef
Bow Reef

Heath Reef
Magpie Reef
Fife Island
Eden Reef
Hannah Island
Stainer Island (Iris Reef)
King Island
Fahey Reef
South Pipon Island
Wharton Reef
Megeara Reef
South Barrow Islet
Howick Island
Watson Island
Coquet Island
Miles Reef
Pethebridge Islets
Palfrey Islet
Decapolis Reef
Maxwell Reef
Three Islands

Grassy Hill
Egret Reef
Cooktown

Archer Point
Bougainville Reef
Pickersgill Reef
Gubbins Reef
Island Point
Low Isles
Port Douglas
Island Point (Historic)
Arlington Reef
Euston Reef
Cairns
Fitzroy Island

Little Fitzroy Island
Russell Island

North Barnard Islands

South Brook Island
Pith Reef
Rib Reef
Albino (White) Rock

Cape Cleveland
Townsville
Cape Bowling Green

Holbourne Island

Eshelby Island
Pinnacle Point

Pacific

Ocean

Gulf of

Carpentaria

Northern

Queensland

211

Booby Island
Torres Strait, Thursday Island Queensland

Ref: 3274   Built: 1890   Elevation: 37   Tower: 18
Range: 39

Located at the western entrance to Torres Strait this island was named by both Captain Cook and Captain Bligh after the booby birds that make the island their home. It was also known as Post Office Island because passing ships would leave messages in a cave on the island. At first they were just a record of the ships passing but eventually sailors left letters that were picked up by ships going in the other direction. To provide sailors with the means for writing letters a supply of ink, pens and paper was stored there, on shelves made from an old puncheon (barrel). This practice that started about 1820 (and made it the second post office in Australia) continued until 1874 when Thursday Island became the major port in Torres Strait. The tower is a galvanised iron clad wood framed tower. Although it still has its 3.1m Chance Brothers lantern the second order lens was replaced by a lamp array when it was converted to solar power in 1991. It was demanned at the same time although there is still a caretaker on the island. The three keepers' houses are in reasonable condition but paint and minor repairs are needed. It is accessible, with difficulty from Thursday Island by boat or helicopter.

On the western side of Cape York in the Gulf of Carpentaria there is only one major lighthouse. That is **Duyfken Point** (Ref: 3297, a GRP hut on a 30m stainless steel frame tower built in 1962) that serves the alumina ore ships entering and leaving Weipa. There used to be the **Carpentaria Shoal lightship** (Ref: 3296, built in 1982) southwest of Booby Island but a buoy has now replaced it. From Booby Island to the west and Bramble Cay to the east of Cape York down to Port Douglas there are a string of lights that mark the passage through Torres Strait and the northern section of the Great Barrier Reef. They allow ships to safely sail through the calm but dangerous waters between Cape York and the outer reef. As they are less than 50km apart there are a large number of them, solar powered lights on low platforms or frame towers marking a passage through the reef like a well-lit highway. The lights through the North East Channel and Torres Strait down to the top of the cape are: **Bramble Cay** (Ref: 3292, a 17m stainless steel frame tower built in 1924); **Dalrymple Islet** (Ref: 3288, a white GRP hut on a 23m stainless steel frame tower built in 1944); **Arden Islet** (Ref: 3285, a 13m metal frame tower built in 1982); **Dove Islet** (Ref: 3284, built in 1957); **Bet Reef** (Ref: 3280, a white GRP hut on a 7m red metal frame tower built in 1944); **Sue Islet** (Ref: 3279, built in 1962); **Kirkcaldie Reef** (Ref: 3278.5, built in 1997); **Harvey Rocks** (Ref: 3278, a white GRP hut on an 8m red metal frame tower built in 1944); **East Cay** (Ref: 3290, a 31m metal frame tower on piles built in 1997); **Hammond Island** (Ref: 3267, built in 1980 - the first light in Australia to be powered by solar panels); **Hammond Rock** (Ref: 3266, built in 1921); **Tuesday Islet** (Ref: 3263, built in 1988); **Wednesday Island** (Ref: 3262, built in 1974); **Twin Island** (Ref: 3260, built in 1945) and **East Strait Island** (Ref: 3258, built in 1945).

Western Hill, Goods Island

Torres Strait, Thursday Island Queensland

**Ref: 3270.1   Built: 1886   Elevation: 105
Tower: 5   Range: 20**

Matthew Flinders named the island after the gardener on his 1802 expedition, Peter Good. For a period it was known as Goode Island and currently it is Good's or Goods Island. The lighthouse, a wooden framed corrugated iron sheathed structure with a Chance Brothers 250mm lens was built under the supervision of G.P. Heath who was responsible for the construction of 12 major (and a total of 33) lights between Brisbane and Booby Island. In total there were seven lights of this type built the others being Grassy Hill (Cooktown), Little Sea Hill, Caloundra Head, Bay Rock (Townsville), North Point (Moreton Island) and Gatacombe Head (Gladstone). Western Hill and the **Goods Island Front Light** (Ref: 3270, built in 1941 and replaced in 1988) at the base of Western Hill are used to mark the entrance to Normanby Sound and the Prince of Wales Channel. They are accessible by boat or helicopter from Thursday Island.

Clustered around the top of Cape York and south to Cape Weymouth there are a number of lights. These are: **Eborac Island** (Ref: 3256, a square concrete tower built in 1921); **Albany Rock** (Ref: 3254, a square concrete tower also built in 1921); **Wyborn Reef** (Ref: 3252, originally built in 1938 and replaced by a 21m stainless steel tower on piles built in 1991); **Cairncross Islets** (Ref: 3250, built in 1934); **Hannibal Islands** (Ref: 3248, originally built in 1921 and replaced by a white GRP hut on a 26m red metal frame tower built in 1990) and **Clerke Island** (Ref: 3244, originally built in 1915 and replaced by a white GRP hut on a 22m red metal frame tower built in 1990). Further down the east coast of Cape York towards Lockhart River there is: **Moody Reef** (Ref: 3243, built in 1980); **Inset Reef** (Ref: 3242.5, built in 1980); **Piper Islands** (Ref: 3242, originally built in 1917 and replaced by a 12m stainless steel tower on piles built in 1991. The 1917 light replaced a lightship that had been there since 1878); **Eel Reef** (Ref: 3241, built in 1952); **Middle Reef** (Ref: 3240.4, built in 1975); and **Wye Reef** (Ref: 3238, built in 1980).

Restoration Rock
Cape Weymouth, Lockhart River Queensland

Ref: 3240 Built: 1986 Elevation: 38 Tower: 5 Range: 17

This white GRP cabinet that replaced the original hut built in 1927, sits on top of a small rugged island off Cape Weymouth. It is typical of the new lights located on elevated rocks or islands along the Great Barrier Reef. It is, with difficulty accessible by boat.

Chapman Reef (Centre)
Cape Direction, Lockhart River Queensland

Ref: 3236 Built: 1991 Elevation: 18 Tower: 14 Range: 20W 13R

This stainless steel tower on concrete piles just offshore from Cape Direction replaced the original light built in 1917. It has a Chance Brothers 250mm catadioptric drum lens. It is typical of the lights on the reefs or low islands along the northern part of the Great Barrier Reef. It is, with difficulty accessible by boat.

From Cape Direction south through Princess Charlotte Bay to Cape Melville the following lights are dotted along the reef: **Waterwitch Reef** (Ref: 3234, originally built in 1918 and replaced by a white GRP hut on a 19m stainless steel tower on piles in 1991); **Bow Reef** (Ref: 3233, built in 1960); **Heath Reef** (Ref: 3232, originally built in 1918 and replaced by a white GRP hut on an 11m metal frame tower built in 1985); **Fife Island** (Ref: 3230, built in 1961); **Magpie Reef** (Ref: 3229, built in 1977); **Hannah Island** (Ref: 3228, a white GRP hut on a 21m red metal frame tower built in 1934); **Stainer Island** (Iris Reef) (Ref: 3227.5, a red GRP hut on piles built in 2000); **Fahey Reef** (Ref: 3227, built in 1961); **Eden Reef** (Ref: 3226.6, built in 1960); **Wharton Reef** (Ref: 3226, a white GRP hut on piles originally built in 1915 and replaced in 1990. The original lighthouse is now in Townsville); **King Island** (Ref: 3225, a white GRP hut on a 17m red metal frame tower built in 1950).

Pipon Island (Bottom)
Cape Melville, Cooktown Queensland

Ref: 3224 Built: 1989 Elevation: 26 Tower: 25 Range: 19W 13R

This light was originally built in 1901 but was replaced by a white GRP hut on a stainless steel frame tower on piles in 1989 just offshore from Cape Melville. It is, with difficulty, accessible by boat.

From Cape Melville to Cooktown the following lights mark the channel along the reef.
South Barrow Islet (Ref: 3222, a white square concrete tower built in 1950); **Watson Island** (Ref: 3221.4, built in 1985); **Megeara Reef** (Ref: 3221, built in 1969); **Howick Island** (Ref: 3220, built in 1969); **Miles Reef** (Ref: 3219.5, built in 1974); **Coquet Island** (Ref: 3219, a white GRP hut on a 22m red galvanised iron lattice tower built in 1915); **Pethebridge Islets** (Ref: 3217, built in 1958); **Palfrey Islet** (Ref: 3216, a white square concrete tower built in 1936); **Maxwell Reef** (Ref: 3215.5, built in 2000. First exhibited in 12/2000 it was the last light built in the twentieth century); **Decapolis Reef** (Ref: 3215, built in 1958 and replaced in 1985) and **Three Isles** (Ref: 3214, a white GRP hut on a 26m red metal frame tower built in 1942 and replaced in 1997).

Grassy Hill
Cooktown Queensland

Ref: **3208**   Built: **1886**   Elevation: **162**   Tower: **6**   Range: **17**

This wooden framed corrugated iron sheathed lighthouse, identical to the Goods Island light is built on a hilltop where Lt Cook once stood looking for a way through the Great Barrier Reef. Its importance as a highway light continued until 1937 when Cooktown became accessible by road. It had a Chance Brothers lantern room and lens but the lens is now in the local James Cook Historical Museum. Originally there was one keeper who not only tended to the light but would also raise a flag whenever a ship was entering the Endeavour River. When the light was automated it was demanned and the keeper's house was demolished. At one stage the light was going to be deactivated but after requests from local fishermen it was decided to keep it operating as a low powered harbour light. Although a sign at the lighthouse says "…and for years was one of only four along the

Queensland coast" there were actually at least sixteen already in the state. It is at the end of Hope Street in Cooktown.

Other lights between Cooktown and Port Douglas are:
Egret Reef (Ref: 3207, built in 1979); **East Diamond Islet** (Ref: 3206.7, a white GRP hut on a 23m frame tower on piles built in 1988); **Lihou Reef** (Ref: 3206.6, a red GRP hut on a 34m stainless steel frame tower on piles built in 1999); **Bougainville Reef** (Ref: 3206, a white GRP hut on a 14m stainless steel frame tower on piles built in 1968) **Gubbins Reef** (Ref: 3196, a GRP hut on a square concrete column built in 1958) and **Pickersgill Reef** (Ref: 3195.9, a GRP hut on a square concrete column built in 1992).

Archer Point
Cooktown Queensland

Ref: 3200 **Built: 1979** **Elevation: 65**
Tower: 6 **Range: 32W 24R 24G**

This grey square concrete tower that replaced the original elegant steel clad tower built in 1883 could easily take the prize as the most unattractive lighthouse in Australia. Its only saving grace is the sweeping views along the coast. It has a Stone Chance 400mm lens with white, red and green sectors that clearly mark the channel along the reef. There is also the remains of a small light on **Rocky Islet** just south of the point that was used as a front leading light for the old tower. Although it was turned off in 1996 it still serves as a daymark. The lights are at the end of the Archer Point 'Road' that turns off the main highway about 15km south of Cooktown.

The picture below shows the base of the original Archer Point tower and in the distance Rocky Islet.

Low Isles
Port Douglas Queensland

Ref: 3194   Built: 1878   Elevation: 20
Tower: 18   Range: 48

The white galvanised iron clad timber framed tower with a red cupola has a Chance Brothers 2.4m lantern although its lens was replaced with a modern ML 300 Tupperware light during conversion to solar power in 1993. When the lightstation was demanned in 1994 it was handed over to the Great Barrier Reef Marine Parks Authority (GBRMPA). The original keepers' houses, replaced in 1963 are now used for staff accommodation. Located on a 2.5 hectare cay 13km from Port Douglas the lighthouse can be reached by cruise boat from Port Douglas. Once there visitors can follow a self-guided path with informative signs through the lightstation.

Island Point

Port Douglas Queensland

NEW: Ref: **3186** Built: **1997** Elevation: **90** Tower: **40** Range: **26W 20R**
OLD: Ref: **** Built: **1879** Elevation: **26** Tower: **6** Range: **0**

The old light may have only been a small concrete tower with a red dome surrounded by lush tropical growth but it was the epitome of a lighthouse in the tropics. Allowing houses to be built around it was, to say the least short sighted. There is a path that leads down to the light but it can be difficult to locate. The new light is attached to the communication tower on Island Point Road at Lookout Point. Unfortunately it was determined that this tower would not survive gale force winds so was replaced in 2001.

Fitzroy Island

Grafton Passage, Cairns Queensland

Ref: **** **Built: 1973** **Elevation: 150** **Tower: 17**
Range: 0

The original tower built in 1943 marked the entrance to the Grafton Passage through the Great Barrier Reef to the Coral Sea.

Since then additional lights at **Euston Reef** (Ref: 3166, built in 1970) and **Arlington Reef** (Ref: 3167, built in 1990) have been built along the passage. Due to restricted visibility a new tower was built in 1973. It was the third, and last manned light constructed by the Commonwealth since 1915. The tiled concrete tower is similar to the tower at Point Cartwright in Mooloolaba although its lantern room, designed by the Department of Transportation is different. It also has a never-used signal station attached to it. Although it was automated and demanned in 1991 the light was turned off in 1992 when a new light on Little Fitzroy Island was commissioned. The keepers' quarters are in excellent condition but are not accessible. Fitzroy Island can be reached by cruise boat from Cairns. The light is then a strenuous uphill walk from the beach.

Little Fitzroy Island (Above)
Grafton Passage, Cairns Queensland

Ref: **3168**   Built: **1992**   Elevation: **33**   Tower: **4**   Range: **28W 22R 22G**

The first light on Little Fitzroy Island was built in 1929 at the request of the Cairns Chamber of Commerce. It was turned off in 1973 when the new Fitzroy Island light was built. When it was decided to extinguish the Fitzroy Island light a new GRP cabinet light was built and lit in 1992. The island can be reached by taking a cruise boat from Cairns to Fitzroy Island and then paddling to it in a kayak.

South Brook Island (Left)
Cardwell Queensland

Ref: **3132**   Built: **1921**   Elevation: **52**   Tower: **18**   Range: **19**

Between Cairns and Ingham there are a number of lights. **Russell Island** (Ref: 3162, a 17m frame tower built in 1929) and **North Barnard Island** (Ref: 3138, a GRP hut on a square concrete tower built in 1988 that replaced one built in 1919) follow the coast while **Rib Reef** (Ref: 3120.7, built in 1979); **Pith Reef** (Ref: 3120.5, a 28m stainless steel frame tower on piles built in 1979) and **Albino (White) Rock** (Ref: 3120, a square concrete tower built in 1940) mark the channel through Palm Passage.
 The Brook Islands consist of three small islands, North, Middle and South. The light is on the highest point of the South Island and is typical of the frame towers built before the advent of stainless steel. Although there is a concrete 'road' leading up to the light that can be used by a LARC if the jungle is hacked back most servicing is done by helicopter. The 'butterfly-infested' island, just north of Hinchinbrook Island is accessible by boat or helicopter.

Cape Cleveland
Townsville Queensland

Ref: **3092.1** Built: **1879**
Elevation: **64** Tower: **11**
Range: **28W 22R**

This timber framed galvanised iron clad light is one of 14 towers of this type built in Queensland. It is identical to the light on Dent Island that was built at the same time. Because the tower is relatively short the weights that powered the clockwork mechanism had to be wound up every 75 minutes making each night a long one for the keepers. After conversion to solar power in 1987 the light was demanned. The keepers' houses are still in reasonable condition even though they are only used intermittently. Although it is close to Townsville the light is only accessible by boat or helicopter.

223

North Reef Lighthouse Queensland

Lihou Reef

East Diamond Islet

Pith Reef

Rib Reef

Great

Albino (White) Rock

Cape Cleveland

Townsville

Cape Bowling Green

Barrier

Holbourne Island

Eshelby Island

Pinnacle Point

White Tip Reef

Little Bugatti Reef

Edward Island

Bugatti Reef

Dent Island

Reef

Coppersmith Rock

Creal Reef

Bailey Islet

Penrith Island

Mackay

Flat Top Island

Pine Peak Island

Vernon Rocks

Pine Islet

Frederick Reef

High Peak Island

Saumarez Reef

Clara Group

South

Swains Reef

Great Keppel Island

North Reef

Pacific

Cape Capricorn

Southern

Gladstone

East Point

Clews Point

Lady Musgrave Islet

Queensland

Bustard Head

Lady Elliot Island

Ocean

Breaksea Spit Lightship-Buoy

South Head

Sandy Cape

Bundaberg

Hervey Bay

Fraser Island

Double Island Point

Point Cartwright

Caloundra Lights

Cape Moreton; North Point

Redcliffe

Moreton Island

Moreton Bay

Brisbane

Point Lookout

Cleveland Point

North Stradbroke Island

Coolangatta

Point Danger

225

Cape Bowling Green (Above)
Upstart Bay, Ayr Queensland

Ref: **3090** Built: **1987** Elevation: **36**
Tower: **32** Range: **20**

The original wood framed, steel sheathed tower was built in 1874. In 1920 it was automated, demanned and the keepers' cottages were demolished. When the new steel lattice tower was built in 1987 the old tower was dismantled and shipped to the Australian National Maritime Museum at Darling Harbour in Sydney. Re-erection was completed in late 1994. Access to the old light in Sydney is easy but to the new one access is difficult.

The old Cape Bowling Green Tower after it was rebuilt at the Australian National Maritime Museum.

Eshelby Island (Opposite, left and bottom)
Proserpine Queensland

Ref: **3068** Built: **1972** Elevation: **56** Tower: **4**
Range: **19**

After Cape Bowling Green there is **Holbourne Island** (Ref: 3069, built in 1963) and then Eshelby Island that is the divergence point for ships going through the Whitsunday Passage and those going around the Whitsunday Islands. Originally built in 1935 it was replaced by a GRP cabinet in 1972. It can be accessed by boat or helicopter.

For ships going around the islands they will come across the **Pinnacle Point** light on Hook Island (Ref: 3067.4, built in 1964) and the **Edward Island** light (Ref: 3066.6, built in 1967) while those going through the passage will encounter Dent Island and then **Coppersmith Rock** (Ref: 3062, built in 1928 and replaced in 1987).

Great Keppell Island (Right)

Gladstone Queensland

Ref: **2997** Built: **1975** Elevation: **52** Tower: **2**
Range: **17**

This small GRP light perched on top of a grassy knoll at North East Point marks the passage through the Keppel Islands. There is an airstrip at the southern end of the island and a track that leads to the light.

Dent Island

Whitsunday Islands, Proserpine Queensland

Ref: **3064**   Built: **1879**   Elevation: **37**
Tower: **10**   Range: **19**

Dent Island is one of the many islands in the Whitsunday Islands. The tower is identical to the timber framed galvanised iron clad Cape Cleveland tower that was built at the same time. It is the southern light for ships travelling through the Whitsunday Passage.

After it was demanned in 1987 the keepers' houses were vandalised. They have since been repaired and are used by people living on the island. The grave is that of a three year old girl who died in 1885. It is accessible by boat from Shutehaven or Hamilton Island.

Just south of Mackay is Point Hay a large coal loading facility. For the ships using the port a new passage through the Great Barrier Reef called Hydrographers Passage was opened and navigation lights built. These were **Bugatti Reef** (Ref: 3056, built in 1990); **White Tip Reef** (Ref: 3054, a 37m steel lattice tower on piles built in 1985 that also has a 10m front lead light); **Little Bugatti Reef** (Ref: 3053, a 24m steel lattice tower on piles built in 1984) and **Creal Reef** (Ref: 3052, a 34m steel lattice tower on piles built in 1984) while closer to shore the existing lights on **Penrith Island** (Ref: 3049, a square concrete tower built in 1963); **Bailey Islet** (Ref: 3048, a square concrete tower built in 1928) and **Flat Top Island** (Ref: 3028, a 10m round metal tower built in 1874) are used. All the lattice towers also have distinctive daymark panels.

Between Mackay and Yeppoon there are a number of small lights that guide ships through the Northumberland Isles. These are the **Vernon Rocks** (Ref: 3023, built in 1967), **Pine Peak Island** (Ref: 3022, built in 1958), **High Peak Island** (Ref: 3018, a square concrete tower built in 1920) and **Clara Group** (Ref: 3017, built in 1987) lights. There is also the **Pine Islet** light (Ref: 3020, a tapered GRP cabinet built in 1985 that replaced the original steel clad, wood framed tower built in 1885). Up until it was extinguished the original light was the last light in Australia using kerosene. The keepers' cottages were demolished but the old tower was dismantled and rebuilt in Mackay where it is now on display. After its removal the work crew inscribed the old base with *Pine Islet Lighthouse Built 18/07/1885 Dismantled 12/11/1986 'REST IN PIECES'*.

North Reef (Also overleaf)
Capricorn Channel, Gladstone Queensland

Ref: **3014**   Built: **1878**   Elevation: **23**   Tower: **24**   Range: **28**

The North Reef Light located at the north end of the Capricorn Group is one of the most interesting lights in Australia. The galvanised iron clad wooden framed tower and residence was built on a reef. The hollow concrete base of the tower was used as a fresh water tank with the circular residence surrounding the tower. Over time the structure has caused sand to build up around the tower so that now it is quite a substantial sand island. The light was converted to solar power in 1987 and demanned. Because of the confined and difficult conditions only bachelors were assigned to the three-keeper station. The lighthouse is 100km offshore from Gladstone and can only be reached by boat or helicopter.

Further east, beyond the Capricorn Channel and the main reef are **Swains Reef** (Ref: 3014.5, built in 1999), **Saumarez Reef** (Ref: 3015, an 18m stainless steel frame tower with a red GRP hut built in 1971 and replaced in 1996) and **Frederick Reef** (Ref: 3016, a 34m round stainless steel tower built in 1968).

North Reef Lighthouse

East Point (Left)

Facing Island, Gladstone Queensland

Ref: **2972**   Built: **1980**   Elevation: **47**
Tower: **10**   Range: **30**

This unattractive stainless steel frame light marks the passage into Boyne Island and the Port of Gladstone. Its FA 251 solar powered Tupperware light with an intensity of 24,000 candelas is typical of the modern lights now used around Australia. It can be reached by boat from Gladstone.

Lady Musgrave Islet (Below)

Bunker Group, Gladstone Queensland

Ref: **2963**   Built: **1974**   Elevation: **21**
Tower: **17**   Range: **24**

Lady Musgrave Islet located within the Great Barrier Reef Marine Park is one of the southern most parts of the reef. The stainless steel frame tower and GRP cabinet at the southwest corner of the islet is typical of the larger towers built along the reef. There are regular boat tours to the surrounding reef operating from Bundaberg.

Cape Capricorn

Curtis Island, Gladstone
Queensland

Ref: **2992.1**   Built: **1964**
Elevation: **93**   Tower: **7**
Range: **30W   22R**

The first light on this spectacular bluff at the north-east end of Curtis Island was built in 1875 based on a design by F.D.G. Stanley. It was replaced in 1936. The current white square concrete block tower was built in 1964. The original oil burner was converted to vaporised kerosene in 1923 and to generator power in 1938. It was converted to solar power during the 1980's and demanned at the same time. The privately leased keepers' houses are in good condition. The light, 24km north of Gladstone can be reached by boat or by a small plane using the beach as a runway.

Bustard Head
Gladstone Queensland

Ref: 2964 **Built:** 1868 **Elevation:** 102
Tower: 17 **Range:** 39

The tower is made of cast-iron panels imported from England, that were bolted together on site. It was the first light built by the Government after Queensland became a state and was also the last light of this type built in Queensland. It has a Chance Brothers 2.9m lantern and a 250mm 8 panel lens with an intensity of 200,000 candelas. A red sector light was added in 1935 but this was removed when it was automated and demanned in 1985. It is also the rear light used in conjunction with a leading light at **Clews Point** (Ref: 2968) for traffic heading south from Gladstone. After demanning the keepers' houses were vandalised but have since been repaired and are available for overnight stays. As there is a significant history associated with this lightstation it is hoped that efforts being made to repair the infrastructure (that includes a cemetery with nine graves dating from 1879 to 1911) are successful. The best way to visit the light is by boat or with 1770 Environmental Tours that run day trips to Bustard Head on a pink LARC from the Town of 1770.

Lady Elliot Island
Bundaberg Queensland

NEW:	Ref: **2962**	Built: **1995**	Elevation: **38**	Tower: **32**
		Range: **37**		
OLD:	Ref: ********	Built: **1873**	Elevation: **22**	Tower: **17**
		Range: **0**		

Lady Elliot Island, named after the first ship to pass by the island, is at the southern extremity of the Great Barrier Reef. It was once inhabited by vast flocks of birds that deposited commercial quantities of guano. As a result the island was mined even before the lighthouse was built. The mining plus introduced goats left the island completely bare. The first light on top of a mast built in 1866, blew away during a gale in 1871. It was replaced by another temporary light until a classical tower, constructed with a hardwood frame and covered with galvanised iron sheets was built in 1873. This was the first of the 14 towers of this type that were constructed in the state. After the mining stopped Don Adams planted casuarinas (she-oaks) and pandanus palms. The trees grew so well that the foliage started to obscure the light. Bureaucracy decreed that the trees could not be trimmed so in 1995 the new steel frame tower was built and the old light extinguished. The island is now a resort accessible by air from Bundaberg or Hervey Bay. The keepers' cottages are in good condition and are used by the resort staff.

South Head

Burnett River, Bundaberg Queensland

Ref: **2956** Built: **1920** Elevation: **20**
Tower: **17** Range: **33**

The current tiled concrete tower replaced a small wooden tower built in 1873 that has been re-erected about a kilometre away. The new tower was manned until 1932. The tower is also used as one of two Australian receiving sites (the other being near Albany in WA) for the Cospas-Sarsat satellite international rescue system. This technology has, or no doubt will be replaced with one based on the GPS navigation system. The light is accessible by road from Bundaberg.

Breaksea Spit

Lightship, Bundaberg Queensland

Ref: 2934   Built: 1982   Elevation: 10   Tower: 10   Range: 0

The two Breaksea Spit lightships (CLS7 and CLS8), positioned 40km NNE of Fraser Island and the two at Carpentaria Shoal were the last lightships on active duty in Australia. A buoy has now replaced the lightships. Prior to 1916 there were a number of manned lightships at various locations around Australia. They were often temporary lights until a permanent lighthouse could be built. In 1916-1918 the first four unmanned light vessels were built. These were replaced in 1981-1982 by the second batch of four. Only two remain, the CLS2 in the Queensland Maritime Museum and the CLS4 in the National Maritime Museum in Sydney. The remainder have been wrecked or scuttled. For a detailed account of lightships see the chapter on 'Australia's Lighthouses'.
Note: Lightships that do not have a crew are technically light buoys or light vessels although they tend to be called lightships like those that are manned.

Sandy Cape

Fraser Island, Hervey Bay Queensland

Ref: **2932**   Built: **1870**   Elevation: **128**   Tower: **33**   Range: **39**

Located at the northern end of the largest sand island on earth this prefabricated cast-iron panel conical tower is the tallest lighthouse in Queensland. The only other tower of this type in Queensland is at Bustard Head. One of its unique features is the entrance to the main part of the tower. The door is at the second level above the storage room and is reached via an external staircase. When converted to electric power in 1930 a fourth order lens replaced the original first order apparatus. The new lens using a 1,000-watt quartz-halogen globe produced an intensity of 1,000,000 candelas that apparently was later raised to 3,000,000 candelas. When a buoy first replaced the lightship at Breaksea Spit it was found that the buoy was not very effective. As a result the first permanent racon in Australia

was installed on the Sandy Cape tower. In the early days supplies were moved from the beach to the lighthouse by horses pulling trolleys along a 1.2km wooden rail line to the base of a nearly vertical section. For this last section a horse powered windlass was used. The station was demanned and automated in 1984. At the same time the light was replaced with a solar powered Vega VRB-25 rotating Tupperware light that produces an intensity of 160,000 candelas. The keepers' cottages that were replaced in 1930 are currently used by the Queensland National Parks Service (QNPS) as staff quarters. The station is accessible with a 4WD provided that the beach is open through the Ngkala Rocks area.

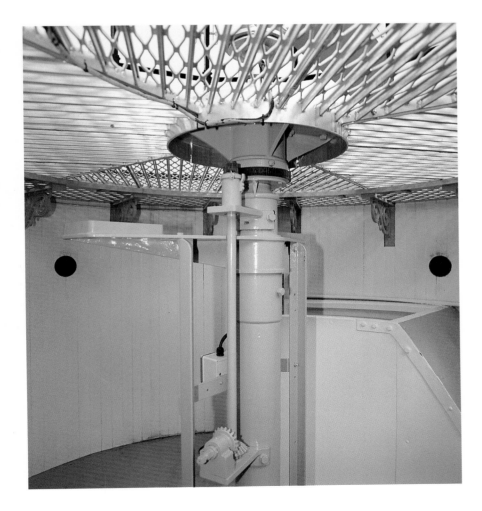

Double Island Point

Rainbow Beach Queensland

Ref: **2912** Built: **1884** Elevation: **96**
Tower: **12** Range: **32**

Double Island Point named by Captain Cook is part of the Capricorn Coast National Park. The steel clad wood framed tower is almost identical to the original Pine Islet light built at the same time. Over the years the Chance Brothers third order light had its intensity increased until by 1980 it was producing 1,000,000 candelas. Although it still has its 2.5m lantern, a Tupperware light with an intensity of only 40,000 candelas replaced the original lens when it was converted to solar power in 1992. The station was demanned at the same time. The two current houses replaced the original three keepers' cottages in 1933 and are used by the QNPS as staff quarters. The tower is accessible by 4WD from Rainbow Beach.

The weather 'shack'.

Caloundra Lights

Caloundra Queensland

Tower One: Ref: **** Built: **1896** Tower: **9** Range: **0**
Tower Two: Ref: **** Built: **1967** Tower: **11** Range: **0**

The first Caloundra light built in 1896 and one of the city's five oldest buildings was a corrugated iron, wood framed tower. As with other similar lights of the era the corrugations tapered synchronously with the taper of the tower so there were the same number at the top as there were at the bottom. It was also the first light in Queensland with an incandescent lamp.

The new concrete tower and signal station was built adjacent to the old tower that was then removed and erected at Golden Beach further down the coast. As the new tower's light became partially obscured by high-rise buildings in the area it was decided to build a replacement coastal light at Point Cartwright 20km to the north. In 1996 when the tower's signal station was decommissioned and although the light is still used as a harbour light it was decided to move the old tower back to its original location. This was completed in 2000. It is planned that both towers will, sometime in the future be opened for tours. They are located on Canberra Terrace in Caloundra.

243

Point Cartwright

Mooloolaba Queensland

Ref: **2907.8**   Built: **1979**
Elevation: **53**   Tower: **32**
Range: **43W   20R**

Similar to the tower at Fitzroy Island the Point Cartwright tower was the third one built for guiding ships into Moreton Bay from the north. The other two were at Caloundra 20 kilometres to the south. The pentagonal (5-sided) tower is made of reinforced concrete with a pre-cast concrete lantern room. An unusual feature is a flush toilet located on the tower's second level. It uses three vertical panels of five 200 watt sealed beam lamps with an intensity of 310,000 candelas. It also has a red sector light that is shown in the photograph on the right. It is accessible from the Pacific Boulevard in Mooloolaba.

Cape Moreton

Moreton Island, Brisbane Queensland

Ref: **2854.1** Built: **1857** Elevation: **122** Tower: **23** Range: **28**

Except for the unlit tower built in 1844 on Raine Island at the northern end of the Great Barrier Reef, Cape Moreton is the only stone lighthouse in Queensland. Built of rough-faced sandstone blocks quarried at the site it was the first highway light built in Queensland. The height of the tower was raised by a few metres in 1928. An unusual feature is the external stairway to the second level of the tower. Its original apparatus was 21 parabolic reflectors each with its own oil wick lamp. In 1930 a Chance Brothers 2.2m 16 sided lantern with a third order dioptric lens was installed. In 1993 a solar powered Tupperware light, with an intensity of only 14,000 candelas replaced the third order lens. The three keepers' houses, rebuilt in the 1920's are used by the QNPS for staff accommodation. The best way to reach the lighthouse is to take a ferry from Scarborough to Bulwer at the northern end of Moreton Island. It is then a 20km trip in a 4WD drive, via the Blue Lagoon and the eastern beaches to the lightstation.

Cape Moreton (Above)

North Point (Right)

Moreton Island, Brisbane Queensland

Ref: **2854**   Built: **1939**   Elevation: **25**
Tower: **7**   Range: **17W 15R**

This square concrete tower at the northern most point of Moreton Island is used as a leading light in conjunction with the Cape Moreton light. It is accessible from the Cape Moreton lightstation.

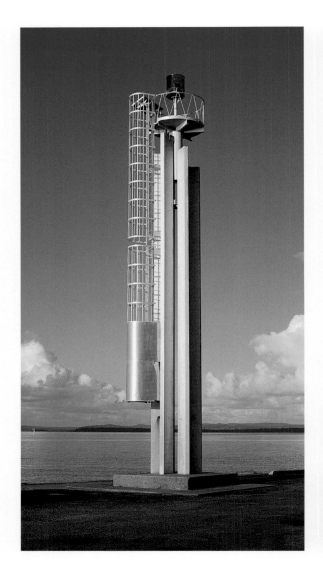

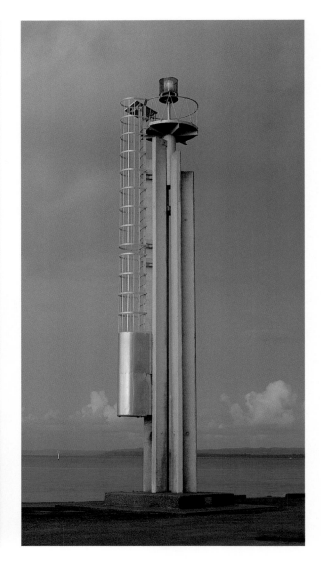

Cleveland Point

Raby Bay, Cleveland Queensland

NEW: Ref: **2898** Built: **1976** Elevation: **14** Tower: **12**
Range: **24W 15R**
OLD: Ref: **** Built: **1864** Elevation: **11** Tower: **9**
Range: **0**

The first light at this site that marks the entrance into Raby Bay and the once thriving port of Cleveland was a light on an open wooden frame built in 1847. It was the first light exhibited in Queensland. In 1864 it was replaced by a hexagonal wood framed structure clad in weatherboards that is now located across the reserve from the current light. Just three keepers kept this light burning during its first 70 years. This included James Troy who was the keeper from 1877 to 1927, an Australian record. The new light is made of exposed aggregate prefabricated concrete columns. The lights are in a park at the end of North Shore Street in Redland.

Point Lookout (Above)

North Stradbroke Island, Brisbane
Queensland

Ref: **2852**   Built: **1932**   Elevation: **78**
Tower: **5**   Range: **28**

The point, a remnant of an old volcano that initiated the formation of the island was named by Lt Cook in 1770. The lighthouse is a square concrete tower that marks the passage into Moreton Bay between North Stradbroke and Moreton Islands. There are car ferries from Cleveland to Dunwich on the island. North Point is at the end of the sealed North Coast Road.

Point Danger (Right)

Captain Cook Memorial, Coolangatta
Queensland

Ref: **2845**   Built: **1970**   Elevation: **45**
Tower: **20**   Range: **35**

This lighthouse was also pictured at the start of NSW because it straddles the Queensland-NSW border (shown in the photo on the right). As a modern light on a memorial for an early mariner it represents the period of the existence of lighthouses in Australia and was an appropriate place to start and finish the images.

Index – Museums

Map	**251**
Introduction	**252**

New South Wales: 253-255

Cape Byron Lightstation (O)
Yamba Historical Society (M)
Coffs Harbour Historical Society And Museum (M)
Smoky Cape Lightstation (O)
Mid North Coast Maritime Museum (M)
Sugarloaf Point Lightstation (O)
Nelson Head Lighthouse Cottage And Reserve (M)
Norah Head Lightstation (O)
Australian National Maritime Museum (M)
Wollongong Harbour Lighthouse (N)
Lady Denman Heritage Complex (M)
Cape St George Lighthouse Ruins (N)
Montague Island Lightstation (O)
Narooma Visitors Centre (M)
Ben Boyd's Tower (N)
Eden Killer Whale Museum (M)
Green Cape Lightstation (N)

Victoria: 256-257

Gabo Island Lightstation (O)
Point Hicks Lightstation (O)
Port Albert Maritime Museum (M)
South East Point Lightstation (O)
Cape Schanck Lightstation (O)
Eastern Light (N)
South Channel Pile (N)
Polly Woodside Maritime Museum (M)
Williamstown Timeball Tower (N)
Queenscliff Maritime Museum (M)
Fort Queenscliff (O)
Point Lonsdale Lighthouse (O)
Split Point Lightstation (O)
Cape Otway Lightstation (N)
Flagstaff Hill Maritime Museum (M)
Portland Maritime Discovery Centre (M)
Cape Nelson Lightstation (O)

Tasmania: 258-259

Deal Island Lightstation (N)
Currie Museum (M)
Swan Island Lightstation (O)
Low Head Lightstation (O)
Low Head Pilot Station And Maritime Museum (M)

Devonport Maritime Museum (M)
Eddystone Point Lightstation (O)
Maritime Museum Of Tasmania (M)
Cape Bruny Lightstation (N)
Maatsuyker Island Lightstation (N)
Stanley Park (M)

South Australia: 260-261

Margaret Brock Reef Centre (M)
Hope Cottage Museum (M)
Cape Willoughby Lightstation (O)
Cape Borda Lightstation (O)
Cape du Couedic Lightstation (O)
South Australian Maritime Museum (M)
Semaphore Timeball Tower (N)
Troubridge Island Lightstation (O)
Point Lowly Lightstation (O)

Western Australia and Northern Territory: 262

Albany Residency Museum (M)
Cape Leeuwin Lightstation (O)
Cape Naturaliste Lighthouse Museum (O)
Western Australian Maritime Museum (M)
Gascoyne Historical Society (M)
Vlaming Head Lighthouse (N)
Jarman Island Lightstation (N)
Cape Don Lightstation (O)

Queensland: 263-265

Torres Strait Historical Museum (M)
James Cook Historical Museum (M)
Courthouse Museum (M)
Low Isles Lightstation (O)
Fitzroy Island Lighthouse (N)
Townsville Maritime Museum (M)
Pine Islet Lighthouse Restoration (M)
Bustard Head Lightstation (O)
Lady Elliot Lighthouse (N)
South Head Lighthouse Restoration (N)
Caloundra Lighthouses (N)
Cleveland Lighthouse Restoration (N)
Queensland Maritime Museum (M)

(M) Regular Museums

(O) Operational Lighthouses

(N) Non-Operational Lighthouses

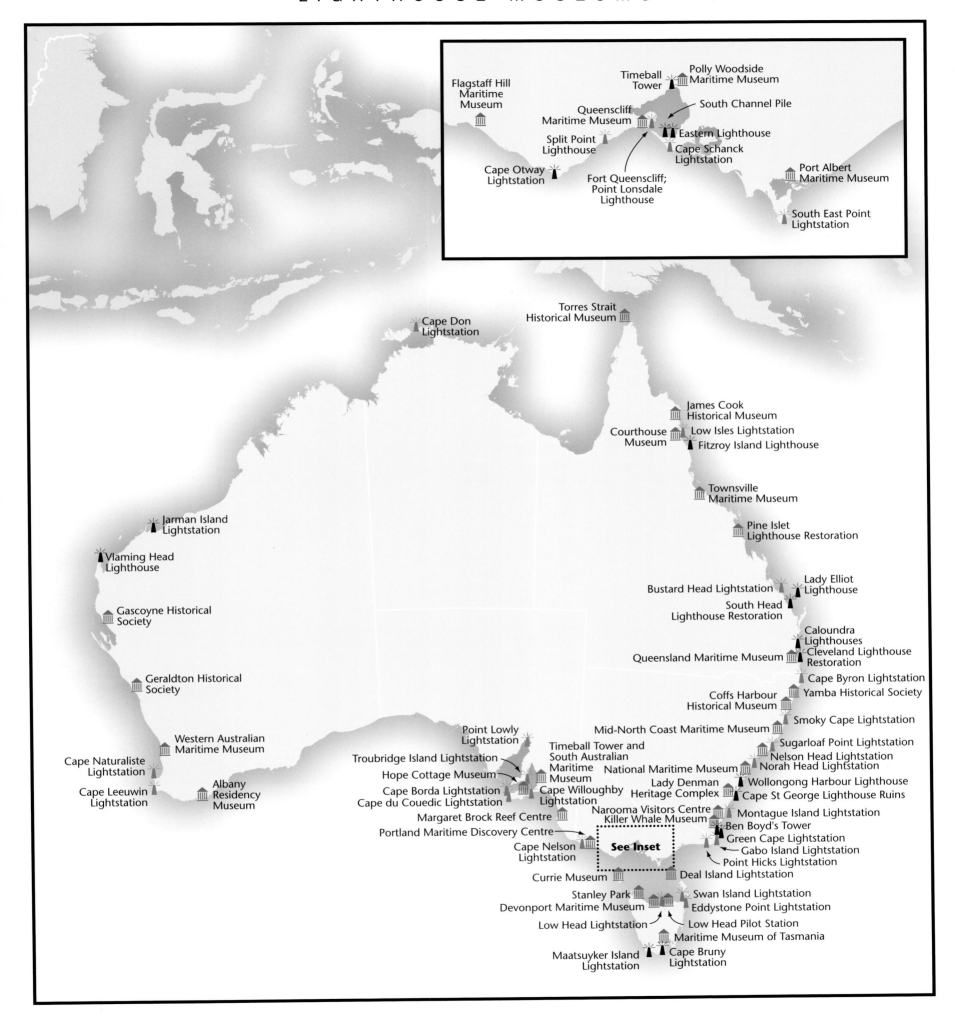

Flagstaff Hill Maritime Museum

Timeball Tower

Polly Woodside Maritime Museum

South Channel Pile

Queenscliff Maritime Museum

Split Point Lighthouse

Eastern Lighthouse

Cape Schanck Lightstation

Cape Otway Lightstation

Fort Queenscliff; Point Lonsdale Lighthouse

Port Albert Maritime Museum

South East Point Lightstation

Cape Don Lightstation

Torres Strait Historical Museum

James Cook Historical Museum

Low Isles Lightstation

Courthouse Museum

Fitzroy Island Lighthouse

Townsville Maritime Museum

Pine Islet Lighthouse Restoration

Jarman Island Lightstation

Lady Elliot Lighthouse

Bustard Head Lightstation

Vlaming Head Lighthouse

South Head Lighthouse Restoration

Gascoyne Historical Society

Caloundra Lighthouses

Cleveland Lighthouse Restoration

Queensland Maritime Museum

Cape Byron Lightstation

Geraldton Historical Society

Yamba Historical Society

Coffs Harbour Historical Museum

Smoky Cape Lightstation

Point Lowly Lightstation

Mid-North Coast Maritime Museum

Sugarloaf Point Lightstation

Western Australian Maritime Museum

Troubridge Island Lightstation

Timeball Tower and South Australian Maritime Museum

Nelson Head Lightstation

Norah Head Lightstation

Cape Naturaliste Lightstation

Hope Cottage Museum

National Maritime Museum

Lady Denman Heritage Complex

Wollongong Harbour Lighthouse

Cape Borda Lightstation

Cape Willoughby Lightstation

Cape Leeuwin Lightstation

Albany Residency Museum

Cape du Couedic Lightstation

Cape St George Lighthouse Ruins

Margaret Brock Reef Centre

Narooma Visitors Centre Killer Whale Museum

Montague Island Lightstation

Ben Boyd's Tower

Portland Maritime Discovery Centre

Green Cape Lightstation

Cape Nelson Lightstation

See Inset

Gabo Island Lightstation

Point Hicks Lightstation

Currie Museum

Deal Island Lightstation

Swan Island Lightstation

Stanley Park

Eddystone Point Lightstation

Devonport Maritime Museum

Low Head Lightstation

Low Head Pilot Station

Maritime Museum of Tasmania

Maatsuyker Island Lightstation

Cape Bruny Lightstation

Lighthouse Museums

Although lighthouses are, in reality no longer needed as aids to navigation they have served the seafarer well over many thousands of years. They have been in part responsible for the successful settlement of places such as the USA and Australia and New Zealand. Their importance to the development of trade throughout the world cannot be underestimated. They were also the momentum behind the research into areas such as optics, glass manufacture, building techniques, lights and automatic controls. There is a wealth of folklore that has built up about the people who developed, built and manned the lights.

As their importance wanes it has become imperative to preserve their history for future generations. This is gradually being recognised throughout the world. In 2000 two conferences were held, one in Norway and one in Canada. The outcome from these meetings was the recognition of the need to establish an International Association for Lighthouse Preservation. This organisation, that would be under the guidance of the International Association of Lighthouse Authorities (IALA) would further the cause for the preservation of lighthouses and their technology. It will also look at alternative viable uses for the existing lightstations.

As the process of demanning and downsizing lightstations in Australia progressed it was recognised that the lightstations, at least the historical ones needed to be transferred to organisations whose focus included preservation. As a result AMSA handed over the significant lightstations to the states who in turn have put them under the control of their Park Authorities. Before handing them over AMSA carried out major maintenance to the stations. As most of the lights at this time are still operational AMSA continues to be responsible for the maintenance of the towers. Exceptions to this situation are where new towers have been built and the old towers are no longer needed as a light. This for example has occurred at Point Perpendicular and Green Cape in NSW, Cape Bruny and Maatsuyker Island in Tasmania and Cape Otway in Victoria.

The following section sets out places in Australia where information and artefacts about lighthouses can be seen and in the case where accommodation is available at the lightstations, experienced.

The 'Lighthouse Museums' in this section belong to one of the following groups:

Regular Museums (M) where lighthouse artefacts are on display. This may include actual lighthouses that have been removed from their original location and rebuilt, lightships, lenses and lantern rooms, light source apparatus, photographs, logbooks, reference data and historical displays.

Operational Lightstations (O) where *organised* access to (the tower) keepers' houses and other buildings is available. Some may also offer accommodation in the keepers' houses and have small museums. This group is subject to change.
Note: At this time Queensland is the only state that does not cater for public accommodation in the state owned lightstations.

Non-Operational Lighthouses (N) that allow self-guided tours or organised access. They may also offer accommodation in the keepers' houses and have small museums.

The museums are listed in the same geographical order as the lighthouses. They start in northern NSW and follow the coast around through New South Wales, Victoria, Tasmania, South Australia, Western Australia, Northern Territory and Queensland.

Burnett River Lighthouse Qld

ORIGINAL LIGHTHOUSE 1873 — 1972

New South Wales:

Cape Byron Lightstation (O)

Lighthouse Road Byron Bay NSW

The lightstation grounds are open for self-guided tours. Overnight accommodation in the keepers' cottages is available.

Yamba Historical Society (M)

Pilot Street Yamba NSW

A replica of the original 1866 light is used as a radio station. The museum has historical photos and a model of the current light.

Coffs Harbour Historical Society And Museum (M)

191a High St Coffs Harbour NSW

A Chance Brothers first order dioptric revolving eight-panel lens from the South Solitary Island lighthouse is prominently displayed.

Smoky Cape Lightstation (O)

Lighthouse Road Smoky Cape South West Rocks NSW

The lightstation grounds are open for self-guided tours. Overnight accommodation in the keepers' cottages is available. The light is in the Hat Head National Park at the end of Lighthouse Road Smoky Cape, South West Rocks.

Mid North Coast Maritime Museum (M)

6 William Street Port Macquarie NSW

The original Chance Brothers lens from the Tacking Point Lighthouse is prominently displayed.

Sugarloaf Point Lightstation (O)

Seal Rocks NSW

The lightstation grounds are open for self-guided tours. The light is accessible by road from the Seal Rocks village.

Nelson Head Lighthouse Cottage And Reserve (M)

Port Stephens Historical Society
Halifax Park Nelson Bay NSW

The lighthouse tower and keeper's cottage are used as a museum and tearooms. The museum houses a number of lighthouse artefacts.

Norah Head Lightstation (O)

Norah Head NSW

The lightstation grounds are open for self-guided tours. Overnight accommodation in the keepers' cottages is available.

Coffs Harbour Museum – South Solitary Island lens
Wollongong Harbour – Harbour Light during and after restoration

253

Australian National Maritime Museum – Carpentaria Shoal Lightship CLS4

Australian National Maritime Museum (M)

Darling Harbour Sydney NSW

The original lighthouse from Cape Bowling Green Queensland, built in 1874 was rebuilt at the museum in 1993. The Carpentaria Light Vessel CLS4, built in 1918 is moored at the wharf while the Chance Brothers first order lens from the Tasman Island light in Tasmania is prominently displayed in the museum.

Wollongong Harbour Lighthouse (N)

Flagstaff Point Wollongong NSW

Self-guided tours around this newly restored non-operational lighthouse can be taken at any time.

Lady Denman Heritage Complex (M)

Dent Street Huskisson NSW

The museum has lighthouse artefacts and historical information about the local lighthouses.

Cape St George Lighthouse Ruins (N)

Jervis Bay National Park, Jervis Bay ACT

Self-guided tours of these non-operational ruins can be taken at any time. The ruins are accessible by road from Nowra.

Montague Island Lightstation (O)

Narooma NSW

Boat tours to the island lightstation are available from Narooma.

Narooma Visitors Centre (M)

Princes Highway Narooma NSW

The Chance Brothers first order lens from Montague Island is prominently displayed in the Visitors Centre.

Eden Killer Whale Museum (M)

Imlay Street Eden NSW

Includes a lighthouse tower with a Chance Brothers first order lens, the clockwork mechanism from Gabo Island and other lighthouse artefacts.

Ben Boyd's Tower (N)

Green Cape Road Ben Boyd NP Eden NSW

Self-guided tours of these non-operational ruins can be taken at any time. To access turn off the Princes Highway 19km south of Eden and drive to the end of Edrom Road.

Green Cape Lightstation (N)

Ben Boyd NP Eden NSW

The lightstation grounds are open for self-guided tours. The operational light is now on a new frame tower next to the old tower. Overnight accommodation in the keepers' cottages is available. To access turn off the Princes Highway 19km south of Eden on to Edrom Road and then turn on to the Green Cape Road.

Narooma – Montague Island lens and the Narooma Visitors Centre

Victoria:

Gabo Island Lightstation (O)

Croajingolong NP Mallacoota Vic

Tours of the lightstation, including the tower are available. There is also overnight accommodation in the keepers' cottages. Access to the island is by small plane or boat.

Point Hicks Lightstation (O)

Croajingolong NP Cann River Vic

Tours of the lightstation including the tower and its spectacular staircase are run daily. Overnight accommodation in the keepers' cottages is available. The lightstation is located at the end of a 47km dirt road originating in Cann River.

Port Albert Maritime Museum (M)

Tarraville Road Port Albert Vic

The collection includes the Cliffy Island Work Boat plus a large number of artefacts from other lighthouses in the area including Wilson's Promontory, Deal Island and the original Citadel Island light.

South East Point (Wilson's Promontory) Lightstation (O)

Tidal River Vic

Once the 18 kilometre hike from trail head near Tidal River has been completed, there are self-guided tours of the lightstation but not the tower. Overnight accommodation in the keepers' cottages or in the camping area is available.

Cape Schanck Lightstation (O)

Cape Schanck Road Cape Schanck Vic

The museum in the head keeper's cottage focuses on light technology. This includes clock mechanisms, acetylene and kerosene burners as well as lenses. Tours of the tower with its Chance Brothers 3.3 metre lantern and a first order 920mm catadioptric lens are held throughout the day on weekends and public holidays. Overnight accommodation in the keepers' cottages is also available. It is accessed from the Rosebud-Flinders Road at the southern tip of the Mornington Peninsula.

Eastern Light (N)

Point Nepean Road McCrae Vic

Self-guided tours of this non-operational light can be taken at any time. It is located on the Point Nepean Road between Rosebud and McCrae.

South Channel Pile (N)

Port Phillip, Rosebud Vic

A trip to this beautifully restored but non-operational light is worthwhile and can be taken at any time. Currently there is no access to the light except sailing around it in a boat but tours may be available in the future.

Polly Woodside Maritime Museum (M)

Lorimer Street East Southbank Melbourne Vic

The museum has a mini tower displaying the Gellibrand light Lantern Room. The light at Gellibrand Point near Williamstown was built in 1906 using the lantern from the lightship it replaced. The four-roomed lighthouse on a pile structure was knocked over by the *Melbourne Trader* on the 22nd June 1976. The next day the structure was burnt. The lens and the lantern room were salvaged.

Polly Woodside Maritime Museum – Gellibrand Lantern
Fort Queenscliff – Signal Station

Williamstown Timeball Tower (N)

Williamstown, Port Phillip Vic

Self-guided tours of this timeball tower (that was previously a light) can be taken at any time. It is located at the end of Nelson Place in Williamstown.

Queenscliff Maritime Museum (M)

Weeroona Parade Queenscliff Vic

The museum's collection includes the lens from the 1930 Wedge light that was replaced in 1993, other Fresnel lenses, sun valves, acetylene burners and two old buoys. Visits to the Point Lonsdale Light are also available.

Fort Queenscliff (O)

Gellibrand Street Queenscliff Vic

The fort is no longer a restricted area so tours of the fort, the old signal station and the lighthouse area are now available. The three front lights can also be viewed from the beach below the fort. The four lights are Shortland Bluff, Murray Tower, Queenscliff Low and the Hume Tower.

Point Lonsdale Lighthouse (O)

Point Lonsdale Vic

Organised tours of the tower, arranged at the Queenscliff Maritime Museum are available on weekends and holidays. Self-guided tours around the tower are available at any time.

Split Point Lightstation (O)

Airey's Inlet Vic

The lightstation grounds are open for self-guided tours. Occasionally the tower is open for inspection. Overnight accommodation in the keepers' cottages is available.

Cape Otway Lightstation (N)

Apollo Bay Vic

The tower with its Chance Brothers first order lens and the lightstation buildings are open for inspection. The operational light is now on a new solar powered Tupperware light next to the old tower. The nearby Signal Station can also be visited. Overnight accommodation in the keepers' cottages is available. The sealed 17km road to the lighthouse turns off the Great Ocean Road 20km west of Apollo Bay.

Flagstaff Hill Maritime Museum (M)

Merri Street Warrnambool Vic

The museum's collection includes the Flagstaff Hill leading lights and keeper's cottage. Tours of the rear light are available.

Portland Maritime Discovery Centre (M)

Lee Breakwater Road Portland Vic

The Discover Centre has the original Cape Nelson Chance Brothers catadioptric holophote lens, manufactured in 1884 on display.

Cape Nelson Lightstation (O)

Portland Vic

The lightstation including the tower are open for inspection. The old stables and storeroom have been beautifully renovated as a café and shop. Overnight accommodation in the keepers' cottages is available. The lightstation is 12km from Portland at the end of the Cape Nelson Lighthouse Road.

Gabo Island, Cape Otway and Cape Nelson – Keepers' Houses

Deal Island Head Keeper's House (Above) **Low Head Pilot Station Houses** (Below)

Tasmania:

Deal Island Lightstation (N)

Deal Island Bass Strait Tas

The head keeper's house is set up as a museum and contains a number of Deal Island lighthouse artefacts.

The steep walk up to the non-operational tower is strenuous but worthwhile. (It's the highest lighthouse site in the southern hemisphere.) Access to the island is by boat or helicopter.

Currie Museum (M)

Currie, King Island Tas

The museum in the keeper's cottage has one panel of the original Cape Wickham Chance Brothers lens on display plus many King Island artefacts.

Swan Island Lightstation (O)

Swan Island Tas

The lightstation is open for inspection by guests staying in the keepers' cottages. Access to this privately owned lightstation is by plane or boat, usually from Cape Portland.

Low Head Lightstation (O)

Lighthouse Road Low Head Tas

The lightstation grounds are open for inspection. It has the only Chance Brothers foghorn in existence that is still capable of being made operational. The foghorn is huge. It has two compressed air tanks that are about five metres high and two metres in diameter. There is an electrically powered compressor as well as a motorised backup. The horn can be heard for about 30km out to sea. There is no access to the tower but access to the foghorn building can be arranged. Overnight accommodation is available at the Tamar River Leading Lights keepers' cottages. Accommodation in the lighthouse keepers' cottages may be available in the future.

Low Head Pilot Station
And Maritime Museum (M)

Lighthouse Road Low Head Tas

This Pilot Station built at the same time as the original lighthouse contains historical lighthouse artefacts and various river and sector lights. Overnight accommodation in the Pilot Station cottages is available.

Devonport Maritime Museum (M)

Victoria Parade Devonport Tas

The museum has historical information about the Mersey Bluff lighthouse.

Eddystone Point Lightstation (O)

Mount William NP Ansons Bay Tas

The lightstation grounds are open for self-guided tours. Accommodation in the keepers' cottages may be available in the future. Access is by road from the St Helens Bridport road.

Maritime Museum Of Tasmania (M)

16 Argyle Street Hobart Tas

The museum has only recently been moved to the old library building that was originally financed by Andrew Carnegie the American philanthropist. All the artefacts are beautifully displayed including the AGA acetylene burners and the Chance Brothers lens from the Goose Island light.

Cape Bruny Lightstation (N)

South Bruny Island Tas

The lightstation grounds are open for self-guided tours from 10:00am until 4:00pm. There is also a small museum in the grounds containing ancillary equipment and information. The operational light is now a new Tupperware light on the next point over from the old tower. Access to the tower and accommodation in one of the keepers' cottages may be available in the future. The lightstation can be accessed by car and car ferry from Hobart.

Maatsuyker Island Lightstation (N)

Maatsuyker Island Tas

The lightstation grounds are open for self-guided tours. Access to the old tower and accommodation in the keepers' cottages may be available in the future. The lightstation can only be accessed by helicopter.

Stanley Park (M)

Stanley Tas

It has a mini tower displaying the 1924 Bluff Point Lantern.

Stanley Park – Highfield Point Lantern (Below)

Cape Jaffa Lighthouse

South Australia:

Cape Jaffa Lighthouse (M)

Marine Parade Kingston SA

The lighthouse from Cape Jaffa SA originally built on the Margaret Brock Reef in 1872 and replaced by the Guichen Bay light in Robe in 1973, was rebuilt at the centre in 1976. Guided tours of the non-operational lighthouse and keepers' quarters are available during the summer and on school and public holidays. The museum is also referred to as the Margaret Brock Reef Centre.

Hope Cottage Museum (M)

Kingscote Kangaroo Island SA

The original Chance Brothers dioptric revolving lens and lantern room from Cape Willoughby was installed on a stub tower at the museum in 1974.

Cape Willoughby Lightstation (O)

Eastern end of Kangaroo Island SA

The lightstation is open for inspection including tours of the tower. One of the keepers' cottages is set up as an information centre. The other two are available for overnight accommodation.

Cape Borda Lightstation (O)

Western end of Kangaroo Island SA

The lightstation is open for inspection including the bottom section of the tower. Overnight accommodation in the keepers' cottages is available.

Cape du Couedic Lightstation (O)

South Western end of Kangaroo Island SA

The lightstation is open for self-guided tours. Overnight accommodation in the keepers' cottages is available.

South Australian Maritime Museum (M)

126 Lipson Street Port Adelaide SA

The lighthouse from South Neptune Island built in 1874 was rebuilt at the museum in the 1980's.

Semaphore Timeball Tower (N)

Semaphore Road Semaphore SA

Located at the end of Semaphore Road it is not far from the Maritime Museum. Although it was never used as a lighthouse the tower, built in 1875 is an integral part of the nineteenth century aids to navigation. Self-guided tours of this tower can be taken at any time. (See page 1)

Troubridge Island Lightstation (O)

Edithburgh SA

Overnight accommodation in the keepers' cottages is available. Boat tours of the island lightstation can be arranged in Edithburgh.

Point Lowly Lightstation (O)

Port Whyalla SA

The lightstation grounds are open for self-guided tours. Overnight accommodation in the keepers' cottages is available. The light is accessible from the Port Bonython Road north of Whyalla.

South Australian Maritime Museum – South Neptune Lighthouse (Above)

Hope Cottage Museum – Cape Willoughby Lantern (Left)

Western Australia and Northern Territory:

Albany Residency Museum (M)
Residency Road Albany WA

The original Chance Brothers first order 920mm lens from Eclipse Island and the Chance Brothers fourth order catadioptric lens from Legendre Island are prominently displayed in the museum. The museum also has other lighthouse artefacts and historical information.

Cape Leeuwin Lightstation (O)
Leeuwin Naturaliste NP Augusta WA

There are daily tours of the lightstation, including the tower. There is a gift shop and overnight accommodation in the keepers' cottages is available. Located in the Leeuwin Naturaliste National Park it is accessible by road from Augusta.

Cape Naturaliste Lighthouse Maritime Museum (O)
Leeuwin Naturaliste NP Dunsborough WA

One of the keepers' cottages is used to house lighthouse artefacts including the original clockwork mechanism for Cape Naturaliste light and the Chance Brothers 500mm lens from Jarman Island. At the entrance to the museum is the acetylene beacon from the Great Sandy Island light. The lightstation is open for inspection. Overnight accommodation in the keepers' cottages is also available. Located in the Leeuwin Naturaliste National Park it is accessible by road from Dunsborough.

Western Australian Maritime Museum (M)
Cliff St Fremantle WA

The documentation from an extensive study of WA Lighthouses is stored at the museum. They also have the original lenses from Breaksea Island, Cape Inscription, Point Quobba, Bedoubt Island, the LBUA 500 gas lantern from Eclipse Island as well as numerous other items from WA lights.

Geraldton Historical Society (N)
Geraldton WA

The society owns the Original Bluff Point rear leading light and keeper's cottage built in 1876. There is also a memorial made from the limestone blocks from the front leading light tower that was destroyed by fire in 1943.

Gascoyne Historical Society (M)
Babbage Island Carnarvon WA

The society, who owns the Babbage Island keeper's cottage also has the original lantern room from the light, with its distinctive red and white striped dome, on display.

Vlaming Head Lighthouse (N)
Exmouth WA

Self-guided tours around this non-operational lighthouse 15km north of Exmouth can be taken at any time.

Jarman Island Lightstation Cossack Historical Port (N)
Cossack WA

Self-guided tours to the Jarman Island non-operational lightstation can be taken at any time. A small boat can be hired in Cossack for access to the island that is 3km from Cossack.

Cape Don Lightstation (O)
Cobourg Peninsula Darwin NT

Tours of this remote lightstation are available for visitors staying in the keepers' cottages. Located 150km NE of Darwin it is accessible by plane for guests. (The landing strip is 15km from the Lightstation so casual fly ins are not feasible).

Albany Residency Museum – Eclipse Island Lens
Cape Naturaliste Lighthouse – Museum Entrance

Queensland:

Torres Strait Historical Museum (M)

Thursday Island Qld

The original Chance Brothers Booby Island lens and the CLS5 Lightship lantern are on display at the museum.

James Cook Historical Museum (M)

Cooktown Qld

The original Chance Brothers Grassy Hill lens is on display at the museum.

Courthouse Museum (M)

Port Douglas Qld

The original Chance Brothers Lowe Isles lens is on display at the museum.

Low Isles Lightstation (O)

Low Isles Port Douglas Qld

Located on a 2.5 hectare cay 13km from Port Douglas the lighthouse can be reached by cruise boat from Port Douglas. Once there visitors can follow a self-guided path with informative signs through the lightstation.

Fitzroy Island Lighthouse (N)

Fitzroy Island Cairns Qld

The light is a strenuous uphill walk from the beach. Once there the grounds around the non-operational tower are open for self-guided tours. Fitzroy Island can be reached by cruise boat from Cairns.

Townsville Maritime Museum (M)

Palmer Street Townsville Qld

The Bay Rock Lighthouse built in 1866 was rebuilt at the museum in 1993. It is a 7m timber framed, corrugated steel clad tower with a lead cupola. The light was manned up until the 1930's when a shark took the last keeper. It was decommissioned in 1992. The museum also has the small lights from the Rib Reef, Penrith Island and Bow Reef lights. The original Wharton Reef Lighthouse, an 11m steel frame tower built in 1915 is located on a roundabout near the museum.

Pine Islet Lighthouse Restoration (M)

Mackay Qld

The original Pine Islet Lighthouse, an 11m timber framed, steel clad tower built in 1885 was moved to Mackay in 1985 after a new GRP tower was built on the islet. Self-guided tours around the tower can be taken at any time.

Bustard Head Lightstation (O)

Bustard Head Qld

There are daylong tours (on a LARC) that travel to Bustard Head from the Town of 1770 although they do not run every day of the week. Once at the lightstation the grounds around the lightstation and cemetery are open for self-guided tours.

Pine Islet Lighthouse Restoration

Lady Elliot Lighthouse (N)

Lady Elliot Island Qld

For guests visiting the island from Bundaberg or Hervey Bay there is a self-guided tour around the old and new towers. The keepers' cottages are not accessible as they are used for staff accommodation. Access to the old tower may be available in the future.

South Head (Burnett River) Lighthouse Restoration (N)

Burnett Heads Qld

The original South Head Lighthouse a 10m timber framed, timber clad tower built in 1873 has been restored and is located in a park next to a campground and not far from the new light built in 1920. The grounds around the non-operational tower are open for self-guided tours.

Caloundra Lighthouses (N)

Canberra Terrace Caloundra Qld

The first and second Caloundra Lighthouses are located on their original sites next to each other. The original tower is an 8m timber framed sheet iron tower built in 1896 that was replaced by a 9m concrete tower in1967. The Point Cartwright lighthouse replaced the concrete tower in 1979. The grounds around the non-operational towers are open for self-guided tours. Occasional access to the towers will be available in the future.

Cleveland Lighthouse Restoration (N)

Cleveland Point, Shore Street Redland Qld

The original Cleveland Point Lighthouse a 10m timber framed, timber clad tower built in 1864 is located close to the new light that was built in 1976. The grounds around the tower are open for self-guided tours.

Queensland Maritime Museum (M)

Corner of Stanley and Sidon Streets South Brisbane Qld

The lighthouse from Bulwer Island, a 16m timber framed corrugated iron sheet clad tower has been rebuilt at the museum. The Carpentaria Shoal Light Ship CLS2, built in 1918 is moored in the Brisbane River. Other artefacts include a bronze buoy, a lantern from the 1970's, Bustard Head's old bulls eye lens and pedestal and a lantern, lantern house and solar panels from a modern acrylic lens.

Townsville Maritime Museum – Wharton Reef Lighthouse (Above)

Queensland Maritime Museum – Carpentaria Lightship CLS2 (Left)

Townsville Maritime Museum – Bay Rock Lighthouse (Opposite)

Chronological List Of Lights:

The information for this chronological list has been obtained from many sources. Some have provided contradictory data. Where possible the year the light was first exhibited has been used which could account for some of the differences that may have been referring to date built. Where multiple lights have been built in a year they are listed alphabetically by state.

Every light built with the exception of most of the modern solar powered lights has gone through some transformation. All lights in Australia are now powered by mains or solar power with the vast majority being solar powered. These kinds of upgrades have not been mentioned.

Some lights that are listed as being replaced in the 1980's and 1990's were possibly only modified but not completely replaced. This applies to lights built prior to 1960 that now include a GRP cabinet that only came into use in the mid 1960's.

1818 Macquarie, Sydney NSW
    Replaced in 1883
1832 Iron Pot Island, Storm Bay Hobart Tas
    Replaced in 1833
1833 Low Head, Tas
    Replaced in 1888
1836 The Lightship Rose, Sydney Harbour
    The first lightship in Australia
    A buoy was installed on the site in 1912
1838 Cape Bruny, South Bruny Island Tas
    Replaced by a GRP cabinet in 1996
    The old tower has been retained
1840 Timeball Tower and Lighthouse Williamstown Vic
    Replaced in 1849 No longer used
1843 Shortland Bluff, Queenscliff Vic
    Replaced in 1863
1844 Raine Island Qld
    No light was ever installed on the tower
1845 Swan Island, Cape Portland Tas
1846 Ben Boyd's Tower, Eden NSW
    The light was never lit
1846 Goose Island, Bass Strait Tas
1847 Cleveland Point, Cleveland Qld
    Replaced in 1864 and again in 1976
1848 Deal Island, Kent Group Bass Strait Tas
    Non-operational Replaced by NE Is.
    and SW Is. in 1992
1848 Cape Otway, Apollo Bay Vic
    Replaced by a GRP cabinet 1994
    The old tower has been retained
1851 Arthur's Head, Fremantle WA
    Replaced in 1878 and
    Demolished in 1904
1851 Rottnest, Rottnest Island Perth WA
    Replaced in 1896
1852 Cape Willoughby, Kangaroo Island SA
1853 Gabo Island, Mallacoota Vic
    Replaced in 1862
1854 Eastern Light, McCrae Vic
    Replaced in 1883 It is no longer used
1854 Queenscliff Low, Queenscliff Vic
    Replaced in 1863
1854 West Channel Lightship, St Leonards Vic
    Replaced in 1881 with a pile light
1854 Bluff Point Leading Lights, Geraldton WA
    The front light was demolished in 1943
    The rear is non-operational
1855 Cape Dombey Obelisk, Robe SA
    Replaced by Robe light in 1972
1856 Troubridge Island, Edithburgh SA
1857 Cape Moreton, Moreton Island Qld
1858 Fort Denison, Sydney Harbour NSW
    Rebuilt in 1913

1858 Hornby, Sydney NSW
1858 Nobby's Head, Newcastle NSW
1858 Cape Borda, Kangaroo Island SA
1858 Breaksea Island, Albany WA
    Replaced in 1901
1858 Point King, Albany WA
    Extinguished in 1911
    Only the ruins of the keepers' cottage remain
1859 Cape Northumberland, Port MacDonnell SA
    Replaced in 1882
1859 Cape Schanck, Flinders Vic
1859 Griffiths Island, Port Fairy Vic
1859 Middle Island, Warrnambool Vic
    Moved to Flagstaff Hill Rear 1871
1859 South East Point, Wilson's Promontory Vic
1859 Whaler Point, Portland Vic
    Moved to its current location in 1889
1860 Cape St George, Jervis Bay NSW
    Only ruins of this light remain
1861 Cape Wickham, King Island Tas
1862 Lookout Point, Eden NSW
    Replaced in the 1970's
1862 Port Stephens, Fingal Bay NSW
1863 Point Lonsdale, Point Lonsdale Vic
    Replaced in 1867 and 1901
1866 Ballina Head, Richmond River NSW
1866 Clarence Head, Yamba NSW
    Replaced in 1955
1866 Tipara Reef Lightship, Wallaroo SA
    Replaced by a lighthouse in 1877
1866 Lady Elliot Island, Gladstone Qld
    Replaced in 1873 and 1995
1866 Woody Island Twin Lighthouses
    Hervey Bay Qld
1867 Fort Denison, Sydney Harbour NSW
1868 Barranjoey Head, Palm Beach NSW
    Replaced in 1881
1868 Bustard Head, Bundaberg Qld
1869 Port Adelaide, Adelaide SA
    Replaced lightships used since 1842
    After being upgraded in 1873 the tower was moved to South
    Neptune Is. in 1901 while the apparatus went to Wonga Shoal It
    is now non-operational
1870 Sandy Cape, Fraser Island Qld
1870 Schnapper Point, Mornington Vic
    Replaced in 1983
1870 Busselton, WA
    Replaced in 1904 and decommissioned in 1933
1870 Casuarina Point, Bunbury WA
    Replaced in 1901, 1904, 1971
1871 Cape Jervis, Fleurieu Peninsula SA
    Replaced in 1972

1871 Flagstaff Hill Front, Warrnambool Vic
    Light added to Obelisk built in 1854
1871 Flagstaff Hill Rear, Warrnambool Vic
    Rebuilt from Middle Island Light
1872 Fingal Head, Fingal NSW
1872 Nelson Head, Port Stephens NSW
1872 Wollongong Harbour, Wollongong NSW
1872 Cape Jaffa, (Margaret Brock Reef) Robe SA
    Replaced by the Guichen Bay light in Robe in 1972
    The original tower was then moved to Kingston. A small light
    on the old platform was moved to a new structure in 2002
1873 Warden Head, Ulladulla NSW
    Moved from Ulladulla Breakwater in 1889
1873 South Head, Bundaberg Qld
    Replaced in 1920
1874 Cape Bowling Green, Ayr Qld
    Replaced in 1987 The old tower is in the
    National Maritime Museum in Sydney
1874 Flat Top Island, Mackay Qld
1874 South Channel Pile, Rye Vic
    Although rebuilt and moved in 1998 it is
    non-operational
1875 Sugarloaf Point, Seal Rocks NSW
1875 Cape Capricorn, Curtis Is. Gladstone Qld
    Replaced in 1936 and 1964
1875 Sea Hill, Cape Capricorn Qld
    Replaced in 1933. Decommissioned in the 1980's
1876 Point Moore, Geraldton WA
    Moved to its current location in 1878
1877 Tipara (or Tiparra) Reef, Wallaroo SA
    Replaced a lightship that had been on the site since 1866
    It in turn was replaced by Warburto Point in 1995
    There is still a small light on the old platform
1878 South Solitary Island, Coffs Harbour NSW
1878 Low Isles, Port Douglas Qld
1878 North Reef, Gladstone Qld
1878 Piper Islands Lightship, Lockhart River Qld
    Replaced by a lighthouse in 1917 and 1991
1878 Penguin Island, Beachport SA
    Replaced by Cape Martin in 1960
1878 Point Malcolm, Lake Alexandria SA
    Australia's only fresh water lighthouse
1879 Crowdy Head, Crowdy Head NSW
1879 Tacking Point, Port Macquarie NSW
1879 Cape Cleveland, Townsville Qld
1879 Dent Island, Proserpine Qld
1879 Island Point, Port Douglas Qld
    Replaced in 1997 and 2001
1879 Althorpe Island, Stenhouse Bay SA
1880 Currie Harbour, Currie King Island Tas
1881 Montague Island, Narooma NSW
1881 West Channel Pile, St Leonards Vic
    Replaced a lightship that had been on site since 1854
1881 Dotterel Point, Port Dalrymple Tas
1881 Middle Channel, Port Dalrymple Tas
1881 She Oak Point, Port Dalrymple Tas
1882 Crookhaven Head, Crookhaven NSW
    Replaced in 1904
1882 Cape Banks, Carpenter Rocks SA
1882 Corny Point, Dunn Point SA
1883 Green Cape, Eden NSW
    Replaced by a steel lattice tower in 1992
    The old tower has been retained
1883 Archer Point, Cooktown Qld
    Replaced in 1979

1883 Rocky Islet (Day Mark at Archer Point) Qld
    Light turned off in 1996
1883 Point Lowly, Port Whyalla SA
    Replaced a lightship
    8 metres were added to the tower in 1909
1884 Vaucluse Bay Front, Sydney Harbour NSW
    Replaced in 1910
1884 Vaucluse Bay Rear, Sydney Harbour NSW
Replaced in 1910
1884 Double Island Point, Rainbow Beach Qld
1884 Cape Nelson, Portland Vic
1884 Cliffy Island, Welshpool Vic
1885 Pine Islet, Mackay Qld
    Replaced in 1985
    The old tower is now in Mackay
1886 Bay Rock, Townsville Qld
    Decommissioned and moved to Townsville
1886 Claremont Light Vessel Qld
    No longer exists
1886 Grassy Hill, Cooktown Qld
1886 Little Sea Hill Qld
1886 Western Hill Goods Is., Torres Strait Qld
1887 Kiama Harbour, Kiama NSW
1888 Table Cape, Wynyard Tas
1888 Jarman Island, Cossack WA
    Non-operational
1889 Eddystone Point, Ansons Bay Tas
1889 Mersey Bluff, Devonport Tas
1890 Shark Island, Sydney Harbour NSW
    Replaced in 1913
1890 Booby Island, Torres Strait Thursday Is. Qld
1890 Point Hicks, Cann River Vic
1891 Smoky Cape, South West Rocks NSW
1891 Maatsuyker Island, Ramsgate Tas
    Replaced in 1996 by a GRP cabinet
    The old tower has been retained
1891 Split Point, Aireys Inlet Vic
1892 Bonnet Islet, Strahan Tas
1892 Entrance Islet, Strahan Tas
1893 Charles Point, Darwin NT
1894 North Point Moreton Island Qld
    Replaced in 1939
1894 Yellow Patch Qld
    No longer used
1896 Caloundra Lights, Caloundra Qld
    Replaced in 1967 and again in 1979
    by Point Cartwright
1896 Babbage Island, Carnarvon WA
    Repaired a number of times after being damaged by fire The
    current tower was built in the early 1960's
1896 Cape Leeuwin, Augusta WA
1899 Point Perpendicular, Jervis Bay NSW
    Replaced by a steel lattice tower in 1993
    The old tower has been retained
1899 Cape Sorell, Strahan Tas
1899 Lagoon Point, Shark Bay WA
1900 Emery Point, Darwin NT
    Replaced in 1917
1900 Gatcombe Head, North Facing Island Qld
    Decommissioned 1980
1900 Bathurst Point, Rottnest Island Perth WA
1900 Broome Jetty Leading Lights, Broome WA
    Demolished and replaced in 1981
1901 Cape Byron, Byron Bay NSW

1901 South Neptune Island, Port Lincoln SA
    Built using the old Port Adelaide light
    After being replaced in 1985 the old tower
    was moved to the SA Maritime Museum
1901 Wonga Shoal, Adelaide SA
    It was replaced by buoy in 1912 after being destroyed by the
    Dimsdale
1901 Pope's Eye Beacon Port Phillip Vic
1901 Esperance Breakwater, Esperance WA
    Replaced c1980
1901 Derby Jetty, Derby WA
1901 Pipon Island, Cooktown Qld
    Replaced the Princess Charlotte Bay Channel
    Rocks lightship that was lost with all hands in 1899
    Replaced in 1980
1902 Eastern Shoal North SA
    Replaced in 1955 but is now non-operational
1902 Woodman Point, Munser WA
1903 Norah Head, Norah Head NSW
1903 North Mole Head, Fremantle WA
1903 South Mole Head, Fremantle WA
1904 Goat Island, Sydney Harbour NSW
    Replaced in 1990
1904 Cape Naturaliste, Dunsborough WA
1905 Bradley's Head, Sydney Harbour NSW
1905 Cape Donington, Port Lincoln SA
    The current lighthouse replaced
    a small temporary light
1905 Burnie Breakwater, Burnie Tas
1905 Gantheaume Point, Broome WA
    Replaced in 1917 and 1984
1906 Yatala Shoal Buoy, Kangaroo Island SA
1906 Tasman Island, Port Arthur Tas
1906 Gellibrand Point Port Phillip Vic
    Replaced lightships that had been on
    site since 1859 Destroyed by the *Melbourne Trader* on the 22nd
    June 1976 The lantern is now in the Polly Woodside Maritime
    Museum
1908 Eastern Channel Pile, Sydney Harbour NSW
    Replaced in 1947
1908 Main Bar Lights, Newcastle NSW
    Replaced in 1990
1908 Cape St Albans, Kangaroo Island SA
1908 Circular Head Tas
    Replaced by Table Cape and Rocky Cape
1909 Cape Du Couedic, Kangaroo Island SA
1909 Wardang Island, Port Victoria SA
    Replaced in 1987
1909 Bedout Island, Port Hedland WA
    Replaced in 1980
1910 Robertson Point, Sydney Harbour NSW
1910 Cape Inscription, Dirk Hartog Is. WA
1910 Point Cloates, Exmouth WA
    Decommissioned after being damaged in the mid 1930's A new
    light on Fraser Is. toppled over when the island blew away The
    current 1966 light is 1km from the original tower
1911 Grotto Point, Sydney Harbour NSW
1911 Parriwi Head, Sydney Harbour NSW
1911 Dangerous Reef Centre, Spencer Gulf SA
    Replaced in 1988
1911 Marion Reef SA
1911 Shoalwater Point, Cowell SA
    Replaced in 1986
1911 Wedge Island, Port Lincoln SA
    Replaced in 1990

1911 Winceby Island, Tumby Bay SA
    Replaced in 1987
1911 South, Cowell SA
1911 Cape Leveque, Broome WA
1911 West Koombanah Bay WA
1912 Middle Bank, Cowell SA
    Replaced in 1985
1912 Entrance Point, Broome WA
    Replaced 1981
1912 Vlaming Head, Exmouth WA
    Replaced in 1967 by NW Cape
1913 Cape Liptrap, Walkerville Vic
    Replaced in 1951
1913 Citadel Island, Glennie Group Vic
    Replaced in 1982
1913 Airlie Island, Onslow WA
    Replaced in 1980
1913 Bessieres Island, Onslow WA
    Previously called Anchor Island
    Demolished c1980 and replaced in 1985
1913 North Sandy Island, Lowendal Islands WA
    Replaced in 1980
1914 Flinders Island, Investigator Group Ellison SA
    Replaced in 1986
1914 Four Hummocks Island, Coffin Bay SA
    Replaced in 1988
1914 Price Island, Ceduna SA
    Extinguished during WWII and never re-lit
1914 Cape Bossut, Broome WA
    Dismantled in 1995
1915 Clerke Island, Lockhart River Qld
    Replaced in 1990
1915 Coquet Island, Cooktown Qld
    Replaced in 1989 and 2004
1915 Wharton Reef, Lockhart River Qld
    Replaced in 1990
1915 Point Marsden, Kangaroo Island SA
    Replaced in 1984
1916 Carpenteria Shoal Light Vessels Qld
    Replaced by new lightships in 1982 and by a buoy in 1999
1916 West Point, Arthur River Tas
    Replaced by Bluff Hill 1982
1917 Cape Don, Darwin NT
1917 Chapman Reef, Cape Direction Qld
    Replaced in 1982
1917 Piper Islands, Lockhart River Qld
    Replaced in 1983 and 1991
1917 Cape Forrestier, Coles Bay Tas
    Replaced in 1971 by Cape Tourville and Point Home
1918 Breaksea Spit Light Vessels, Qld
    Replaced by new lightships in 1982
    and then by a buoy in 1999
1918 Heath Reef, Lockhart River Qld
    Replaced in 1983 and 1985
1918 Little Sea Hill, Bustard Head Qld
    Non-operational
1918 Waterwitch Reef, Lockhart River Qld
    Replaced in 1983
1919 Carpentaria Light Vessel, Cape York Qld
    CLS2 is now in the Queensland Maritime Museum, Brisbane
    and CLS4 is in the National Maritime Museum, Sydney
    Replaced by two new lightships in 1983 that were, in turn
    replaced by a buoy
1919 North Barnard Islands Qld
    Replaced in 1988

1919 Point Grant, Phillip Island Vic
    Replaced in 1947
    Replaced by Round Island in 1997
1920 High Peak Island, Mackay Qld
1921 Albany Rock, Bamaga Cape York Qld
1921 Eborac Island, Bamaga Cape York Qld
1921 Hammond Rock, Torres Strait Qld
    Replaced in 1989
1921 Hannibal Island, Bamaga Cape York Qld
    Replaced in 1990 and 2004
1921 Wednesday Island (Ince Point), Torres Strait Qld
    Replaced in 1974 and 1989
1921 South Brook Island, Cardwell Qld
    Replaced in 1988
1921 Mount Blaze, Port Hedland WA
    Demolished c1950
1923 Point Boston, Port Lincoln SA
    Replaced in the 1990's
1923 Round Hill Point, Burnie Tas
1923 Mount Barkly, Jemmys Point Lakes Entrance Vic
1924 Western Channel Pile, Sydney Harbour NSW
    Replaced in 1947
1924 Archer Point Auxiliary, Cooktown Qld
1924 Bramble Cay, Great NE Channel Qld
    Replaced in 1973, Upgraded 1987
1924 Eastern Shoal South SA
    No longer operational
1924 St Francis Island, Denial Bay Ceduna SA
    Replaced in 1986
1924 Cape Rochon, Three Hummock Island Tas
    Replaced by a GRP cabinet 1983
1924 Highfield Point, North Point Stanley Tas
    Replaced in 1981
1924 Hunter Island (Cuvier Bay), Smithton Tas
    Replaced in 1984
1924 Fawkner Beacon, Sandringham Vic
    Rebuilt in 1965, 1981
1924 Hovell Light, Dromana Vic
    Rebuilt in 1939
1924 Hume Tower, Queenscliff Vic
1924 Port Melbourne Front, Port Melbourne Vic
1924 Port Melbourne Rear, Port Melbourne Vic
1925 Long Spit, Port Wakefield SA
    Replaced in 1987 and 2002
1925 Orontes Bank, Oyster Bay SA
    Replaced in 1986
1926 Eclipse Island, Albany WA
1927 Restoration Rock, Cape Weymouth Qld
    Replaced in 1986
1927 Sandy Cay Qld
1927 Legendre Island, Dampier WA
    Replaced in 1963 and 1989 (twice)
1928 Cape Hotham, Darwin NT
1928 East Vernon Island, Darwin NT
    Replaced in 1986
1928 Bailey Islet, Mackay Qld
1928 Coppersmith Rock, Mackay Qld
    Replaced in 1987
1928 Cape Woolamai, Phillip Island Vic
1929 Little Fitzroy Island, Cairns Qld
    Replaced in 1992
1929 Russell Island, Innisfail Qld
    Replaced in 1989
1930 Monash Light, Point Nepean Vic
1930 Wedge Light, Queenscliff   Vic
    Replaced in 1993

1930 Escape Island, Jurien WA
    Replaced in 1980
1931 Prince George Shoal, Port Arlington Vic
    Replaced in the mid 1990's
1932 Blues Point, Sydney Harbour NSW
    Replaced in 1993
1932 Point Lookout, North Stradbroke Island Qld
1934 Cairncross Islets, Bamaga Cape York Qld
    Replaced in 1996
1934 Hannah Island, Lockhart River Qld
1935 Bustard Head Auxillary, Bundaberg Qld
1935 Clews Point, Bundaberg Qld
1935 Eshelby Island, Proserpine Qld
    Replaced in 1972 and 1985
1935 Mary Anne Island, Onslow WA
    Replaced maybe 6 times through 1993
1936 Fraser Island, Ningaloo WA
    See Point Cloates 1910
1936 Palfrey Islet, Cooktown Qld
1936 Frazier Island Qld
1936 Saddle Island Qld
1937 Wollongong Head Wollongong NSW
1938 Wyborn Reef, Bamaga Cape York Qld
    Replaced in 1981
1938 Hamelin Island Augusta WA
    Replaced by Foul Bay in 1967
1940 Albino (White) Rock, Ingham Qld
    Replaced in 1984
1941 Goods Island Front, Torres Strait Qld
    Replaced in 1988
1941 Low Head Auxillary, Low Head Tas
1942 Three Isles, Cooktown Qld
    Replaced in 1997
1943 Fitzroy Island, Grafton Passage Cairns Qld
    Replaced in 1973 Non-operational
1944 Bet Reef, Great NE Channel Qld
    Replaced in 1975
1944 Dalrymple Islet, Great NE Channel Qld
    Moved in 1959 and replaced in 1981
1944 Harvey Rocks, Great NE Channel Qld
1944 Lighthouse Point, Corner Inlet Vic
1945 Cape Fourcroy, Bathurst Island NT
1945 East Strait Island, Torres Strait Qld
    Replaced in 1991
1945 Twin Island, Torres Strait Qld
    Replaced in 1989
1945 Browse Island, Derby   WA
    Replaced in 1958 and 2003
1947 Coles Light, Queenscliff Vic
1950 Cape Bailey, Kurnell NSW
1950 King Island, Cooktown Qld
    Replaced in 1996
1950 South Barrow Islet, Cooktown Qld
1950 Cape Spencer, Stenhouse Bay SA
    Replaced in 1975
1950 Point Quobba, Shark Bay Carnarvon WA
1951 Yarraville Shoal, Cowell Spencer Gulf SA
    Replaced in 1986
1951 Stokes Point, Seal Bay King Island Tas
    Replaced in 1971
1951 Adele Island, Derby WA
    Replaced in 2002
1951 Tanner Island, Derby   WA
    Formerly called More Island
1952 Eel Reef, Lockhart River Qld

1952 Rundle Island, Qld
     Decommissioned 1987
1953 Sandy Cape, Kenneth Bay West Coast Tas
1955 Henry Head, Botany Bay La Perouse NSW
1957 Dove Islet, Great NE Channel Qld
1958 South West Vernon Island, Darwin NT
1958 Decapolis Reef, Cooktown Qld
     Replaced in 1972
1958 Gubbins Reef, Cooktown Qld
1958 Pethebridge Islets, Cooktown Qld
     Replaced in 1974 and 1990
1958 Pine Peak Island, Mackay Qld
1958 Shoal Point, Port Gregory WA
1959 Great Sandy Island, Onslow WA
     Replaced in 1986
1960 Bow Reef, Lockhart River Qld
1960 Eden Reef, Lockhart River Qld
1960 Cape Martin, Beachport SA
     Replaced the Penguin Is. light
1960 Entrance Front, Devonport Tas
1960 Entrance Rear, Devonport Tas
1960 Portland Breakwater, Portland Vic
1960 Degerando, Derby WA
1960 D'Entrecasteaux Point, Windy Harbour WA
1960 Imperieuse Reef, Port Hedland WA
     Replaced in 1970
1960 Steep Point, Shark Bay Denham WA
     Replaced in 1984
1961 Fahey Reef, Lockhart River Qld
     Replaced in 1980
1961 Fife Island, Lockhart River Qld
1961 Cape Ronsard, Bernier Island Carnarvon WA
1961 Lacrosse Island, Wyndham WA
1962 New Year Island, Mingilang NT
     Replaced in 2002
1962 Duyfken Point, Albatross Bay Weipa Qld
     Replaced in 1984
1962 Sue Islet, Great NE Channel Qld
1962 Marino Rocks, Marino Adelaide SA
     Replaced the Wonga Shoal light
1963 Holbourne Island, Proserpine Qld
1963 Penrith Island, Mackay Qld
1963 Low Rocky Point, Elliot Bay Tas
1963 Lesueur Island, Wyndham WA
     Replaced in 2000
1964 Pinnacle Point, Hook Island Qld
1964 Cape Bauer, Streaky Bay SA
1964 Evans Island, Denial Bay Ceduna SA
1964 Williams Island, Spencer Gulf SA
1965 Althorpe Island Front, Stenhouse Bay SA
1965 Cumberland, Grassy King Island Tas
1965 Hogan Island, Hogan Group Bass Strait Tas
1965 St Kilda False Light, St Kilda Vic
     This is not a real lighthouse
1965 Cull Island, Esperance WA
     Formerly called Gull Island
1965 Figure Of Eight Island, Esperance WA
1965 Rosemary Island, Dampier WA
1966 Brady Rock, Groote Eylandt NT
1966 Cape Wessel, Wessel Islands Nhulunbuy NT
1966 Connexion Islet, Groote Eylandt NT
     Replaced in 1997
1966 North East Islet, Groote Eylandt NT
1966 Bristow Island Thursday Island
     Handed over to New Guinea in 1971
1966 Cape Conran, Orbost Vic

1967 Brush Island, Bawley Point NSW
1967 Edward Island, Proserpine Qld
1967 Vernon Rocks, Mackay Qld
1967 Cape Barren, Cape Barren Island Tas
1967 Cat Island, Flinders Island Tas
1967 Holloway Point, Flinders Island Tas
1967 Caffarelli Island, Broome WA
1967 Foul Bay, Augusta WA
     Replaced Hamelin Island
1967 North Island (Houtman Abrolhos),
     Geraldton WA
1967 North West Cape, Exmouth WA
     Replaced Vlaming Head
1968 Bougainville Reef, Cooktown Qld
     Replaced in 1986
1968 Frederick Reef, Mackay Qld
1968 Pearson Isles, Investigator Group Ellison SA
1968 Rocky Cape, Detention River Tas
1968 East Lacepede Island, Broome WA
     Replaced in 1987
1968 North West Island, Monte Bello Islands WA
1968 Red Bluff, Broome WA
     Replaced in 1987
1968 Trimouille Island, Monte Bello Islands WA
1969 Howick Island, Cooktown Qld
1969 Megeara Reef, Cooktown Qld
     Replaced in 2000
1970 Point Danger, Tweed Heads NSW/
     Coolangatta Qld
1970 Euston Reef, Grafton Passage Cairns Qld
     Replaced in 1990
1970 Chicken Point, Schouten Island Coles Bay Tas
1970 Waterhouse Island, Tomahawk Tas
1971 Saumarez Reef, Mackay Qld
     Replaced in 1996
1971 Cape Tourville, Coles Bay Tas
1971 Point Home Lookout, Triabunna Tas
1971 Cape St Cricq, Dorre Island Carnarvon WA
1971 McKenna Point, Bunbury WA
1972 Bolingbroke Point, Tumby Bay SA
1973 Guichen Bay, Robe SA
     Replaced the Cape Jaffa
     (Margaret Brock Reef) light
1974 Burrewarra Point, Tomakin NSW
1974 Gneering Shoal Buoy, Bundaberg Qld
1974 Lady Musgrave Islet, Gladstone Qld
1974 Miles Reef, Cooktown Qld
1974 Councillor Island, King Island Tas
1974 Ile Du Nord Island, Triabunna Tas
1974 Pelsaert Island, Brolhos Island Geraldton WA
1975 North Solitary Island, Coffs Harbour NSW
1975 Bickerton Island, Groote Eylandt NT
1975 Truant Island, Nhulunbuy NT
1975 Great Keppel Island, Yeppoon Qld
1975 Middle Reef, Lockhart River Qld
1975 Murray Tower, Queenscliff Vic
1976 Evans Head, Evans Head NSW
1976 Bass Strait Oil Platform Kingfish B, Vic
1976 Cave Point, Albany WA
     Non-operational
1977 Magpie Reef, Lockhart River Qld
1977 Cervantes Island, (Front and Rear) WA
1978 Snapper Point, Kangaroo Island SA
     Decommissioned in 2003
1979 Egret Reef, Cooktown Qld
1979 Pith Reef, Ingham Qld

1979 Point Cartwright, Mooloolaba Qld
      Replaced the 1896 and 1967 towers
      in Caloundra
1979 Rib Reef, Ingham Qld
1979 Sphinx Island, Hays Point Qld
      Decommissioned 1984
1980 East Point, Facing Island Gladstone Qld
1980 Hammond Island, Torres Strait Qld
      The first light in Australia to be
      powered by solar panels
1980 Inset Reef, Lockhart River Qld
1980 Moody Reef, Lockhart River Qld
1980 Wye Reef, Lockhart River Qld
1980 South Page Island, Kangaroo Island SA
1980 Troubridge Hill, Edithburgh SA
1980 West Cape, Stenhouse Bay SA
1980 Bass Strait Oil Platform Tuna, Welshpool Vic
1981 Craggy Island, Bass Strait Tas
1981 Cape Cuvier, Shark Bay Carnarvon WA
1981 Cape Peron, Shark Bay Denham WA
1982 Veronica Islet, Nhulunbuy NT
1982 Arden Islet, Great NE Channel Qld
      Replaced in 2002
1982 Tapley Shoal, Port Giles SA
1982 Taylor Island, Port Lincoln SA
1982 Bluff Hill, Arthur River Tas
      Replaced the West Point lighthouse
1982 Omega Facility, Darriman Vic
      Decomissioned in 1997 and
      taken over by the Australian Navy
1983 North Neptune Island, Port Lincoln SA
      Decommissioned 2003
1983 Sibsey Island, Port Lincoln SA
1983 Troubridge Hill Auxiliary, Edithburgh SA
1983 Waterhouse Point, Thistle Island SA
1983 East Moncoeur Island, Tas
1984 Stevens Island, Nhulunbuy NT
1984 Warnawi Island, Nhulunbuy NT
1984 Creal Reef, Hydrographers Passage Mackay Qld
1984 Guilderton, Guilderton WA
1984 Port Walcott Buoys C1-C13, Wickham WA
      Upgraded to LED lights in 10-2003
1985 Abbott Shoal NT
1985 Little Bugatti Reef, Hydrographers Passage Qld
1985 Watson Island, Cooktown Qld
1985 White Tip Reef, Hydrographers Passage Qld
1985 Plank Shoal, Cowell SA
1985 Western Shoal, Cowell SA
1986 Steelworks Channel Directional Light,
      Newcastle NSW
1986 Bass Strait Oil Platform Flounder A, Vic
1986 Hillarys Boat Harbour, Wanneroo WA
1986 Port Hedland Buoys C1-C14, Port Hedland WA

1987 Haul Round Island, Maningrida NT
1987 North West Vernon Island, Darwin NT
1987 Clara Group, Mackay Qld
1987 North East Island, Kent Group Bass Strait Tas
1987 South West Island, Kent Group Bass Strait Tas
1988 Cape Croker, Mingilang NT
1988 East Diamond Islet, Cooktown Qld
1988 Tuesday Islet, Torres Strait Qld
1990 Arlington Reef, Grafton Passage Cairns Qld
1990 Bugatti Reef, Hydrographers Passage Mackay Qld
1990 North West Reef, Torres Strait Qld
1992 Pickersgill Reef, Cooktown Qld
1992 Outer Sister Island, Tas
1993 Little Rame Head, Mallacoota Vic
      Built to supplement Gabo Island
      and Point Hicks
1995 Warburto Point, Wallaroo SA
      Replaced Tipara Reef
1997 Boot Reef, Great NE Channel Qld (Never Built)
1997 East Cay, Great NE Channel Qld
1997 Halfway Island Great NE Channel Qld (Never Built)
1997 Kirkcaldie Reef, Great NE Channel Qld
1997 Marsden Island, Great NE Channel Qld (Never Built)
1997 Round Island, Phillip Island Vic
      Replaced Point Grant
1998 Whale Head, SE Cape Ramsgate Tas
      Built to supplement Cape Bruny
1999 Lihou Reef, Cooktown Qld
      The last lighthouse built in the
      1990's (13-10-1999)
1999 Point Cartwright Auxiliary, Mooloolaba Qld
1999 Swains Reef, Mackay Qld
2000 Stainer Island, Lockhart River Qld
2000 Maxwell Reef, Cooktown Qld
      The last lighthouse built in the
      20th Century (12-2000)
2002 Marion Reef, Edithburgh SA
2003 Sugar Ran Reef, Great NE Channel Qld
2003 Smith Cay Light, Great NE Channel Qld
2004 Nardana Patches, Torres Strait Thursday Is. Qld
      Replaces a buoy
2004 LADS Passage/Fairway Channel, Princess Charlotte Bay Qld
      (9 fixed structures and 5 buoys; The beacons are:)
2004 LADS Passage Colclough Reef
2004 LADS Passage Diamond Reign
2004 LADS Passage Fairway
2004 LADS Passage First Three Mile
2004 LADS Passage Frederick Patches
2004 LADS Passage Robin Reef
2004 LADS Passage South Creech
2004 LADS Passage Sunk Reef
2004 LADS Passage Thirteen South Rock

Glossary

The following is a glossary of terms associated with lighthouses. Where a definition has been built up from a number of sources the source has been arbitrarily given as (Ibbotson)

Acetylene:

Acetylene is a colourless hydrocarbon gas (C_2H_2) produced when calcium carbide and water are mixed. Although discovered in 1836 it was not until the technique of dissolving it under pressure in acetone was perfected (by Gustav Dalen) that it became a viable fuel for lighthouses. (Ibbotson)

Aids to Navigation:

See Navigation Aids.

AMSA:

The **Australian Maritime Safety Authority** (AMSA) that commenced operation in January 1991 is the current Commonwealth Authority responsible for the construction, maintenance, and upgrading of aids to navigation as well as for ship surveys and regulatory matters, crewing, safety, protecting the marine environment and co-ordinating marine search and rescue operations. (AMSA, Ibbotson)

Apparatus:

The equipment needed for a particular purpose or function. For lighthouses this includes the lantern room, lens, lens rotational mechanism, power source, light source (lamp), lamp changer, flasher, daylight control switch, lantern control switch. (Oxford, Ibbotson)

Astragals:

Brass or bronze rails and mullions that secure the glass panes in the lantern room. (Ibbotson)

Auxiliary Light:

The auxiliary or subsidiary light is a light placed on or near a main light and has a special use in navigation. Also see Main Light. (Vol K)

Balcony:

The exterior walkway around the lantern room or watch room of the lantern. Also see Gallery Deck (Historic Lighthouse Resources)

Beacon:

A generic term for lighthouses, buoys, beacons or lightships.
A distinctly marked and shaped non-floating device rigidly fixed to the seabed and sometimes carrying a light, whistle or bell that marks a channel or obstruction. (Ibbotson)

Buoy:

A distinctly marked and shaped anchored float, sometimes carrying a light, whistle or bell, marking a channel or obstruction. (Macquarie)

Caisson:

A watertight enclosure inside which underwater construction work can be done.
A lighthouse type, so called because a caisson was used during the construction of the lighthouse's foundation. (Historic Lighthouse Resources)

Candelas:

The SI base unit of luminous intensity; the luminous intensity, in a given direction of a source that emits monochromatic radiation with a frequency of 540x10 to the twelfth hertz and has a radiant intensity in that direction of 1/683 watt per steradian. (Macquarie)

From a practical point of view a typical car headlamp on high beam produces 75,000 - 95,000 candelas.

Candlepower:

The luminous intensity (of a light) or the illuminating capacity of a lamp or other device, measured in candelas. (Macquarie)

Catadioptric:

This is where light is refracted as it enters or leaves a prism and is also reflected within the prism. Also see Dioptric. (Ibbotson)

Catoptric:

This is where light is reflected from a polished surface or from within a prism so that it does not pass through a particular side of that prism. (Ibbotson)

Character:

The flashing of a light, either in the light source or by a rotating beam, gives an identifying signal known as its character. The colour of the light is usually white but red and green are also used. By international agreement the number of characters that may be used is limited.
A fixed light is where a constant light is displayed.
A flashing light is where a single flash is repeated every few seconds.
A group-flashing light is where a long eclipse separates a group that is made up of a number of flashes with a short eclipse between each flash.
An occulting light that may also occur in groups is where the flash is longer than the eclipse.
(From Dusk Till Dawn)

CLS:

The **Commonwealth Lighthouse Service** (CLS) was established under the Lighthouse Act of 1911 and came into effect in 1915. The CLS was given the responsibility for coastal and landfall lights while the states retained the responsibility for Harbour lights. (Ibbotson)

Coastal Lights:

Coastal or Highway lights are those that assist mariners navigate along an open coastline. They will include those identifying shoals, reefs or dangerous waters. (Also see Harbour Lights and Landfall Lights) (Ibbotson)

Daymark:

A distinctive pattern painted on the exterior of a lighthouse or other aid to navigation, and used for identification purposes during daylight hours. In many cases the lighthouse structure itself is considered a daymark. (Historic Lighthouse Resources)

Differential GPS (DGPS):

Differential GPS includes access to a fixed ground station that allows minor errors (satellite range corrections), inherent in the moving satellites, to be calculated and used to adjust the GPS reading. This provides the users position with an accuracy of less than ten metres. Also see Global Positioning System. (Ibbotson)

Dioptric:

This is where light entering or leaving a prism is refracted (bent). (Ibbotson)

Eclipse:
This is the dark period between flashes (Ibbotson)

Exhibited:
A term used to describe when a light is turned on. (Ibbotson)

Focal Plane:
The level plane at which the lighthouse's lens is focused; the height of this plane is measured from mean sea level. (Historic Lighthouse Resources)

Fog Signals:
A device used to produce a distinct and repetitive sound that can be heard over a large distance (up to 40km). The signal is produced by many types of emitters such as diaphones, sirens or reeds (using compressed air), horns (using compressed air or electricity to vibrate a diaphragm), bells, gongs, whistles or even explosives. (Vol K, Ibbotson)

Fresnel Lens:
A compound lens having axial symmetry, whose surface is a series of concentric rings and shaped steps and is widely used in headlights and in the optical apparatus of lighthouses (La Rousse).

The Fresnel lens was perfected in 1822 by a French optician Augustin Fresnel (Fray-NELL). Originally there were six orders of lens. The first order was the largest, (1.8m in diameter, 2.6m high and weighing four tonnes), the sixth order the smallest (30cm in diameter and 40cm high). The lenses were made in both rotating and stationary models. The lens, which resembles a beehive, is made up of lenses and prisms that focus a central light into a strong horizontal beam. It consists of tiers of dioptric prisms above and below a central lens. These prisms refract the light and direct it outward through a central magnifying lens that further intensifies the light. Above and below the dioptric prisms are catadioptric prisms that capture the oblique rays from the light source and reflect and refract them so they also become part of the horizontal beam.

Chance Brothers in England who were a leading manufacturer of lenses established the following standard lens orders based on the lens's focal distance, which is the distance from the light source to the lens:

Hyper-radial:	1330mm
Meso-radial:	1125mm
First order:	920mm
Second order:	700mm
Third order:	500mm
Fourth order:	250mm
Fifth order:	187.5mm
Sixth order:	150mm

There was also a seventh order 375mm lens that was referred to as a three-and-a-half-order lens or a Third order (small type). (Ibbotson)

Front Light:
The closer of two lights (the front and the rear), that when in line with the rear light indicates that the ship is in the middle of a navigable channel. At times there are three front lights with the outer two being red or green. When an outer front red or green light is lined up with the rear light it indicates the ship is at the edge of the navigable channel. (Ibbotson)

Gallery Deck:
The exterior walkway outside the lantern. Also see Balcony. (Historic Lighthouse Resources)

Geographical Range:
This is the maximum distance at which light from a light can theoretically reach an observer, as limited only by the curvature of the earth, the refraction of the atmosphere and by the elevation of the light and the height of the eye of the observer. (Vol K)

Glass:
A hard, brittle, usually transparent or translucent substance produced by the fusion of mutually dissolved sand, soda and lime and sometimes with other ingredients. Ordinary, crown or low dispersion glass is made without lead or iron oxides in it and is used for windows, bottles and optical purposes etc. Flint glass (originally made from flint) is a colourless high dispersion variety that contains lead oxide and is used for quality glassware (crystal) and for optical purposes. (Oxford/Macquarie)

Glass Reinforced Plastic (GRP) Cabinet:
First used in 1965-66 the majority of lighthouses constructed today consist of or include a GRP cabinet. They are made of a number of pre-cast fibreglass panels (4 walls, a door and a roof) that are bolted together and mounted on a base that is usually a concrete pad or a platform on a frame tower. A standard cabinet is one metre by one metre and two metres high. When a taller tower is required multiple cabinets are bolted together. If the light is mounted on the roof, the cabinet is equipped with a ladder and roof top handrails. All the metal fittings are stainless steel. The cabinet is used to house the storage batteries and electronics needed for controlling the light. Solar cells are often mounted on the railings. The cabinets that are usually white but are sometimes red may also serve as a day-mark. (Ibbotson)

Global Positioning System (GPS):
The Global Positioning System is a computerised navigation system based on 24 satellites that provides precise position (including altitude), velocity and time information to ships, planes, vehicles or people anywhere on earth with an accuracy of about 15 metres. Usually readings from four satellites are needed if altitude is needed but ships only require three because altitude is not a factor. Also see Differential GPS. (Ibbotson)

Harbour Lights:
These are lights that assist mariners navigate safely into or within a bay or harbour. (Also see Coastal Lights and Landfall Lights). (Ibbotson)

Hygroscopic:
Absorbing or attracting moisture. (Macquarie)

IALA:
This is the **International Association of Lighthouse Authorities** that is responsible for the overall worldwide standards for navigation aid placement and identification. The 1955 Scheveningen Lighthouse Conference resulted in IALA being created in 1957 with 20 member nations. It now represents 80 countries worldwide. (Ibbotson)

Illuminant:
The fuel used for generating the light. Illuminants that have been used in lighthouses include wood, coal, candles, whale oil (usually spermaceti from the head of sperm whales), various other oils (lard or colza), kerosene (mineral oil), town gas, acetylene and electricity (from mains power, generators, batteries or solar panels). (Ibbotson)

Kilometre:
A metric unit of measurement for distance. It is equal to 1,000 metres or one ten thousandth of the distance between the equator and the North Pole. It is also equal to 0.5397 nautical miles or 0.6210 statute miles. (Macquarie)

Landfall Lights:
Landfall lights are those that provide a point of reference to mariners approaching land from the open ocean. (Also see Harbour Lights and Coastal Lights.) (Ibbotson)

Lantern:
A chamber on top of a lighthouse surrounding the light. (Macquarie)

Lantern Deck:
The deck inside the lantern of first through third order lenses that encircles the lens to provide access for maintenance and cleaning. (Historic Lighthouse Resources)

LARC:
The **Lighter Amphibious Resupply Cargo** vessel (LARC) is an amphibious vehicle, originally built for the US military in the 1940's through the 1960's. They are used to ferry supplies from the lighthouse tender to lights that are located on small islands, rocks, reefs or on difficult terrain. (Ibbotson)

Leading Lights:
Two or more lights associated so as to form a leading line to be followed. Individually referred to as the Front and the Rear lights (Vol K).

Lens:
A piece of transparent substance usually glass or high quality plastic having two (or two main) opposite surfaces, either both curved or one curved and one plane, used for the concentrating or dispersing light rays. (Macquarie/Oxford)

Light:
This is the actual source of the light such as wick or electric light bulb although it can also include the lenses and other apparatus. (Ibbotson)

Lighthouse:
A structure, usually a tower built on shore or in shallow water to support a light used as an aid to marine coastal navigation. From the sea a lighthouse may be identified during daylight hours by the distinctive painting of the structure and at night by the colour coding, flashing or occulting of its light. (Encyclopaedia Britannia)

From the purist or romantic point of view lighthouses are tall and graceful but solid structures, perched precariously but with a sense of strength, on remote and desolate headlands or wave swept rocks. Their tones are original rock or white, or white with stripes of red or black. They are manned by hardy souls who ensure the tree thick beams of light are always reaching out into the darkness.

In preparing this book a broader definition has been used.
A lighthouse is any structure that is or has been used to provide an illuminated point of reference to mariners and which is historically important, structurally interesting or is located in a spectacular or interesting setting. (Ibbotson)

Lighthouse Tender:
A ship used to supply the lighthouses, maintain buoys and service lightships. (Historic Lighthouse Resources)

Lightship:
A ship anchored in a specific location and displaying a light or lights for the guidance of mariners. Also see Light Vessel. (Macquarie)

Lightstation:
This is the infrastructure associated with a lighthouse. It will include the lighthouse or tower and any storage sheds, fuel tanks, solar panel arrays, keepers' cottages, helipads, jetties, haulage ways, signal masts or weather measuring apparatus associated with the lighthouse. (Ibbotson)

Light Vessel:
The correct term for lightships that do not have a crew is light float or light vessel. (Duvoisin)

Loom:
The diffused glow observed from a light below the horizon or hidden by an obstacle, due to atmospheric scattering. (Vol K)

Luminous Range:
This is the maximum distance that a light can be seen at a given time, as determined by the intensity of the light and the meteorological visibility prevailing at the time. It takes no account of elevation, observer's height of eye or the curvature of the earth. (Vol K)

Main Light:
The major of two or more lights situated on the same support or neighbouring supports. Also see Auxiliary Light. (Vol K)

Metre:
A metric unit of measurement for distance. The SI base unit of measurement of length equal to the distance travelled by electromagnetic radiation through a vacuum in 1/299792458 seconds and is approximately equal to 1.094 yards (39.384 inches). Originally it was defined as one ten millionth of the distance between the equator and the North Pole measured on a meridian. (Macquarie)

Mullion:
A slender, vertical dividing bar between the lights or panes of windows, doors etc. (Historic Lighthouse Resources)

Nautical Mile:
The nautical or sea mile equals one sixtieth of a degree of latitude and varies in length depending on the latitude. The standard distance used (also known as the Admiralty Measured Mile) is 6,080 feet. This is equal to 1.151 statute miles or 1.853 kilometres. (A Dictionary of Sea Terms)

Navigation Aid:
A navigation aid or nav aid is any device that is available to, or used by ships for navigational purposes. It includes lighthouses, beacons, buoys, landmarks, radar, racons, GPS, DGPS, fog signals and printed and computerised navigation charts. Technically 'Navigation Aids' are on the ships and are used to access 'Aids to Navigation' but common usage uses Nav Aids for both. (Ibbotson)

Nominal Range:
This is the luminous range when the meteorological visibility is 10 sea miles (19 km). (Vol K)

Occulting:
To hide or shut off (an object) from view.
To shut off (a light) periodically as in lighthouses. In the case of lighthouses the light is on longer than it is off. (Macquarie)

Period:
The interval during which a light repeats its sequence. Also see Character. (From Dusk Till Dawn).

Pharology:
The science of lighthouses from '*pharos*' the original Greek word for lighthouse or beacon (Ibbotson).

Pile Light:
This describes the way in which a lighthouse was constructed, usually in open water with a sandy or muddy bottom. It involved driving wooded or iron piles into the sea floor that were then used to support a platform, tower and possibly living quarters. (Ibbotson)

Pointing:
In masonry, the final treatment of joints by the trowelling of mortar into the joints between masonry units (bricks, stones etc). (Historic Lighthouse Resources)

Racon:
A small radar transponder that reacts to impulses from ship borne radar by returning a stronger and specifically identified signal (From Dusk Till Dawn).

Range:
See Geographical Range, Luminous Range, Nominal Range and Loom.

Rear Light:
The more distant of two lights (the front and the rear), that when in line with the front light indicates that the ship is in the middle of a navigable channel. At times there are three front lights with the outer two being red or green. When an outer front red or green light is lined up with the rear light it indicates the ship is at the edge of the navigable channel. (Ibbotson)

Screw Pile Light:
This describes the way in which a lighthouse was constructed, usually in open water with a sandy or muddy bottom. It involved putting a helical fluke or screw-blade (usually 1.2 m diameter) on the end of an iron pile and winding it down into the sea floor like a giant auger. Generally there was one central and eight outer piles, in an octagonal pattern that supported a platform, tower and possibly living quarters. (Ibbotson)

Sector Light:
A light presenting different appearances, either of colour or character, over various parts of the horizon of interest to maritime navigation. (Vol K)

Tower:
The portion of a lighthouse that supports the lantern. (Historic Lighthouse Resources)

Tupperware Light:
This is a tongue-in-cheek name given to any of the modern acrylic lights (such as the APRB-251, FA-251 or the ML-300) that are currently used in lighthouses, particularly those that are solar powered. They are injection moulded in precision dies from high strength, high purity acrylic and have the dioptric and catadioptric elements included as part of the cast shape. They are typically half a metre high, a third of a metre in diameter and weigh ten kilograms. Some are cast as complete units while others are made up of multiple cast panels. Their bases are usually aluminium covered with epoxy enamel. A powerful Tupperware light can be seen for up to 50 kilometres. (Ibbotson)

Ventilation Ball:
The perforated spherical ball at the apex of the lantern roof that originally provided ventilation for the oil fired illuminant. (Historic Lighthouse Resources)

Mullions

Pile Light

Appendix III   Conversion from Kilometres to Nautical Miles and Statute Miles

Kilometres 3281' 1000m km=nm*1.853 km=sm*1.609	Nautical Miles 6080' or 1853m nm=km*0.5397 nm=sm*0.8684	Statute Miles 5280' or 1609m sm=nm*1.1515 sm=km*0.6210	Kilometres 3281' 1000m km=nm*1.853 km=sm*1.609	Nautical Miles 6080' or 1853m nm=km*0.5397 nm=sm*0.8684	Statute Miles 5280' or 1609m sm=nm*1.1515 sm=km*0.6210
1	0.54	0.62	51	27.52	31.67
2	1.08	1.24	52	28.06	32.29
3	1.62	1.86	53	28.60	32.91
4	2.16	2.48	54	29.14	33.53
5	2.70	3.11	55	29.68	34.16
6	3.24	3.73	56	30.22	34.78
7	3.78	4.35	57	30.76	35.40
8	4.32	4.97	58	31.30	36.02
9	4.86	5.59	59	31.84	36.64
10	5.40	6.21	60	32.38	37.26
11	5.94	6.83	61	32.92	37.88
12	6.48	7.45	62	33.46	38.50
13	7.02	8.07	63	34.00	39.12
14	7.56	8.69	64	34.54	39.74
15	8.10	9.32	65	35.08	40.37
16	8.64	9.94	66	35.62	40.99
17	9.17	10.56	67	36.16	41.61
18	9.71	11.18	68	36.70	42.23
19	10.25	11.80	69	37.24	42.85
20	10.79	12.42	70	37.78	43.47
21	11.33	13.04	71	38.32	44.09
22	11.87	13.66	72	38.86	44.71
23	12.41	14.28	73	39.40	45.33
24	12.95	14.90	74	39.94	45.95
25	13.49	15.53	75	40.48	46.58
26	14.03	16.15	76	41.02	47.20
27	14.57	16.77	77	41.56	47.82
28	15.11	17.39	78	42.10	48.44
29	15.65	18.01	79	42.64	49.06
30	16.19	18.63	80	43.18	49.68
31	16.73	19.25	81	43.72	50.30
32	17.27	19.87	82	44.26	50.92
33	17.81	20.49	83	44.80	51.54
34	18.35	21.11	84	45.33	52.16
35	18.89	21.74	85	45.87	52.79
36	19.43	22.36	86	46.41	53.41
37	19.97	22.98	87	46.95	54.03
38	20.51	23.60	88	47.49	54.65
39	21.05	24.22	89	48.03	55.27
40	21.59	24.84	90	48.57	55.89
41	22.13	25.46	91	49.11	56.51
42	22.67	26.08	92	49.65	57.13
43	23.21	26.70	93	50.19	57.75
44	23.75	27.32	94	50.73	58.37
45	24.29	27.95	95	51.27	59.00
46	24.83	28.57	96	51.81	59.62
47	25.37	29.19	97	52.35	60.24
48	25.91	29.81	98	52.89	60.86
49	26.45	30.43	99	53.43	61.48
50	26.99	31.05	100	53.97	62.10

Select Bibliography

AMSA, (Australian Maritime Safety Authority) Aids to Navigation Schedules through 2000
AMSA, (Australian Maritime Safety Authority) Numerous Pamphlets
AMSA, (Australian Maritime Safety Authority) Safety Aboard Newsletter 1993 – 2000
AMSA, (Australian Maritime Safety Authority) The First Decade 2001
Australia Maritime Safety Division, Hydrographers Passage Sailing Directions 1984
British Admiralty, List of Lights and Fog Signals Volume K Indian and Pacific Oceans South of the Equator 1993, 1995, 2001
Buchanan, Stuart, Lighthouse of Tragedy 1999
Buchanan, Stuart, The Lighthouse Keepers 1994
Clark, Mary and Jack, Lighthouses of the NSW Coast, Sydney Afloat 6/1996 - 6/1997
Commonwealth Department of Transport (Gordon Reid), From Dusk Till Dawn A History of Australian Lighthouses 1988
Commonwealth of Australia, LIGHTHOUSES: Do we keep the keepers? 1984
Commonwealth of Australia, Lighthouses in Australia A Guide to the Records Held by the Australian Archives. 1993
Commonwealth of Australia (Commander Brewis RN), Reports on the Lighting of the Australian Coastline (7) 1912 – 1913
Cumming Denis, Lighthouses of Western Australian Coast and Offshore Islands 1995
Curtain, Cyril, Prism Official Newsletter of the Australian Lighthouse Association 1998 - 2001
Douglas, Elizabeth, Leading Lights The Story of the Warrnambool Lighthouses and Lighthouse Keepers 1998
Edgecombe, Jean, Discovering King Island and Western Bass Strait 1993
Edgecombe, Jean, Flinders Island and Eastern Bass Strait 1986
England, Naomi, The Story of a Lighthouse South Solitary 1982
Fleming Alexander, The Illawarra Lighthouses 1972
Fremantle Maritime Museum WA, Various Information Sheets
Harris, Jill, Swan Island Retreat Visions from the Past 1995
Henderson, Captain C.W.T., The Origin of Some Sydney Harbour Place Names c1965
Holland, F. Ross, Lighthouses 1995
Hydrographer of the Navy Australian Pilot Volume I 1992
Hydrographer of the Navy Australian Pilot Volume II 1982
Hydrographer of the Navy Australian Pilot Volume III 1973
IALA Lighthouses of the World 1996
Leading Lights, The International Lighthouse Journal, Great Britain 1995-2001
Lighthouse Book Committee, A Remarkable Point (Corny Point Lighthouse SA)
Lighthouse Digest International Lighthouse Magazine, USA 1992-2001
McDonald, Malcolm, Lighthouses of Australia Project – website www.lighthouse.net.au
McGregor and Chester, Australia's Wild Islands 1997
McLaren, Verne, The Cape Jaffa Lighthouse Story 1977
Maizels, Grant & Tracy – website www.nu/lights/
Marine Board of Queensland, Sailing Directions for the Ports and Harbours of Queensland 1940
Maritime Services Board of NSW, Sailing Directions: NSW Coast 1983
Nelson Head Lighthouse Museum, The Guiding Light 1998
NSW Dept. of Navigation, Sailing Directions: NSW Coast 1930
Noble, Captain John, Australian Lighthouses 1967
Ocean Vision VI.36
Pacey, Laurelle, The Lure of Montague 1991
Parsons, Ronald, Lighthouses of South Australia 1985
Phillips, Valmai, Romance of Australian Lighthouses 1977
Queensland Government, Queensland Heritage Act Register 1992
Queenscliff Maritime Museum Vic, Various Information Sheets
Raison, E.T. (Ray), Lighthouses at Port Phillip Heads 1996
Royal Australian Historical Society, Vol 20 1934
Scott, Nuala, Eclipse Island Lighthouse1988
Smith, Dacre, The Lighthouses of Victoria 1979
Sparks, Jervis, Tales From Barrenjoey 1992
Stanley, Kathleen M., Guiding Lights Tasmania's Lighthouses and Lighthousemen 1991
Stephensen, P.R., The History and Description of Sydney Harbour 1966
Striker, Charles, Sydney Harbour Sketchbook 1968
Sutton-Jones, Kenneth, Pharos The Lighthouse Yesterday To-day and To-morrow 1985.
Sydney Maritime Museum NSW, Various Information Sheets
The Keepers Log, The Official publication of the US Lighthouse Society, 1985-2001
Thurston and Barrett, Against Darkness and Storm – Lighthouses of the Northeast 1993
Toghill, Jeff, Circumnavigating Australia's Coastline 1988
Toghill, Jeff, Circumnavigating Australia's Coastline The Ports and Anchorages -2- 1989
U-Light Reports from the Motor Vessel Cape Morton (MVCM) 1969-1992
Victoria Ports and Harbours Division, Sailing Directions Including Bass Strait 1970
Walker, Donald, Beacons of Hope An Early History of Cape Otway and King Island Lighthouses 1981
Whitney, Dudley, The Lighthouse 1975

Index

Abrolhos Islands 187
Acetylene - Glossary, 6, 11
Acrylic 11
Adele Island 202
AGA 6
Aids to Navigation - Glossary
Airlie Island 194
Albany Residency Museum 175, 262
Albany Rock 214
Albino (White) Rock 222
Althorpe Island Front 158
Althorpe Island Rear 158-159
AMSA - Glossary, 10
Apparatus - Glossary
Archer Point 217
Archer, Lee 138
Arden Islet 213
Argand, Aime 4
Arlington Reef 221
Astragals - Glossary
Australian Maritime Safety Authority –
    Glossary, 10
Australian Maritime Systems 16
Australian National Maritime Museum 124, 226, 254-255
Auxiliary Light – Glossary

Babbage Island 192-193
Backstairs Passage 148
Bailey Islet 229
Balcony - Glossary
Ballina Head 23, 26-27
Banks Strait 112, 115
Barnet, James 9, 29, 30, 35, 40, 42, 51, 67
Barrenjoey Head 42
Bass and Flinders 9, 25, 32, 178, 214
Bass Strait 9, 78-79, 82, 108-118
Bathurst Point 185
Bay Rock 263, 265
Beacon - Glossary
Bedout Island 196
Ben Boyd's Tower 65, 255
Bessieres Island 194
Bet Reef 213
Bickerton Island 209
Blow Hole Point 57
Blues Point 49
Bluff Hill 132
Bluff Point Leading Lights 188
Bolingbroke Point 167
Bonnet Islet 131
Booby Island 212-213
Botany Bay 52
Bougainville Reef 216
Bow Reef 215, 263
Boyd, Benjamin 9, 65
Bradleys Head 47
Brady Rock 209
Bramble Cay 213
Breaksea Island 9, 172-173
Breaksea Spit Lightship 14, 239-240, Cover
Browse Island 203
Brush Island 28, 65
Buccaneer Archipelago 203

Bugatti Reef 229
Built 19
Bulwer Island 264
Bunker Group 233
Buoy - Glossary
Burnett River 238, 252, 264
Burrewarra Point 64-65
Bustard Head 235, 263

Caffarelli Island 202-203
Cairncross Islets 214
Caisson - Glossary
Caloundra Lights 243, 264
Candelas - Glossary
Candlepower - Glossary
Cape Bailey 52-53
Cape Banks 143
Cape Barren 113
Cape Barren Island 113
Cape Bauer 167
Cape Borda 9, 150, 261
Cape Bossut 196
Cape Bowling Green 226, 255
Cape Bruny VI, 4, 9, 126-129, 259
Cape Byron 24-25, 253
Cape Capricorn 234
Cape Cleveland 223, 228
Cape Conran 76
Cape Croker 209
Cape Direction 215
Cape Dombey Obelisk 146
Cape Don 204, 209, 262
Cape Donington 165
Cape du Couedic 149, 261
Cape Everard (See Point Hicks)
Cape Forrestier 122
Cape Fourcroy 206
Cape Grafton 12-13
Cape Hatteras (USA) 4
Cape Hotham 208
Cape Howe (See Gabo Island)
Cape Inscription 10, 190-191
Cape Jaffa Lighthouse 146, 260-261
Cape Jervis 151
Cape Leeuwin 9, 178-179, 262
Cape Leveque 10, 200-201
Cape Liptrap 83
Cape Martin 145
Cape Melville 215
Cape Moreton 9, 246-247
Cape Naturaliste 10, 177, 262
Cape Nelson 11, 105, 257
Cape Northumberland 9, 142
Cape Otway 3, 9, 100-101, 116, 257
Cape Rochon 132
Cape Ronsard 192
Cape Schanck 84-85, 256
Cape Sorell 130
Cape Spencer 156-157
Cape St Albans 148
Cape St Cricq 190
Cape St George 9, 58-59, 255
Cape Tourville 122, 132

Cape Wessel 209
Cape Weymouth 214-215
Cape Wickham 100, 116-117
Cape Willoughby 9, 146-147, 261
Cape Woolamai 82
Cape York 213-214
Capricorn Channel 230
Captain Cook Memorial 22, 249
Carpentaria Lightship 14, 213, 254, 264
Carpenter Rocks 143
Casuarina Point 180
Cat Island 113
Catadioptric - Glossary
Catoptric - Glossary
Cave Point 7, 174-175
Chance Brothers (Robert and James) 5, 273
Chapman Reef 215
Character - Glossary
Charles Point 9, 206-207
Chicken Point 122
Citadel Island 79, 82-83, 109
Clara Group 229
Clarence River 23, 25, 54
Clerke Island 214
Cleveland Lighthouse Restoration 264
Cleveland Point 9, 248, 264
Clews Point 235
Cliffy Island 16, 78-79, 82
CLS - Glossary, 10
Coastal Lights - Glossary
Cobourg Peninsula 209
Coffs Harbour Historical Museum 29, 253
Coles Light 94
Colossus of Rhodes 2
Commonwealth Lighthouse Service 10, 16
Commonwealth Navigation Act 9
Connexion Islet 209
Cook, James 9, 22, 213
Coppersmith Rock 226
Coquet Island 215
Corny Point 160
Cossack 262
Councillor Island 118
Courthouse Museum 263
Craggy Island 109, 116
Creal Reef 229
Crookhaven Head 58
Crowdy Head 23, 33
Cull Island 172
Cumberland 116, 118
Currie Harbour 118
Currie Museum 259
Curtis Island 234
Cuvier Bay 132

Dalen Flasher 6, 11
Dalen, Gustav VI, 4, 6, 11
Dalrymple Islet 213
Dangerous Reef Centre 164-165
Davidson, Clive V
Dawson, Alexander 37
Daymark - Glossary
De Ville 143, 147

De Vlamingh, William 184
Deal Island 9, 17, 110-112, 124, 258-259
Decapolis Reef 215
Decca Navigation Chain 10
Degerando Island 203
Demanning 11
Denison, William 9
Dent Island 228-229, 223
D'Entrecasteaux Point 176
Derwent Light 119
Devonport Enterance Lights 135
Devonport Maritime Museum 259
DGPS - Glossary, 7, 16
Differential GPS (DGPS) - Glossary, 7, 16
Dioptric - Glossary
Dirk Hartog Island 190-191
Double Island Point 242
Dove Islet 213
Duyfken Point 213

East Cay 213
East Diamond Islet 216
East Lacepede Island 199
East Moncoeur Island 108-109
East Point 233
East Strait Island 213
East Vernon Island 208
Eastern Channel Pile 45
Eastern Light 9, 88, 256
Eborac Island 214
Eclipse - Glossary
Eclipse Island 175, 262
Eddystone (England) 2
Eddystone Point 120-121, 259
Eden Killer Whale Museum 255
Eden Reef 215
Edward Island 226
Eel Reef 214
Egret Reef 216
Elevation 19
Emery Point 208
Entrance Front Devonport 135
Entrance Islet 131
Entrance Rear Devonport 135
Escape Island 187
Eshelby Island 226-227
Euston Reef 221
Evans Head 167
Evans Island 28
Exhibited - Glossary
Eyre Peninsula 10, 161-162, 165, 167

Facing Island 233
Fahey Reef 215
Fawkner Beacon 88
Festu, Maurice 44, 46
Fife Island 215
Figure Of Eight Island 172
Fingal Head 23
Fitzroy Island 221-222, 244, 263
Flagstaff Hill Front 102
Flagstaff Hill Maritime Museum 102, 257
Flagstaff Hill Rear 102
Flagstaff Point 54-55
Flat Top Island 229

Fleurieu Peninsula 151
Flinders Island 113, 116
Flinders Island Light 167
Focal Plane - Glossary
Fog Signals - Glossary
Foghorns 6, 138
Fort Denison 9, 48-49
Fort Queenscliff 96, 256-257
Foul Bay 176
Four Hummock Island 167
Fraser Island Qld 239-240
Fraser Island WA 194
Frederick Reef 230
Fremantle 262
Fresnel Lens - Glossary, 2
Fresnel, Jean Augustin 5
Freycinet Peninsula 122
Front Light - Glossary
Furneaux Group 113

Gabo Island 9, 70-71, 256
Gages Road 181
Gallery Deck - Glossary
Gantheaume Point 10, 198-199
Gascoyne Historical Society 262
Gellerstad, Robert 4
Gellibrand Light 256-257
Genoa (Italy) 2
Geographe Channel 192
Geographical Range - Glossary
Geraldton Historical Society 262
Glass - Glossary, 5
Glass Reinforced Plastic Cabinet - Glossary, 4
Glennie Group 82
Global Positioning System - Glossary, 7, 16
Goat Island 48-49
Goods Island 214
Goose Island 6, 9, 112, 115
GPS - Glossary, VI, 7, 16
Grafton Passage 221
Grassy Hill 216
Great Barrier Reef 10
Great Keppel Island 227
Great NE Channel 213
Great Sandy Island 194
Green Cape 66-67, 255
Greenway, Francis 9, 51
Griffith Island 103
Groote Eylandt 209
Grotto Point 44
Group Flashing Lens 5
GRP Cabinet - Glossary, 4
Gubbins Reef 216
Guichen Bay 146
Guilderton 186
Gulf of Capentaria 213
Gulf of St Vincent 152-155
Gull Island (See Cull Island)

Hamelin Island 176
Hammond Island 6, 11, 213
Hammond Rock 213
Hannah Island 215
Hannibal Islands 214
Harbour Lights - Glossary

Harding, Charles 25
Harvey Rocks 213
Haul Round Island 209
Heath George Poynter 214
Heath Reef 215
Hells Gate 131
Henry Head 52
High Peak Island 229
Highfield Point 132, 259
Hillarys Boat Harbour 186
Hixson, Francis 9
Hogan Group 108
Hogan Island 108-109
Holbourne Island 226
Holloway Point 113
Hope Cottage Museum 147, 261
Hopkinson, John 5
Hornby 9, 42-43, 136
Hovell Light 86
Howick Island 215
Hume Tower 97
Hunter Island 132
Hutchinson William 4
Huxson, Robert 138
Hydrographers Passage 229
Hygroscopic – Glossary

IALA - Glossary, 252
Ile Du Nord Island 122
Illuminant - Glossary
Imperieuse Reef 196
Ince point (See Wednesday Island)
Inchcape Rock (Scotland) 2
Inset Reef 214
Inside Passage 10
Investigator Strait 157-158
Iris Reef 215
Iron Pot Island 9, 119
Island Point 220

James Cook Historical Museum 216, 263
Jarman Island 194-195, 262
Jemmy's Point 76
Jervis Bay 58, 60

Kangaroo Island 146-150
Kent Group 109-112
Kiama Harbour 57
Kilometre – Glossary, 276
King George Sound 173
King Island 116-118
King Island Light 215
Kingscote 147-151, 261
Kingston 146, 260-261
Kirkcaldie Reef 213

La Jument (France) 2
Lacrosse Island 203
LADS Passage 271
Lady Denman Heritage Complex 255
Lady Elliot Island 236-237, 264
Lady Musgrave Islet 233
Lake Alexandrina 144
Landfall Lights - Glossary
Lantern - Glossary

Lantern Deck - Glossary
LARC - Glossary, 235
Leading Light Townsville 210
Leading Lights - Glossary
Legendre Island 194, 262
Lens - Glossary, 5
Lesueur Island 203
Light - Glossary
Light Vessel - Glossary
Lighthouse - Glossary
Lighthouse Point 76
Lighthouse Tender - Glossary, 12
Lighthouse Tender 20's - Cape Leeuwin 12
Lighthouse Tender 20's - Cape Otway 12
Lighthouse Tender 20's - Cape York 12
Lighthouse Tender 60's - Cape Don 12
Lighthouse Tender 60's - Cape Morton 12
Lighthouse Tender 60's - Cape Pillar 12
Lighthouse Tender 90's - Cape Grafton 12-13
Lighthouse Tender Southern Supporter 12-13
Lightship - Glossary, 4, 14-15
Lightship Bramble 9
Lightship Fitzjames 9
Lightship Lady Wellington 9
Lightship Rose 9
Lightship Ville de Bordeaux 9
Lightstation - Glossary
Lihou Reef 216
Little Brewster Island (USA) 4
Little Bugatti Reef 229
Little Fitzroy Island 221-222
Little Rame Head 72
Long Spit 152
Lookout Point 64-65
Loom - Glossary
Low Head 9, 138, 259
Low Head Pilot Station 258 -259
Low Isles 218, 263
Low Rocky Point 130
Luminous Range – Glossary

Maatsuyker Island 129, 259
Macquarie lighthouse 8-9, 50-51
Macquarie Harbour 130-131
Macquarie, Lachlan 9, 51
Magpie Reef 215
Main Bar Lights 38
Main Light - Glossary
Margaret Brock Reef Centre 146, 260-261
Marino Rocks 152
Maritime Museum of Tasmania 259
Mary Anne Island 194
Maxwell Reef 10, 215
McCrae light (See Eastern Light)
McKenna Point 180
Megeara Reef 215
Mersey Bluff 136-137
Metre - Glossary
Middle Bank 162
Middle Channel 106, 139
Middle Reef 214
Mid-North Coast Maritime Museum 253
Miles Reef 215
Mitchell, Alexander 2
Monash Light 86
Montague Island 62-63, 255

Moody Reef 214
Moreton Island 246-247
Moriarty, Edward 56-57
Mount Barkly 76
Mullion - Glossary
Murray Tower 97

Narooma Visitors Centre 255
Nautical Mile – Glossary, 276
Navigation Aid - Glossary
Nelson Head 36, 253
Nelson Head Lighthouse Cottage 253
New Year Island 209
Nobby's Head 9, 39
Nominal Range - Glossary
Norah Head 40-41, 253
North Barnard Islands 222
North East Island 109, 111
North East Islet 209
North Island 187
North Mole Head (red) 182-183
North Neptune Island 168-169
North Point 247
North Reef 224, 230-232
North Sandy Island 194
North Solitary Island 28
North Stradbroke Island 249
North West Cape 2, 196-197
North West Island 194
North West Vernon Island 208

Occulting - Glossary
O'Connor, Cy 183
Omega Facility 7, 10, 77
Orontes Bank 152
Outer Sister Island 113
Outsourcing 16

Palfrey Islet 215
Parabolic 4
Parriwi Head 44
Pearson Isles 167
Pelsaert Island 187
Penguin Island 145
Penrith Island 229
Period - Glossary
Pethebridge Islets 215
Pharology - Glossary, 2
Pharos - Glossary, 2
Phillip Island 82
Pickersgill Reef 216
Pile Light – Glossary
Pinchgut (see Fort Denison)
Pine Islet 229, 263
Pine Islet Lighthouse Restoration 263
Pine Peak Island 229
Pinnacle Point 226
Piper Islands 214
Pith Reef 222
Plank Shoal 162
Point Boston 161
Point Cartwright 243, 244-245
Point Cloates 192, 194
Point Danger 22, 249
Point Grant 82

Point Hicks 72-75, 256
Point Home Lookout 122-123, 132
Point King 9, 172
Point Lonsdale 95-96, 257
Point Lookout 249
Point Lowly 140, 162-163, 261
Point Malcolm 144
Point Marsden 151
Point Moore 170, 188-189
Point Nepean 86
Point Perpendicular 60-61
Point Quobba 192-193
Pointing - Glossary
Polly Woodside Maritime Museum 256-257
Pope's Eye Beacon 94
Port Adelaide 152, 169
Port Albert Maritime Museum 256
Port Hedland Buoys 196
Port Jackson 45
Port Melbourne Front 90-91
Port Melbourne Rear 91
Port Phillip 86-97
Port Stephens 36-37
Port Stephens Historical Society 37, 253
Port Walcott Buoys 194
Portland Maritime Discovery Centre 257
Prince George Shoal 93

Queenscliff Low 97
Queensland Maritime Museum 264

Racon - Glossary, 7
Radio Beacons 6
Rainbow Beach 242
Raine Island 65, 246
Range - Glossary, 19
Rear Light - Glossary
Red Bluff 199
Ref 19
Restoration Rock 215
Rib Reef 222, 263
Richmond River (See Ballina Head)
Richter, Chris 11, 80
Robe 146, 151
Robertson Point 48
Rocky Cape 133
Rocky Islet 217
Roebuck Bay 199
Rosemary Island 194
Rottnest 9, 184
Rottnest Island 184-185
Round Hill Point 133
Round Island 82
Rudyerd, John 2
Russell Island 222

Sandy Cape Qld 240-241
Sandy Cape Tas 132
Saumarez Reef 230
Schanpper Point 88
Schouten Island 122
Scott, Peter 101
Screw Pile Light - Glossary, 2
Seal Islands 79
Seal Rocks 35

Sector Light - Glossary
Shark Bay 190, 192
Shark Island 47
She Oak Point 139
Shoal Point 187
Shoalwater Point 162
Shortland Bluff 9, 96
Sibsey Island 167
Smeaton, John 2
Smoky Cape 30-31, 253
Snapper Point 148
Sostratus 2
South 162
South Australian Maritime Museum 168-169, 261
South Barrow Islet 215
South Brook Island 222
South Bruny Island 126-129
South Channel Pile 87, 256
South East Point 9, 80-81, 256
South Head 238, 252, 264
South Head Lighthouse Restoration 264
South Head Sydney 9, 50-51
South Mole Head (green) 182-183
South Neptune Island 152, 168-169, 261
South Page Island 148
South Pipon Island 215
South Solitary Island 5, 28-29, 253
South West Island 109, 111-112
South West Vernon Island 208
Southern Supporter 12-13
Sow and Pigs 9, 14, 45
Spencer Gulf 166-167
Split Point 68, 98-99, 257
St Francis Island 167
St Kilda False Light 89
St Vincent Gulf 152,154
Stainer Island 10, 215
Stanley Park 259
Star Buoys 194
Steelworks Channel 38
Steep Point 192
Stevens Island 209
Stevensons 2, 5
Stokes Point 118
Storm Bay 9,119
Sue Islet 213
Sugarloaf Point IV, 34-35, 253
Sun Valve 6, 11
Swains Reef 230
Swan Island 9, 14, 112, 114-115, 259
Sydney Harbour 9, 42-49

Table Cape 134
Tacking Point 23, 32
Tamar River Leading Lights 139
Tanner Island 203
Tapley Shoal 152
Tasman Island 9, 124-125
Taylor Island 166
Telescopic Tower 4
Thistle Island 166
Three Hummock Island 132
Three Isles 215
Thursday Island 213-214
Timeball Tower Semaphore 1, 261
Timeball Tower Williamstown 9, 92, 257

Tiparra or Tipara Reef 147, 161
Torres Strait 9-10, 212-214
Torres Strait Historical Museum 263
Tower – Glossary, 19
Tower of Hercules (Spain) 2
Townsville Maritime Museum 263-264
Trimouille Island 194
Troubridge Hill 152-153
Troubridge Island/ Shoal 9, 154-155, 261
Truant Island 209
Tuesday Islet 213
Tupperware Light - Glossary, 4, 6, 11, etc
Twin Island 213

Vaucluse Bay Front 46
Vaucluse Bay Rear 46
Ventilation Ball - Glossary
Vernon Rocks 229
Veronica Islet 209
Vlaming Head 10, 196-197, 262

Warburto Point 161
Wardang Island 160
Warden Head 62
Warnawi Island 209
Waterhouse Island 113
Waterhouse Point 166
Waterwitch Reef 215
Watson Island 215
Wedge Island 167

Wedge Light 94
Wednesday Island 213
Wessel Islands 209
West Cape 157
West Channel Pile 93
West Point Light 132
Western Australian Maritime Museum 262
Western Channel Pile 45
Western Hill, Goods Island 214, 216
Western Shoal 162
Whaler's Bluff Cover, I, 104
Whales Head 126, 129
Wharton Reef 215, 264
White Lady (See Split Point)
White Tip Reef 229
Whitsunday Islands 226, 228
Williams Island 167
Wilson's Promontory 9, 79-81, 256
Winceby Island 167
Winstanley, Henry 2
Wollongong Harbour 56-57, 253, 255
Wollongong Head 20, 54-55
Wonga Shoal 152
Woodman Point 181
Wyborn Reef 214
Wye Reef 214

Yamba Historical Society 253
Yarraville Shoal 162
Yorke Peninsula 156-157, 160

Quick Facts

First DGPS station	Cape Schanck Vic (1996)
First light (a bonfire)	South Head Sydney NSW (Jan 1793)
First regular light (a fire)	South Head Sydney NSW (1794)
First lighthouse	Macquarie Lighthouse NSW (30th Nov 1818)
First lightship	The *Rose* Sydney Harbour NSW (1836)
First electric powered light	Macquarie Lighthouse NSW (1887)
First solar powered light	Hammond Island Qld (1980)
Highest (non-operational light)	Deal Island Tas (305m, 1001ft)
Highest (operational light)	Tasman Island Tas (276m, 906ft)
Last lighthouse Keeper	Chris Richter, Maatsuyker Island Tas (27th Aug 1996)
Last 20th century lighthouse	Maxwell Reef Qld (Dec 2000)
Last lightship	*CLS8 Breaksea* Qld (1999)
Most Northerly lighthouse	Bramble Cay Qld (lat 9-08.6 long 143-52.6)
Most Southerly lighthouse	Maatsuyker Island Tas (lat 43-39.4 long 146-16.4)
Most Easterly lighthouse	Frederick Reef Qld (lat 20-56.5 long 154-24.0)
Most Westerly lighthouse	Cape Inscription WA (lat 25-28.9 long 112-58.3)
Most powerful light	Cape Byron NSW (2,200,000 candelas)
Oldest light still operating	Iron Pot Hobart Tas (1833)
Tallest classical tower	Cape Wickham King Island Tas (48m, 148ft)
Tallest light specific tower	Steelworks Channel Directional light (60m, 197ft)
Tallest navigational structure	Omega Tower Darriman Vic (427m, 1401ft)
Tallest structure with a light	Tower 11 Northwest Cape Exmouth WA (304m, 996ft)

Eddystone Point – Tasmania

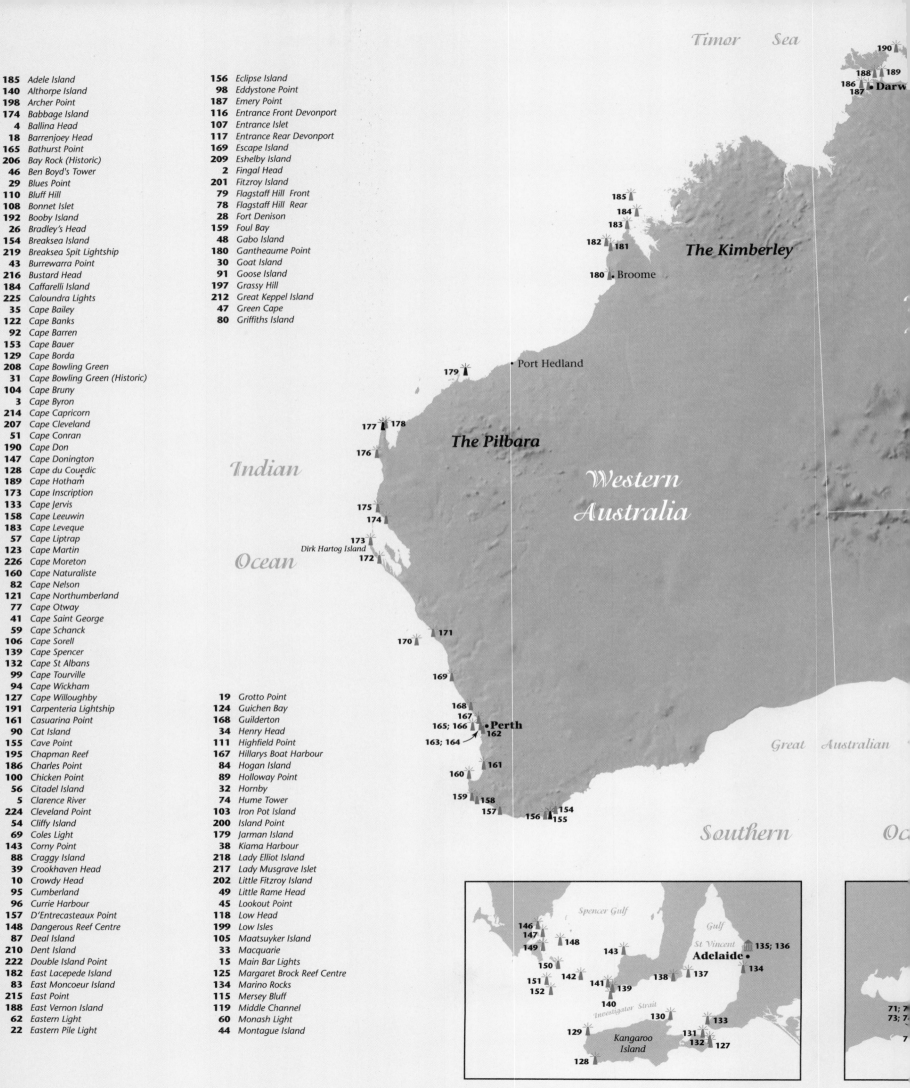

185 Adele Island
140 Althorpe Island
198 Archer Point
174 Babbage Island
4 Ballina Head
18 Barrenjoey Head
165 Bathurst Point
206 Bay Rock (Historic)
46 Ben Boyd's Tower
29 Blues Point
110 Bluff Hill
108 Bonnet Islet
192 Booby Island
26 Bradley's Head
154 Breaksea Island
219 Breaksea Spit Lightship
43 Burrewarra Point
216 Bustard Head
184 Caffarelli Island
225 Caloundra Lights
35 Cape Bailey
122 Cape Banks
92 Cape Barren
153 Cape Bauer
129 Cape Borda
208 Cape Bowling Green
31 Cape Bowling Green (Historic)
104 Cape Bruny
3 Cape Byron
214 Cape Capricorn
207 Cape Cleveland
51 Cape Conran
190 Cape Don
147 Cape Donington
128 Cape du Couedic
189 Cape Hotham
173 Cape Inscription
133 Cape Jervis
158 Cape Leeuwin
183 Cape Leveque
57 Cape Liptrap
123 Cape Martin
226 Cape Moreton
160 Cape Naturaliste
82 Cape Nelson
121 Cape Northumberland
77 Cape Otway
41 Cape Saint George
59 Cape Schanck
106 Cape Sorell
139 Cape Spencer
132 Cape St Albans
99 Cape Tourville
94 Cape Wickham
127 Cape Willoughby
191 Carpenteria Lightship
161 Casuarina Point
90 Cat Island
155 Cave Point
195 Chapman Reef
186 Charles Point
100 Chicken Point
56 Citadel Island
5 Clarence River
224 Cleveland Point
54 Cliffy Island
69 Coles Light
143 Corny Point
88 Craggy Island
39 Crookhaven Head
10 Crowdy Head
95 Cumberland
96 Currie Harbour
157 D'Entrecasteaux Point
148 Dangerous Reef Centre
87 Deal Island
210 Dent Island
222 Double Island Point
182 East Lacepede Island
83 East Moncoeur Island
215 East Point
188 East Vernon Island
62 Eastern Light
22 Eastern Pile Light

156 Eclipse Island
98 Eddystone Point
187 Emery Point
116 Entrance Front Devonport
107 Entrance Islet
117 Entrance Rear Devonport
169 Escape Island
209 Eshelby Island
2 Fingal Head
201 Fitzroy Island
79 Flagstaff Hill Front
78 Flagstaff Hill Rear
28 Fort Denison
159 Foul Bay
48 Gabo Island
180 Gantheaume Point
30 Goat Island
91 Goose Island
197 Grassy Hill
212 Great Keppel Island
47 Green Cape
80 Griffiths Island

19 Grotto Point
124 Guichen Bay
168 Guilderton
34 Henry Head
111 Highfield Point
167 Hillarys Boat Harbour
84 Hogan Island
89 Holloway Point
32 Hornby
74 Hume Tower
103 Iron Pot Island
200 Island Point
179 Jarman Island
38 Kiama Harbour
218 Lady Elliot Island
217 Lady Musgrave Islet
202 Little Fitzroy Island
49 Little Rame Head
45 Lookout Point
118 Low Head
199 Low Isles
105 Maatsuyker Island
33 Macquarie
15 Main Bar Lights
125 Margaret Brock Reef Centre
134 Marino Rocks
115 Mersey Bluff
119 Middle Channel
60 Monash Light
44 Montague Island